COMMON MENTAL DISORDERS IN PRIMARY CARE

Common Mental Disorders in Primary Care brings together distinguished clinicians and researchers from a range of professions – psychiatrists, psychologists, social workers, sociologists and general practitioners – providing an authoritative and updated review of diagnosis, treatment and management of common mental disorders in primary care.

Looking at the theoretical considerations, scientific studies and service evaluation research in the field, the book offers data and information necessary to help those working in a variety of mental health and primary care settings. It is divided into five main sections:

The nature of the problem
Teamwork in primary care
Improving management
Training in mental health skills in primary care
The interface between primary care and specialist mental health services

Published to mark the retirement of Professor Sir David Goldberg, *Common Mental Disorders in Primary Care* will prove accessible and highly relevant to all those working in mental health and primary care settings.

Michele Tansella is Professor of Psychiatry and Director of the Department of Medicine and Public Health at the University of Verona. He is also Head of the South-Verona Community-based Mental Health Service.

Graham Thornicroft is Professor of Community Psychiatry and Director of the Section of Community Psychiatry (PRISM) at the Institute of Psychiatry, London.

Professor Sir David Goldberg

COMMON MENTAL DISORDERS IN PRIMARY CARE

Essays in honour of
Professor Sir David Goldberg

*Edited by Michele Tansella
and Graham Thornicroft*

London and New York

First published 1999
by Routledge
11 New Fetter Lane, London EC4P 4EE

Simultaneously published in the USA and Canada
by Routledge
29 West 35th Street, New York, NY 10001

Routledge is an imprint of the Taylor & Francis Group

© 1999 Michele Tansella and Graham Thornicroft, selection and editorial
matter; individual chapters, the contributors

Typeset in Garamond by
BC Typesetting, Bristol
Printed and bound in Great Britain by
St Edmundsbury Press, Bury St Edmunds, Suffolk

British Library Cataloguing in Publication Data
A catalogue record for this book is available from the British Library

Library of Congress Cataloging in Publication Data
Common mental disorders in primary care: essays in honour of
Professor Sir David Goldberg/edited by Michele Tansella and Graham
Thornicroft.
p.   cm.
Includes bibliographical references and index.
ISBN 0–415–20572–7 (hbk.)
1. Psychiatry.   2. Primary care (Medicine).   I. Tansella, Michele.
II. Thornicroft, Graham.   III. Goldberg, David P.
RC454.4.C655   1999
616.89–dc21   99-24250
                                                              CIP

ISBN 0–415–20572–7

CONTENTS

v

CONTENTS

CONTENTS

ILLUSTRATIONS

Figures

Tables

CONTRIBUTORS

Gavin Andrews is Professor of Psychiatry at the University of New South Wales at St Vincent's Hospital, Sydney and Head of the WHO Collaborating Centre in Mental Health and Substance Abuse, Australia. His research and professional interests are the treatment of anxiety disorders, the education of mental health professionals and models of health care delivery.

Jesús Artal Simón is Head of Mental Health for the Autonomic Government of Cantabria and Head of the Cantabria Programme for Mental Health and Psychiatric Care. His main research interest is in the field of primary care and psychiatric services evaluation.

J.F. William Deakin is Professor of Psychiatry and Director of the Neuroscience and Psychiatry Unit at the University of Manchester, and of the Wellcome Trust Clinical Research Facility. His current research interests developed from work on animals and include: the role of 5HT in affective and impulse control disorders; and schizophrenia and the glutamate system.

Aant (Peter) de Jong is Senior Researcher in eipdemiology and psychology at the Department of Psychiatry of the University of Groningen and Clinical Researcher at the University Hospital. He has been involved in several WHO studies on schizophrenia and related disorders, in particular the development and underlying basic mechanisms of the disability resulting from these illnesses. He is the author of the International Classification of Mental Health Care (ICMHC). He acted as editor-in-chief of the *Reference Book in Psychiatric Epidemiology*, published (in Dutch) in March 1999.

Linda Gask is Reader in Psychiatry in the Department of Community Psychiatry and National Primary Care Research and Development Centre at the University of Manchester. She completed her PhD research into the training of GPs in mental health skills under the supervision of Professor Sir David Goldberg in Manchester. She is now a mental health researcher jointly appointed to a multidisciplinary Department of

Health-funded research unit and a general psychiatrist at the Royal Preston Hospital, working closely with primary care.

Kevin Gournay is Professor of Psychiatric Nursing at the Institute of Psychiatry, London. His previous research has included trials with Community Nurses, cognitive behavioural treatments and economic analyses. He currently has the largest portfolio of psychiatric nursing research in Europe, including studies, systematic reviews and trials in primary care, dual diagnosis, training evaluations, medication management, forensic care and body image disorders. He provides policy advice to the British Government and is involved in various National Standards of Care Groups. He also runs various educational programmes for mental health workers and has developed a range of evidence-based training packages which are now used in other countries.

Scott Henderson is Director of the National Health and Medical Research Council's Psychiatric Epidemiology Research Centre at the Australian National University, Canberra, and Clinical Adviser in Mental Health, Commonwealth Department of Health and Aged Care. His research interests include epidemiology of common mental disorders; the social environment; mental disorders in later life; and molecular genetics in epidemiology.

Andrés Herrán is Associate Professor in the Department of Psychiatry at Cantabria University, a Psychiatrist at the University Hospital 'Marqués de Valdecilla', and a research worker in the Clinical and Social Psychiatry Research Unit of the WHO Collaborating Centre. His main research interests are mental health in primary care; biological and clinical correlates of depression and schizophrenia.

Caroline Hunt is a Lecturer in the School of Psychiatry at the University of New South Wales at St Vincent's Hospital, Sydney. Her research and professional interests are in the education of mental health professionals; generalized anxiety disorder; and the determination of clinical significance of treatment.

Peter Huxley is Professor of Psychiatric Social Work at the University of Manchester. He arrived at Manchester University as a student the same year as Sir David Goldberg went there as Senior Lecturer, and they later enjoyed a productive working relationship, publishing two influential books together (*Mental Illness in the Community*, Tavistock, 1980, and *Common Mental Disorders*, Routledge, 1992). Since then his main research interests have been the quality of life of people with severe mental illness, the impact of socio-economic changes on mental health and the quality of life.

Rachel Jenkins is Director of the WHO Collaborating Centre at the Institute of Psychiatry, London. Her work programme includes collaborating with WHO and other international organisations on the new UN programme 'Nations for Mental Health', as well as on epidemiology, outcome measurement, primary care guidelines and the International Classification of Disability.

Glyn Lewis is Professor of Community and Epidemiological Psychiatry in the Division of Psychological Medicine at the University of Wales College of Medicine. His previous research has included the study of the measurement of common mental disorders and the development of the revised clinical interview schedule. He has been involved in both observational studies, randomised controlled trials and systematic reviews. His current research includes randomised controlled trials in mild depression and development of computerised guidelines.

Elizabeth Hiok-Boon Lin is a Scientific Investigator in the Center for Health Studies of the Group Health Cooperative of Puget Sound, Seattle, and is a practising family physician. She has conducted research on improving care for depressed patients in the general health care setting. The specific focus of these randomised trials included high users of medical services, collaborative care to achieve treatment guidelines, patient adherence to pharmacotherapy, physician education, and using an individualised stepped care strategy to prevent depression persistence and relapse.

Ita Lyons is a Clinical Research Fellow in the Division of Psychological Medicine at the University of Wales College of Medicine. She is currently coordinating a randomised controlled trial of computer decision support in the management of common mental disorders in primary care. Her other research interests include the psychological effects of head injury.

Anthony Mann is Professor of Epidemiological Psychiatry and Head of the Section of Old Age Psychiatry at the Institute of Psychiatry, London. His research interest and publications include: the epidemiology of old age psychiatric disorders; primary health care studies – in particular, the outcome of common mental disorders and the role of the practice nurse in mental illness work; personality disorders – their assessment and epidemiology. He is currently developing primary care research studies in India and Sri Lanka.

Malik Hussain Mubbashar is Professor and Director of the Institute of Psychiatry and WHO Collaborating Centre for Mental Health Research and Training, Rawalpindi Medical College, National Coordinator of the Mental Health Programme for Pakistan and member of WHO Expert Advisory Panels of Mental Health and Substance Abuse, and Dean of the Faculty of Psychiatry, College of Physicians and Surgeons, Pakistan. He is currently Honorary Visiting Professor at the Institute of Psychiatry, London. His research interests include mental health in primary care and promotion of mental health. He has been visiting professor at various universities around the world and is external examiner to the Universities of London and Manchester.

Johan (Hans) Ormel is Professor of Social Psychiatry (in particular psychiatric epidemiology) at the University of Groningen and Professor of Social Psychiatry, Institute of Psychiatry and MRC Centre for Social, Genetic and Developmental Psychiatry, London. He is currently leading randomised trials of relapse/recurrence prevention and of effective treatment of depression in cardiovascular patients and their long-term effects on mental health and quality of life. His etiologic work is increasingly targeting broader developmental issues linking child and adolescent psychopathology with adult mental health and functioning. He now studies pathways of vulnerability and resilience to non-psychotic mental disorder within a dynamic stress–vulnerability paradigm.

Norman Sartorius is Professor at the Department of Psychiatry of the University of Geneva, and at other universities in Europe, USA and China. A past Director of the Division of Mental Health of the WHO in 1977, he is now President of the World Psychiatric Association. He is an honorary fellow or member of numerous professional associations, both national and international, and a member of the editorial and advisory boards of many scientific journals.

Deborah Sharp is Professor of Primary Care at the University of Bristol. Her early studies focused on postnatal depression, but subsequently she has developed a wider perspective on mental health problems in primary care, most recently in the area of guideline development and implementation. She also works as a GP.

Gregory E. Simon is an Investigator in the Center for Health Studies of the Group Health Cooperative of Puget Sound, Seattle, and Research Associate Professor in the Department of Psychiatry and Behavioral Sciences, University of Washington. He completed his speciality training in internal medicine and psychiatry, and his current clinical practice concentrates on psychiatric consultation in primary care. His main research interests include: epidemiology of common mental disorders; management of mental disorders presenting in primary care; and the cost-effectiveness of mental health treatments.

Michele Tansella is Professor of Psychiatry, Director of the Department of Medicine and Public Health and Director of the Postgraduate School in Psychiatry at the University of Verona; he is also Head of the South-Verona Community-based Mental Health Service (WHO Collaborating

Centre for Research and Training in Mental Health and Service Evaluation). He has conducted research at the Institute of Psychiatry, London, in the General Practice Research Unit (GPRU) directed by Professor Michael Shepherd, and in other units. His main research interests are in epidemiological psychiatry and include service evaluation, evaluation of outcome and costs of mental disorders, and mental disorders in primary care settings.

Graham Thornicroft is Professor of Community Psychiatry and Director of the Section of Community Psychiatry (PRiSM), Institute of Psychiatry, London. Professor Thornicroft's research interests cover a wide range in mental health service evaluation, and he has published extensively in this field.

Andre Tylee is Director of the RCGP Mental Health Unit, Institute of Psychiatry, London, a unit that he himself established. He is also a GP principal with a practice in Sutton, Surrey. He has also created the national 'Teach the Teachers' courses for paired GP/nurse tutors and is now focused on commissioning skills training and mental health strategy development, based on patient needs. He was involved in organising the UK 'Defeat Depression Campaign' and now the 'National Depression Campaign'. He is an adviser to WHO and to the National Schizophrenia Fellowship, and is a member of both the RCGP Mental Health Task Group and the Royal College of Psychiatrists.

José Luis Vázquez-Barquero is Head Professor of the Department of Psychiatry of Cantabria University, and Director of the Clinical and Social Psychiatry Research Unit (WHO Collaborating Centre). His research interests are in the field of social and clinical psychiatry; he is a principal investigator in projects related to primary care, schizophrenia, depression and disabilities, participating in various international BIOMED projects. He is the author of over a hundred articles and books and is a member of the editorial committees of several Spanish and international psychiatric journals.

Michael Von Korff is a Senior Investigator in the Center for Health Studies of the Group Health Cooperative of Puget Sound, Seattle. His research concerns the management and outcomes of depression and common chronic pain disorders (back pain, headache) in primary care settings, focusing on behavioural effects (disability, healthcare use, medicine use) of these common episodic illnesses. He has carried out large randomised controlled trials evaluating practical psychological interventions for primary care patients, assessing effects on symptoms, disability and use of health care services.

FOREWORD 1

The contribution of David Goldberg: a British perspective

Rachel Jenkins

I first met David Goldberg in the late 1970s when he delivered a character-istically brilliant evening lecture to the Institute of Psychiatry that simul-taneously enlightened, inspired and made us laugh. Since then I have had ample evidence that this was not a unique occasion but rather what David does every day after breakfast.

Scott Henderson's Foreword draws attention to David Goldberg's 'three distinct contributions' of devising the General Health Questionnaire (GHQ) and the Clinical Interval Schedule (CIS), conducting research in primary care, and his influence overseas, and briefly mentions that Goldberg's work, demonstrating that GPs can be trained to function more effectively, is now a matter of interest to many Ministries of Health. In this Foreword I would like to take the opportunity to expand a little on the way in which Goldberg's work has made major contributions to the evidence and thinking underpinning the various essential elements of mental health policy and practice which need to be considered by Governments wishing to protect, promote and improve the mental health of their populations.

The contribution of epidemiology to mental health policy

Central to the creation of mental health policy is an understanding of the high prevalence and disability of mental disorders, an understanding of the path-ways to care of mental disorders, and an understanding of the multi-factorial nature of the causation, consequences and treatment of mental disorders. Both Goldberg's own research and his writings for medical students have contributed to this understanding.

Because of the high public health burden of mental disorders, which David's epidemiological and methodological contributions have done much to underpin, it is essential that every country create a strategic mental health policy which is well integrated with its overall health policy at ministerial, ministry, regional and local levels, and which covers the three broad tasks of first, community action to promote mental health; second, primary care of mental disorders for prevention and prompt and efficient treatment of common mental disorders; and third, specialist services (as local as is affordable) to support those clients in greatest need and to support and sustain expertise in primary care. A mental health policy also needs to include attention to some generic issues such as the information strategy, the research and development strategy and the human resources strategy. It also needs to cover some specific vital issues such as the precise funding streams for mental health and the organisational structure for policy implementation. Goldberg has made significant contributions to each of these areas.

David Goldberg has contributed to epidemiological knowledge about the frequency of mental disorders across the world both by devising the epidemiological instruments necessary to measure accurately mental disorder and by planning and running epidemiological surveys in the various levels of care. His major contributions to psychiatric epidemiological method have stimulated the impressive body of knowledge which we now have on the prevalence of mental disorders around the world and made it possible for mental disorders to be properly included in the recent World Bank estimates of the Burden of Disease which helped to trigger United Nations' action on world mental health.

Primary care

Goldberg's research has made it clear that mental disorder is so common that, no country, however rich it might be, can afford anything approaching sufficient specialist personnel to see and care for everyone with a mental disorder. Rather, most people with mental disorders will need to be seen and cared for by members of the primary health care unit, and it is therefore essential to strengthen the basic and continuing training of the various members of the primary health care unit by knowledge of assessment, diagnosis, management and criteria for referral of people with mental disorders to secondary care. This is as essential in the developed world as it is in low income countries.

Goldberg and Huxley's masterly (1980) exposition of the pathways to care of the common mental health disorders, and its subsequent elaboration in 1992 has been a key plank in understanding access to care, and in developing ways to strengthen the effectiveness of primary health care teams.

Besides the use for the GHQ as a screening test, Goldberg also developed its use as a tool to describe mental health characteristics of GPs (Goldberg and Huxley 1980) and, more recently, as the tool that produces the groups of 'high 11' and 'low 11' doctors, so that it is then possible to study the 'cue releasing qualities' of various medical behaviour. This has been an important achievement of Goldberg' s teaching of medical interviewing (Goldberg and

Huxley 1992) and with others, Goldberg has produced a series of papers on teaching medical interviewing to medical students, vocational GPs, experienced GPs and postgraduate psychiatrists. With Peter Maguire, Goldberg showed that the training lasted.

Goldberg set up innovative training courses for GPs in Manchester which still go on, and was assisted by Linda Gask and Francis Creed. Goldberg was strongly influenced in this by Art Lesser, the Canadian psychiatrist, who visited Manchester and worked with Goldberg and Gask. There are now large numbers of excellent GPs around Manchester who have been trained by Goldberg and who shine like beacons to their fellows.

Goldberg was a major contributor to the construction of the ICD10 Primary Care Guidelines which are an expert consensus-based system for assessment, diagnosis, management and criteria for referral for the different mental disorders in ICD10. These guidelines have been piloted in a number of countries and are being widely disseminated across the world. Goldberg's research on the determinants of somatisation, its frequency and GPs' ability to detect it led to the development of techniques for teaching GPs to assess and manage somatising patients.

Specialist care

However rich a country may be, specialist mental health staff will nonetheless be in relatively short supply and therefore policy is needed to ensure their efficient deployment. In low income countries specialist services are usually in extremely short supply, and therefore it is even more important to use them to best effect: one of Goldberg's Maudsley Discussion papers tackles this issue for the UK (Goldberg and Gournay 1997).

In most countries the distribution of psychiatrists is inequitable with most concentrated in the capital city. In his time at Manchester, David Goldberg showed that it was possible to build up a centre of excellence away from the capital, with world renowned training programmes and research programmes.

From the point of view of good outcomes, people with severe mental illness should be cared for as close to home as is compatible with health and safety of the individual and the safety of the public, in as least restrictive an environment as possible, with due regard to their rights as a human being and respect for their dignity, religion and culture. The precise service structure and configuration needs to be determined in the context of local needs, culture and resources. Services may include a small flexible mixture of acute inpatient beds (with bed management strategies to keep the number of required beds as small as possible), half-way houses, respite houses, outpatient clinics, occupational rehabilitation, day care, occupational therapy and social activities aimed at promoting each individual's self-determination and personal responsibility in order to achieve the highest attainable level of health and wellbeing. It is particularly important to emphasise rehabilitation back into the normal pattern of daily activities of the rest of the population.

David Goldberg's research into the relative value of the District General Hospital (DGH) psychiatric unit and the mental hospital was the first health economic study in the UK to fully evaluate mental health services. The technique used was devised by Goldberg and Norman Glass, then the economist at the Department of Health (Glass and Goldberg 1977). The Manchester Schizophrenia studies showed that the health and social outcomes in the DGH were better than outcomes in the mental hospital four years into the illness and the effect was even stronger 12 years into the illness. The studies showed both economic savings and enormous benefits in terms of better social adjustment, fewer negative symptoms, more patients symptom-free and treatment preferred by both users and carers.

David pioneered the implementation of the concept of hospital hostels, now known as 24-hour nursed care, and demonstrated their cost-effectiveness by a comparison of health and social outcomes and costs in Douglas House, a converted Victorian house, compared with the local DGH unit (Goldberg et al. 1985).

Primary care and secondary care are more efficient and effective if there is good communication between them, agreed criteria for referral and discharge, agreed guidelines and mutual support. This is likely to entail regular meetings between primary health care teams and specialist staff to discuss criteria for referral, discharge letters, shared care procedures, need for medicines, information transfer and any other co-ordination issues, training, good practice guidelines and consideration of appropriate research. David Goldberg evaluated the impact of this in his Pathways to Care project in Manchester.

Further contributions to medical education

Goldberg has inspired people around him to produce two standard books – *Psychiatry in Medical Practice* (Goldberg et al. 1994) which outsells all other undergraduate medical texts; and the new 'Orange Book' for postgraduates (Goldberg 1997). Goldberg was responsible for many of the original ideas in the undergraduate book, much of which was written by experts including Francis Creed and Sydney Benjamin, and finally edited by Goldberg himself.

Goldberg, assisted by Digby Tantam and Richard Gater, also made major contributions to the training of overseas medical graduates by setting up the Manchester training course for them which runs to this day. This course encouraged the Royal College to start its Overseas Doctors Training Scheme two years later. The course did not aim to provide a second-rate training in mental health for foreign doctors – rather it inspired and taught them how to innovate in mental health service delivery; how to make themselves known to their Ministry of Health; and how to influence local administrators.

Each trainee developed a project for changing their mental health system when they returned to their countries. Most of these trainees now hold senior positions in their countries. This course (originally awarding a Diploma, now a Manchester MSc) trained many psychiatrists in Pakistan and Nigeria, most of the indigenous psychiatrists in Ethiopia, and a number of others from all anglophile African countries.

Research and development

All countries need to establish a sustainable research and development strategy to support its policy development and implementation programme. In the UK, Goldberg was invited to chair the NHS Research and Development Committee on research priorities in mental health which set the research agenda for mental health for the decade and was the first of its kind. He had previously been an active member of the Department of Health's Research Liaison Committee.

Human resources and contributions to medical education

Similarly, countries need a sustainable human resources strategy to carry out the implementation of policy and the delivery of services. Low income countries will have difficulty in meeting all their training requirements for health and social care professionals. They will therefore need a sustainable plan for production and continuing development both at home, and elsewhere, of primary and secondary care staff. David Goldberg has made significant contributions over his working life to the training of medical students, general practitioners and psychiatrists in the United Kingdom and in developing countries and many of his trainees are running training departments of their own.

Involvement of non-governmental organisations and users and carers

People with mental illness, their carers and the community are the 'customers' of the services. Their involvement can greatly improve the planning and delivery of services as they can spot gaps and problems as well as comment on what is working well. Pump priming the non-governmental organisation (NGO) can be a cost-effective way of achieving progress. 'Mental Health in the City' was a conference with a vision in London 1997 which drew users and professionals from all over the world to contribute to a discussion of mental health provision in a range of cities in rich and low income countries (Goldberg and Thornicroft 1998).

Public health measures to reduce suicide and homicide by mentally ill people

Suicide is the tenth leading cause of death in the world, and is thus a significant mortality in most countries. It is nearly always linked to mental illness – the so-called rational suicide is extremely rare. Suicide is therefore preventable in many cases. A number of countries are now developing national suicide prevention policies, and David Goldberg was a key advisor to the UK Government's health strategy to improve health outcomes and reduce mortality.

Strategy to reduce mortality from physical illness in mentally ill people

People with severe mental illness in relatively well off countries tend to have a higher mortality than the general population from cardiovascular disease, respiratory disease and malignancy. Relevant studies have not to my knowledge been done in developing countries. In low-income countries, there is also an enhanced risk of mortality from infectious diseases. It is therefore extremely important to ensure adequate physical health care and health promotion to people with mental illness, particularly those being looked after by the hospital. This has always been an important element of Goldberg's teaching to medical students and young doctors.

I hope I have managed to convey a small flavour of David's immense contributions to mental health policy both in this country and abroad. We can see so far because we are standing on the shoulders of giants. Here indeed is a giant.

References

Glass, N.J. and Goldberg, D. (1977) Cost-benefit analysis and the evaluation of psychiatric services. *Psychological Medicine* 7, 701.707.
Goldberg, D. (1997) *Maudsley Handbook of Practical Psychiatry*. Oxford University Press, Oxford.
Goldberg, D. and Gournay, K. (1997) *The General Practitioner, the Psychiatrist and the Burden of Mental Health Care*. Maudsley Discussion paper No.1, Institute of Psychiatry, London.
Goldberg, D. and Huxley, P. (1980) *Mental Illness in the Community*. Tavistock, London.
Goldberg, D. and Huxley, P. (1992) *Common Mental Disorders. A Bio-Social Model*. Routledge, London.
Goldberg, D. and Thornicroft, G. (eds) (1998) *Mental Health in Our Future Cities*. Psychology Press, Hove.
Goldberg, D., Bridges, K., Cooper, W., Hyde, C., Sterling, C. and Watt, R. (1985) Douglas House: a new type of hostel ward for chronic psychotic patients. *British Journal of Psychiatry* 147, 383–388.

Goldberg, D., Benjamin, S. and Creed, F. (1994) *Psychiatry in Medical Practice.* Routledge, London.

World Health Organization (1996) *Diagnostic and Management Guidelines for Mental Disorders in Primary Care ICD-10 Chapter V Primary Care Version.* Hogrefe and Huber, Göttingen.

FOREWORD 2

The contribution of David Goldberg: an overseas perspective

Scott Henderson

When I first met David Goldberg in 1968, he was working in Michael Shepherd's General Practice Research Unit in London. He shared a room with Robin Eastwood and was working on a new instrument with the innocuous name of the General Health Questionnaire (GHQ) (Goldberg, 1972). Thirty years on, this man's work has had an exceptional influence on world psychiatry. In examining that contribution, it is now possible to see its evolution and to recognise a continuity with his own father's work in public health. One indicator of its significance is the impact it has had on the literature. The Science and Social Science Citation Indexes taken together tell us that Goldberg's work has been cited in more than 6,000 publications by other researchers. Few individuals have had an impact of that magnitude.

Viewed from outside Europe, Goldberg has made three distinct contributions. First is the GHQ itself. Consider how many dissertations, theses and publications have used the GHQ as a core measure. It has been used in large population surveys, in primary care research and in innumerable clinical studies. Most medical students know about it. The GHQ has been translated into the European languages but also into Hebrew, Arabic, Urdu, Hindi, Cantonese, Vietnamese, Japanese and Bahasa Indonesia. One of our own postgraduate students, an Indonesian psychiatrist, successfully used the 30-item version in the Indonesian island of Sumatra, an environment that is distinctly different from Camberwell (Bahar *et al.* 1992). Is there any other instrument that has been taken up so widely?

The intention behind the construction of the GHQ is an example of its author's perspicacity, his capacity to select a useful long-term direction for his efforts. In the mid-1960s, Goldberg knew that a screening instrument would be very useful for the work being tackled in Shepherd's Unit. I think he knew at the same time that the psychological phenomena he was tapping were likely to be ubiquitous, transcending all cultures. He was therefore making an instrument not only for use in South London, but one of some international relevance. The GHQ is certainly remarkable for its cultural portability. Whatever version is used, few of the items need to be changed in their real meaning during translation. One amusing exception is the item, 'Have you been managing as well as most people would in your shoes?' In many parts of the world, shoes are uncommon, but the notion of not coping with daily life is universal. The psychometric properties of the GHQ, together with its acceptability in the community, have made it a major resource for 'the detection of psychiatric illness by questionnaire'. That was the title of its author's Maudsley Monograph (Goldberg, 1972) and the basis of his Doctorate of Medicine at Oxford. The GHQ is a remarkable resource.

In his years with Shepherd, Goldberg was the principal architect of another instrument, less well known but one which has recently played a part in a significant development in research methods. This is the Clinical Interview Schedule (CIS), a systematic psychiatric interview developed for use by clinicians (Goldberg *et al*. 1970). It was revised by Lewis *et al*. (1992) and later used in the National Psychiatric Morbidity Surveys of Great Britain (Jenkins *et al*. 1997). What is now emerging is the extent of the technical problems that have to be confronted when diagnostic interviews, semi-structured or fully structured, are used in unreferred samples of the general population (Brugha *et al*. in press). They produce different estimates and even identify different individuals as cases. So in making a semi-structured clinical interview in the 1960s, Goldberg has provided material for research problems that now have to be confronted. Their resolution will be of fundamental significance for psychiatric epidemiology.

Goldberg's second achievement is his research on mental disorders in primary care. From an overseas perspective, his research on what happens to mental disorders in that setting is considered to be the original uncovering of a pattern that occurs universally. Essentially, it says that a large proportion of people consulting doctors and health workers have psychological problems; only a proportion of them are recognized by doctors to have these; but this proportion can be altered by a systematic training package to improve the doctors' knowledge base and their behaviour in an interview. On an international front, Goldberg and his collaborators have now confirmed this ubiquitous pattern in the WHO Project on 'Psychological Problems in Primary Health Care' (Sartorius *et al*. 1993). The notion of filters along the pathway to care (Goldberg and Huxley, 1980) is a useful model for understanding what happens to people with psychological symptoms or common mental disorders. Some authors have since pointed out that the model is incomplete, being constructed from a medical perspective in which the sufferer is passive. It does not include the effects of mental health literacy on what happens to the sufferer or family. The latter can play a part in the process if they know a little about mental health. This is good research: the original model has helped other workers generate hypotheses, prompting a new generation of studies on the effect of mental health literacy on the use, or non-use, of services and on outcome (Jorm *et al.* 1999).

For administrative purposes, the part that appeals most strongly in Goldberg's work on general practice is where he has shown that some GPs can be trained to function much more effectively. This is now a matter of great interest to many Ministries of Health and the policy makers for mental health services. There is indeed more to it than recalibrating GPs' diagnostic capabilities and teaching them some basic counselling. There are other issues of equal importance for some countries, such as the problem of time and remuneration, or the effective use of other health workers alongside GPs.

In the course of his work on general practice, particularly in Manchester and with collaborating groups in other countries, Goldberg has amassed a great deal of data on symptoms. Sometimes he has had an opportunity to stand back from this corpus and to ask some fundamental questions about the manner in which common symptoms are distributed. It has been one of this writer's pleasures to have Goldberg come to our Centre to work on the application of latent trait analysis to these data with Paul Duncan-Jones and David Grayson. In their meetings, Goldberg's first degree in psychology revealed itself as he effortlessly absorbed the statistical principles. Their latent trait analyses of the general practice data led them to conclude that 'GPs underestimate the extent of psychiatric morbidity and their low slopes show that, even then, they are very unreliable. There is clearly much that psychiatric researchers can contribute in a primary care setting' (Grayson *et al.* 1987). The same data set showed that anxiety and depression are highly correlated, so 'there is an unbroken continuum of cases with various combinations of these two affects' (Goldberg *et al.* 1987, 1988). This is an aspect of Goldberg's research that stands apart from the rest because it leaves the domain of service operation and goes to the core issues of nosology. My impression is that he enjoyed that excursion. This theoretical work, linked as it was to Duncan-Jones' hypothesis about 'movers and stayers' (Duncan-Jones, 1987; Duncan-Jones *et al.* 1990), led to the attractive notion of destabilisation and restitution, together with identification of some factors at play in these shifts (Goldberg *et al.* 1990; Goldberg and Huxley, 1982). These are ideas that deserve to be taken further.

The third of Goldberg's contributions is that he has made face-to-face contact with so many across the world in the community of academic psychiatry. He is one of the best known figures in both hemispheres, a status earned not only through his scientific reputation but also by his having been to where people work. As with Frans Hals' 'Verdonck', none is spared his critical scrutiny, so this always brings extra zest to symposia. It has made him a key contributor at the Section of Epidemiology and Public Health in the World Psychiatric Association and the European Psychiatric Association. Goldberg has made himself travel widely. I think this is because he has wanted to learn about the needs for basic mental health care in other countries; because he correctly feels he has something to offer; and because his wife Ilfra and he have plenty of drive. Goldberg is a scientific colleague to many in North America, India, Pakistan, Burma, Singapore, Hong Kong, China, Japan and certainly in Australia and New Zealand. In many of these countries, there are psychiatrists and psychologists who have worked under him either in Manchester or London, some going on to hold influential chairs in medical schools. In our celebrating the impact that a person has made in professional life, this altricial component deserves special recognition. It is so enduring. Regarding Goldberg's drive, it was on one of his visits to Canberra that he said to me over breakfast, 'So what time is blast-off?' That is how he goes to work in the mornings. When he leaves the wheel-house on Denmark Hill, we hope he will continue to put some of his energy towards the vast agenda of psychiatry in public health.

References

Bahar, E., Henderson, A.S. and Mackinnon, A.J. (1992). An epidemiological study of mental health and socio-economic conditions in Sumatra, Indonesia. *Acta Psychiatrica Scandinavica* 85, 257–263.

Brugha, T., Bebbington, P. and Jenkins, R. (in press) 'A difference that matters: comparisons of structured and semi-structured psychiatric diagnostic interviews in the general population'. *Psychological Medicine*.

Duncan-Jones, P. (1987). Modelling the aetiology of neurosis: long-term and short-term factors. In B. Cooper (ed.) *Psychiatric Epidemiology: Progress and Prospects.* Croom Helm, London.

Duncan-Jones, P., Fergusson, D.M., Ormel, J. and Horwood, L.J. (1990). A model of stability and change in minor psychiatric symptoms: results from three longitudinal studies. *Psychological Medicine* 18, 1–28.

Goldberg, D.P. (1972). *The Detection of Psychiatric Illness by Questionnaire.* Oxford University Press, London.

Goldberg, D.P. and Huxley, P. (1980). *Mental Illness in the Community: The Pathway to Psychiatric Care.* Tavistock Publications, London.

Goldberg, D. and Huxley, P. (1982). *Common Mental Disorders: A Bio-Social Model.* Tavistock/Routledge, London.

Goldberg, D.P., Cooper, B., Eastwood, M.R., Kedward, H.B. and Shepherd, M. (1970). A standardized psychiatric interview for use in community surveys. *British Journal of Preventive and Social Medicine* 24, 18–23.

Goldberg, D.P., Bridges, K., Duncan-Jones, P. and Grayson, D. (1987). Dimensions of neuroses seen in primary care settings. *Psychological Medicine* 17, 461–470.

Goldberg, D., Bridges, K., Duncan-Jones, P. and Grayson, D. (1988). Detecting anxiety and depression in general medical settings. *British Medical Journal* 297, 897–899.

Goldberg, D., Bridges, K., Cook, D., Evans, B. and Grayson, D. (1990). The influence of social factors on common mental disorders: destablisation and restitution. *British Journal of Psychiatry* 156, 704–713.

Grayson, D.A., Bridges, K., Duncan-Jones, P. and Goldberg, D.P. (1987). The relationship between symptoms and diagnoses of minor psychiatric disorder in general practice. *Psychological Medicine* 17, 933–942.

Jenkins, R., Lewis, G., Bebbington, P., Brugha, T., Farrell, M., Gill, B. and Meltzer, H. (1997). The National Psychiatric Morbidity Surveys of Great Britain – initial findings from the household survey. *Psychological Medicine* 27, 775–789.

Jorm, A.F., Korten, A.E., Rodgers, B., Pollitt, P., Jacomb, P.A., Christensen, H. and Jiao, Z. (1997). Belief systems of the general public concerning the appropriate treatments for mental disorders. *Social Psychiatry and Psychiatric Epidemiology* 32, 468–473.

Jorm, A.F., Angermeyer, M. and Katschnig, H. (1999). Public knowledge and attitudes about mental disorders: A limiting factor in the optimal use of treatment services. In G. Andrews and A.S. Henderson (eds) *The Unmet Need for Treatment*. Cambridge University Press, Cambridge.

Lewis, G., Pelosi, A.J., Araya, R. and Dunn, G. (1992). Measuring psychiatric disorder in the community: a standardized assessment for use by lay interviewers. *Psychological Medicine* 22, 465–486.

Sartorius, N., Üstün, T.B., Costa e Silva, J.-A., Goldberg, D., Lecrubier, Y., Ormel, J., Von Korff, M. and Wittchen, H.-U. (1993). An international study of psychological problems in primary care. *Archives of General Psychiatry* 50, 819–824.

Part I

THE NATURE OF THE PROBLEM

EPIDEMIOLOGY OF MENTAL DISORDERS IN THE COMMUNITY AND PRIMARY CARE

José Luis Vázquez-Barquero, Andrés Herrán and Jesús Artal Simón

Primary care has become the centrepiece of programmes for managing mental health problems. Recent studies have found that 10 per cent of the general population consult their general practitioner (GP) for a new illness, and that one out of five of such consultations can be attributed to the presence of mental illness. However, less than 50 per cent of psychiatric disorders are detected by the GP, and only a minority of patients is ever seen by a mental health specialist. In addition, it has been recently established that the disabilities generated by mental illness are as severe, or even more so, than those derived from major medical conditions (Murray and Lopez, 1997). These findings have contributed to a renewal of research interest in this field, and stimulated the development of epidemiological studies and programmes focusing on the management of mental illness by the GP. In order to explore how these aims are achieved, we will analyse the epidemiology of mental disorders in both the community and primary care, following Goldberg and Huxley's innovative model (1980) which describes the extent and nature of mental illness in the community and in the different levels of care. We will, therefore, analyse in this chapter: the distribution of psychiatric morbidity in the general population; the process of establishing medical contact with the GP; the characteristics of mental illness in primary care services; and the detection and management of mental illness by the GP.

The epidemiology of mental illness in the community

Prevalence rates in the community show, even in the most recent surveys, a high degree of variation. This is undoubtedly due to the existence of methodological differences, especially those involving variations in the instruments used for psychopathological assessment. Instruments for the study of mental disorders fall into two main categories: symptom scales

Table 1.1 Prevalence of mental disorders in the community

Author(s)	Instrument	n	Place	Prevalence of mental illness (%)		
(Duration of prevalence rates)				Male	Female	Total
Vázquez-Barquero et al., 1987 (One month)	PSE-ID	1,223	Spain	8.1	20.6	14.3
Canino et al., 1987 (Six months) (Lifetime)	DIS	1,513	Puerto Rico	18.7 34.0	13.4 22.8	16.0 28.1
Regier et al., 1988 (One month)	DIS	18,571	USA	14.0	16.6	15.3
Bland et al., 1988 (Six months)	DIS	3,258	Edmonton, Canada	18.9	15.3	17.1
Lehtinen et al., 1990 (One month)	PSE-ID	742	Finland	6.9	12.4	9.7
Kessler et al., 1994 (One year) (Lifetime)	UM-CIDI	8,098	USA	27.7 48.7	31.2 47.3	29.5 48.0
Offord et al., 1996 (One year)	UM-CIDI	9,953	Ontario, Canada	17.9	19.4	18.6

Notes
DIS   Diagnostic Interview Schedule
PSE   Present State Examination
UM-CIDI University of Michigan Composite International Diagnostic Interview

and psychiatric interviews. While symptom scales are generally used to quantify a previously diagnosed disorder, or to identify the probability that a person meets 'caseness' criteria, standardised psychiatric interviews, e.g. the Schedules for Clinical Assessment in Neuropsychiatry (SCAN) (Wing et al. 1990; Vázquez-Barquero et al. 1994), are always used for establishing a diagnosis. A symptom scale that is often used (e.g. in two-phase psychiatric epidemiological surveys) to identify those in the sample who have a high or low probability of presenting a mental disorder is the General Health Questionnaire (GHQ) (Goldberg and Williams, 1988). We have, for example, recently explored the extent and the nature of mental illness in four primary care services by using GHQ in the first phase of a two-phase design, and the SCAN in the second phase (Vázquez-Barquero et al. 1997).

In two-phase designs, the psychiatric interview introduced in the second phase constitutes the gold standard for psychiatric diagnosis. It should be noted, however, in view of their methodological implications, that there are two main types of standardised psychiatric interviews. The first is represented by semi-structured interviews which, like the SCAN or its predecessor the Present State Examination (PSE), are designed for being applied by trained research clinicians. The second type has been developed for use by non-specialists, featuring closed questions, and with only a very few of the items calling for any judgement. The Diagnostic Interview Schedule (DIS) (Robins et al. 1981) and the Composite International Diagnostic Interview (CIDI) (Robins et al. 1988) are the best known examples of this second type of interview. The methodological implications of this new generation of instruments are derived from the fact that they ensure the minimisation of the information and criterion variance. However, it should be recognised that the selection of either of these two types of instruments has an impact over the prevalence rates detected for each of the different disorders. Examples of surveys conducted over the last decade in the general population, using this design and these instruments, are shown in Table 1.1.

The prevalence rates of reported mental disorders range from 10-30 per cent, with most studies showing higher rates for females. There is now a great deal of evidence indicating that women's higher psychiatric morbidity is due mainly to their higher prevalence of common disorders, e.g. minor depressive and anxiety disorders. In the case of men, the rate of other disorders such as substance abuse or antisocial personality disorder, tends to be much higher. This is clearly shown in the survey conducted by Canino et al. (1987), which concludes that the male predominance of psychiatric morbidity is due to their higher prevalence of alcohol-related problems. The way in which socio-demographic variables condition the prevalence of mental disorders in each gender is cultural in nature, and should be interpreted in the light of each community's idiosyncrasies (Vázquez-Barquero, 1990).

The prevalence of specific mental disorders is shown in Table 1.2. In the 'Epidemiologic Catchment Area Survey' (ECA), conducted by the National

Table 1.2 Prevalence of specific mental disorders in the community

| Author(s) (Place) | Instrument (Duration of prevalence rates) | Prevalence (%) | | | | | | | |
| | | Affective disorders | | Anxiety disorders | | Schizophrenia non-affective psychoses | | Alcohol/other substances abuse | |
		M	F	M	F	M	F	M	F
Mavreas et al., 1986 (Athens)	PSE	4.3	10.1	3.9	12.1	0.4	0.0		
Canino et al., 1987 (Puerto Rico)	DIS (Six months)	2.4	3.4	4.7	9.9	2.1	1.3	10.0	0.5
Bland et al., 1988 (Edmonton, Canada)	DIS (Six months)	3.8	7.6	5.0	8.0	0.4	0.2	10.5	2.1
Regier et al., 1988 (USA)	DIS (One month)	3.5	6.6	4.7	9.7	0.7	0.7	5.0	0.9
Bebbington et al., 1981 (England)	PSE (One month)	4.8	9.0	1.0	4.5	0.3	0.0		
Kessler et al., 1994 (USA)	CIDI (One year)	8.5	14.1	11.8	22.6	0.5	0.6	14.1	5.3
Offord et al., 1996 (Ontario, Canada)	CIDI (One year)	2.8	5.4	5.4	7.9			8.2	2.1

Notes
CIDI   Composite International Diagnostic Interview
DIS   Diagnostic Interview Schedule
PSE   Present State Examination
M   Males
F   Females

Institute of Mental Health (Regier *et al.* 1988), the main goal was to determine the prevalence of mental disorders as defined by the third edition of the Diagnostic and Statistical Manual of Mental Disorders (DSM-III). Symptoms were assessed by lay interviewers, using the DIS. The principal findings were that rates of depression were twice as high for females as for males; that males were more likely to present alcohol dependence; and that substance abuse was more common in people under 30 years old. Later surveys, such as the one that we conducted in northern Spain, have confirmed that the higher female morbidity is due to a significant rise in detected phobic, anxiety, and depressive disorders (Vázquez-Barquero *et al.* 1987).

In addition, the findings of the *'National Comorbidity Survey'* (Kessler *et al.* 1994) revealed that the prevalence of psychiatric disorders was much greater than previously believed. They also found that psychiatric morbidity was concentrated in one-sixth of the population, comprising individuals with a history of three or more comorbid disorders. Major depression, alcohol dependence and anxiety were the most prevalent diagnoses. It is noteworthy that even among those people with a lifetime history of three or more comorbid mental disorders, the proportion who ever obtained mental health treatment at the specialised level of care was less than 50 per cent. This clearly indicates the importance of developing strategies to act on the barriers to patients' help-seeking behaviour.

The act of contacting primary care settings (and related delays)

We recently conducted a research project at different primary care centres from two provinces in the north of Spain (Vázquez-Barquero *et al.* 1997), and found that 10.9 per cent of men and 15.0 per cent of women from the general population consulted their GP for a new illness. These figures are much lower than our previous findings, from the Cantabria Community Survey (Vázquez-Barquero *et al.* 1987), also conducted in northern Spain, in which we detected a contact rate of 23.1 per cent for males and of 33.9 per cent for females. The more recent lower rates may be due to the fact that in the Cantabria Survey we included all types of consultation, and not only those related to new illnesses.

Although physical problems are the principal cause of consultation, it has been shown that the presence of psychiatric illness doubles the probability of consulting a GP. Likewise, we have demonstrated in our studies that approximately 15.5 per cent of consultations by men and 20.3 per cent of consultations by women can be attributed to the presence of psychiatric disorders, i.e. they would not have occurred in the absence of mental illness. In addition to the presence of physical and mental illness, sociodemographic factors also play a relevant role in promoting GP consultations. The most firmly established sociodemographic factor refers to gender differences

(Goldberg and Huxley, 1980; Williams *et al.* 1990), women being more likely to establish medical contact than men. The incidence of consultation also tends to rise with advancing age. The influence of other sociodemographic factors appears to be less important in consultation, and conflicting results have been reported in the recent literature.

Physician utilisation is determined by societal, systemic, and individual factors. Societal factors include aspects such as attitudes and beliefs about illness. Systemic factors are related to health service structure and organisation, and other aspects of that nature. Individual variables include those related to the illness itself, predisposing variables (how disposed is a person to establish medical contact), and enabling variables (conditions that facilitate or inhibit the use of resources) (Vázquez-Barquero, 1990). More recent studies, however, have not confirmed the relevance of this set of variables to consultation. In fact, in these studies most of the variance could be explained by illness-related variables, with predisposing and enabling variables being least relevant to help-seeking behaviour. Accordingly, Goldberg and Huxley (1992) conclude their review of this topic by indicating that higher scores on the GHQ double the chance of a GP consultation, and that 20 per cent of consultations could be attributable to mental disorders.

A recent area of research on the process by which psychiatric patients establish contact with services is represented by the study of the pathways to psychiatric care conducted by the WHO in different countries (see: Gater *et al.* 1991; Vázquez-Barquero *et al.* 1993). In this study, it was found that in the industrialised countries (mainly in Europe), between two-thirds and four-fifths of patients established first contact with a GP. In less-developed countries, on the other hand, the pathways were less well defined, and the contact tended to be established with religious leaders and hospital physicians, while only one-quarter of patients established first contact with a GP. The same study found that delays were remarkably short in all centres regardless of psychiatric resources, although longer delays were found at some centres involving native healers. A major finding of this project was that services with more psychiatrists were associated with predominantly medical referral pathways. In addition, there was no evidence that having more staff resulted in less delay in obtaining care. Finally, although somatic symptoms were the most common initial presentation, patients with these problems did seem to be referred on more slowly at some centres. In Cantabria, we found that in a rural health area the majority of newly referred patients established first contact with a GP, and to a lesser extent with a hospital doctor. On the other hand, in an urban health area there was a greater tendency to contact first with specialised medical and psychiatric services. A representation of the pathways in this study is represented in Figure 1.1.

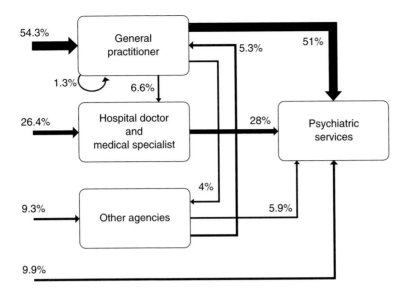

Figure 1.1 Main pathways to psychiatric care in Cantabria (*Source:* adapted from Vázquez-Barquero *et al.* 1993)

The extent and nature of mental illness in primary care settings

Many studies have investigated the extent and nature of mental illness in primary care settings. These studies, which were originally conducted in Western countries with well-developed healthcare systems, have recently been extended to countries with less advanced healthcare systems, thus offering the opportunity for comparisons between different systems and levels of care.

In primary care settings, the analysis of the prevalence of mental disorders could be performed by applying any of the following three strategies of psychopathological evaluation: identification of psychiatric disturbance by the attending GP; evaluation of psychiatric 'caseness' by the administration of screening instruments; and psychiatric evaluation using a diagnostic interview. We will therefore analyse the prevalence rates found in primary care settings according to each of these psychiatric identification strategies.

Mental disorders in primary care as diagnosed by the GP

Several recent studies have analysed the prevalence of mental disorders in primary care settings according to GP diagnosis. An important, and well known, study is the international multi-centre project conducted by the WHO at 15 centres in 14 countries (Sartorius *et al.* 1993; Üstün and

Sartorius, 1995). This two-phase study evaluated more than 25,000 primary care patients in the first phase, using the GHQ-12 as the screening instrument. In the second phase, 5,000 patients were evaluated, using the primary care version of the CIDI. In the 12-month follow-up, the prevalence of mental disorders identified by the primary care physician was 23.4 per cent. It is noteworthy, however, that the prevalence figures varied widely across centres, from 5.4 per cent in Shanghai to 58.5 per cent in Santiago (Goldberg and Lecrubier, 1995). Similar figures have also been found in other recent studies. For example, Commander *et al.* (1997) studying 823 cases in Birmingham, found that GPs diagnosed 23 per cent of patients with psychological problems, and Al-Jaddou and Malkawi (1997), in northern Jordan, showed that GPs identified psychiatric illness in 24 per cent of their patients. Similarly, at four primary care centres in northern Spain, we found a prevalence of mental disorders, according to GP criteria, of 33 per cent (Vázquez-Barquero *et al.* 1997).

Thus, we can arrive at two major conclusions: first, in recent surveys GPs have identified mental illness in approximately one-fourth of their patients; and second, the rate of mental disorders diagnosed by primary care physicians varies a great deal, with the most recent studies showing higher prevalence figures. The differences across studies (from 5 per cent to 40 per cent) probably reflects variations in methodology, rather than real differences in morbidity. We have to recognise, however, that this argument has yet to be verified, in view of the fact that even in studies using a uniform methodological design (e.g. the WHO survey), there are still wide differences across the different populations.

A related area of research that has been promoted in the last few years, and which we will analyse further in a later part of this chapter, is directed at comparing the rates of mental disorders detected by the GP, and those found by diagnostic instruments. This is, we will see, an important area, because it tends to incorporate the explorations of the factors that influence primary care physicians' recognition of mental disorders.

Mental disorders diagnosed by screening and diagnostic instruments

Screening instruments have often been used to assess psychiatric morbidity in primary care, the reason being that they are easy to administer and therefore constitute an inexpensive case detection strategy. The screening instrument most frequently applied in recent studies is the General Health Questionnaire (GHQ). The prevalence figures for probable psychiatric morbidity detected across different studies with this instrument are around 40 per cent. However, this 'probable prevalence' must be considered merely as an estimate of the 'real' prevalence of mental disorders, which in fact should be verified during the second phase of the survey by a structured psychiatric interview. Thus, in primary care surveys, psychiatric evaluation by structured interviews remains the most reliable method. The prevalence figures for mental illness detected with structured psychiatric interviews in some of the most relevant recent surveys conducted in primary care settings are shown in Table 1.3.

An example of the prevalence rates detected for the different disorders can be seen in Table 1.4, showing the prevalence rates that we found in four primary care centres from northern Spain. The rates detected in other recent surveys are generally similar.

The identification and management of mental illness in primary care

An important objective of research in this area has been the study of GPs' ability to correctly diagnose and treat psychiatric disorders. Recent studies tend to indicate that GPs vary considerably in their ability to detect psychiatric illness and that, in general, they do not recognise a substantial proportion of these health problems. The prevalence figures reported by most studies range from 14.3 per cent to 42 per cent. Such rates imply that the GP only identifies around 50 per cent of the patients detected by questionnaires such as the GHQ, or by psychiatrists using standardised diagnostic interviews (Higgins, 1994). As Docherty (1997) has recently pointed out, barriers to recognition and diagnosis in primary care could be divided into 'patient barriers' and 'physician barriers'. The first group includes lack of awareness regarding the nature of depression, and variations in clinical presentation, such as comorbidity with medical illness, degree of somatisation, and feelings of shame or guilt. Physician barriers to recognition of mental illness in primary care would include beliefs and attitudes (e.g. self-confidence and comfort with psychological issues), and knowledge and skills (including the ability to direct and systematically inquire about mood disturbance and to accurately assess non-verbal signs). In addition, the studies of Goldberg and colleagues (e.g. Goldberg et al. 1993) have shown which physician behaviours influence the rates at which patients emit cues that could lead to a diagnosis. These findings have had a decisive impact on programmes directed at improving recognition by GPs.

Studies on GPs' management of primary care patients have focused mainly on the pharmacological treatments that they prescribe. In Spain, we found that 7 per cent of the population was receiving psychotropics. The figures were higher for females, and were also associated with patients' health (Vázquez-Barquero et al. 1989). In a meta-analysis of studies comparing the effects of psychiatric treatments prescribed by mental health professionals and GPs in general practice settings, Balestrieri and colleagues found that although psychiatrists had a higher success rate, the difference was slight,

Table 1.3 Recent surveys of mental health in primary care

Author(s)	Place	n	First-stage instrument	Second-stage instrument	Psychiatric prevalence (%)
Von Korff et al. (1992)	USA	1,242	GHQ-28	DIS	25
Barret et al. (1988)	USA	1,055	SCL-S	SADS	26.5
Dhadphale et al. (1989)	Kenya	881	SRQ	SPI	25
Martínez et al. (1993)	Spain	500	GHQ-28	PSE	19
Ormel et al. (1990)	Netherlands	1,450	GHQ-30	PSE	15
Fink et al. (1995)	Five Nordic countries	1,309	SCL-25	PSE	26
Chocrón et al. (1995)	Spain	400	GHQ-28	CIS	38.8
Goldberg and Lecrubier (1995)	14 countries	26,442	GHQ-12	CIDI	24
Vázquez-Barquero et al. (1997)	Spain	823	GHQ28	SCAN	31.5

CIDI	Composite International Diagnostic Interview
CIS	Clinical Interview Schedule
DIS	Diagnostic Interview Schedule
GHQ	General Health Questionnaire
PSE	Present State Examination
SADS	Schedule for Affective Disorders and Schizophrenia
SCAN	Schedules for Clinical Assessment in Neuropsychiatry
SCL-25	Hopkins Symptom Checklist
SCL-S	20-Item Depression Scale
SPI	Standardised Psychiatric Interview
SRQ	Self-Reporting Questionnaire

Table 1.4 Prevalence of different diagnoses using the SCAN system

Diagnosis	Prevalence % (s.e.)	
	Males	Females
Psycho-organic (F02, F07.0)	1.9 (1.1)	1.4 (0.7)
Psychosis (F20.3, F28)	4.7 (4.0)	0.3 (0.3)
Depression (F33.2, F32.0, F32)	2.5 (1.3)	7.1 (2.6)
Dysthymia (F34.1)	1.2 (0.9)	3.6 (1.2)
Cyclothymia (F34.0)	1.2 (0.9)	0.0 (0.0)
Panic attacks (F41.0, F42.1)	0.6 (0.6)	0.7 (0.5)
General anxiety (F41.1)	1.9 (1.1)	18.5 (4.5)
Obsessive-compulsive disorder (F42.1)	0.6 (0.6)	0.3 (0.3)
Anorexia nervosa (F50.1)	0.0 (0.0)	2.3 (2.3)
Alcoholism (F10.10)	1.2 (0.9)	0.7 (0.5)
Alcohol dependence (F10.40, F10.33)	5.3 (4.0)	0.0 (0.0)
Alcohol abstinence (F15.10, F11.10)	0.6 (0.6)	0.0 (0.0)
Phobia (F40)	0.0 (0.0)	1.4 (0.7)
Total psychiatric pathology	22.3 (6.2)	36.7 (5.5)

Source: Vázquez-Barquero *et al.* 1997

being only 10 per cent higher than the one obtained by GPs (Balestrieri *et al.* 1988).

The importance of these findings lies in recognising: (1) that the correct identification and management of mental illness in these settings has a major impact, not only on mitigating patients' suffering, but also on reducing their consumption of health resources; however, there is still a certain amount of controversy on this point (Tiemens and Ormel, 1996), and (2) that with the development of adequate educational strategies, the doctor's ability to reach a correct psychiatric diagnosis and to perform an appropriate treatment for these disorders could be improved.

It is therefore easy to understand why a large proportion of recent studies in this area include, as one of their objectives, the study of GPs' ability to identify and manage psychiatric pathology, and also why they are often linked to the development of programmes directed at improving GPs' ability to manage mental illness. A good example of the combination of these different objectives is the work conducted over the years by the Manchester Group (Goldberg, 1995). As shown by Higgins (1994) in his recent review of the literature, most training programmes are effective in improving the detection

of mental illness by the GP. This review also indicates that educational programmes are the ideal method for improving recognition and management of
mental illness in primary care.

References

Al-Jaddou, H. and Malkawi, A. (1997) Prevalence, recognition and management of
mental disorders in primary care in Northern Jordan. *Acta Psychiatrica Scandinavica*
96, 31–35.

Balestrieri, M., Williams, P., Wilkinson, G. (1988) Specialist mental health treatment in general practice, a meta-analysis. *Psychological Medicine* 18, 711–717.

Barret, J.E., Barret, J.A., Oxman, T.E., Gerber, P.D. (1988) The prevalence of
psychiatric disorders in primary care practice. *Archives of General Psychiatry* 45,
1100–1106.

Bebbington, P.E., Hurry, J., Tennant, C. (1981) The epidemiology of mental disorders in Camberwell. *Psychological Medicine* 11, 561–580.

Bland, R.C., Newman, S.C., Orn, H. (1988) Period prevalence of psychiatric disorders
in Edmonton. *Acta Psychiatrica Scandinavica* 77 (suppl 338), 33–42.

Canino, G.J., Bird, H.R., Shrout, P.E., Rubio-Stipec, M., Bravo, M., Martínez, R.,
Sesman, M., Guevara, L.M. (1987) The prevalence of specific psychiatric disorders
in Puerto Rico. *Archives of General Psychiatry* 44, 725–735.

Chocrón, L., Vilalta, J., Legazpi, I., Auquer, K., Franch, L. (1995) Prevalencia de
psicopatología en un centro de Atención Primaria. *Atencion Primaria* 16, 586–593.

Commander, M.J., Sashi, S.P., Odell, S.M., Surtees, P.G. (1997) Access to mental
health care in an inner-city health district. I: pathways into and within specialist
psychiatric services. *British Journal of Psychiatry* 170, 312–316.

Dhadphale, M., Cooper, G., Cartwright-Taylor, L. (1989) Prevalence and presentation
of depressive illness in primary health care setting in Kenya. *American Journal of
Psychiatry* 146, 659–661.

Docherty, J.P. (1997) Barriers to the diagnosis of depression in primary care. *Journal
of Clinical Psychiatry* 58 (suppl 1), 5–10.

Fink, P., Jensen, J., Borgquist, L., Brevik, J.I., Dalgard, O.S., Sandager, I., Engberg,
M., Hansson, L., Holm, M., Joukamaa, M., Karlsson, H., Lehtinen, V., Nettelbladt,
P., Nordström, G., Steffanson, C.G., Sørensen, L. and Munk-Jørgensen, P. (1995)
Psychiatric morbidity in primary public health care, a Nordic multicentre
investigation. *Acta Psychiatrica Scandinavica* 92, 409–418.

Gater, R., de Almeida e Sousa, B., Barrientos, G., Caraveo, J., Chandrashekar, C.R.,
Dhadphale, M., Goldberg, D., Al Kathiri, A.H., Mubbashar, M., Silhan, K.,
Thong, D., Torres-Gonzales, F. and Sartorius, N. (1991) The pathways to psychia-
tric care, a cross-cultural study. *Psychological Medicine* 21, 761–774.

Goldberg, D. (1995) Epidemiology of mental disorder in primary care settings.
Epidemiologic Review 17, 182–190.

Goldberg, D. and Huxley, P. (1980) *Mental Illness in General Practice.* London,
Tavistock.

—— (1992) *Common Mental Disorders. A bio-social model.* London, Tavistock/
Routledge.

Goldberg, D.P. and Lecrubier, Y. (1995) Form and frequency of mental disorders
across centres. In: T.B. Üstün and N. Sartorius (eds) *Mental Illness in General
Health Care. An international study.* Chichester, Wiley.

Goldberg, D. and Williams, P. (1988) *A User's Guide to the GHQ*. London, NFER Nelson.

Goldberg, D.P., Jenkins, L., Millar, T. and Faragher, E.B. (1993) The ability of trainee general practitioners to identify psychological distress among their patients. *Psychological Medicine* 23, 185–193.

Higgins, E.S. (1994) A review of unrecognised mental illness in primary care. *Archives of Family Medicine* 3, 908–917.

Kessler, R.C., McGonagle, K.A., Zhao, S., Nelson, C.B., Hughes, M., Eshleman, S., Wittchen, H.U. and Kendler, K.S. (1994) Lifetime and 12-month prevalence of DSM-III-R psychiatric disorders in the United States. Results from the National Comorbidity Survey. *Archives of General Psychiatry* 51, 8–19.

Lehtinen, V., Lindholm, T., Veijola, J., Väisänen, E. (1990) The prevalence of PSE-Catego disorders in a Finnish adult population cohort. *Social Psychiatry and Psychiatric Epidemiology* 25, 187–192.

Martínez, J.M., Marijuán, L., Retolaza, A., Duque, A. and Cascán, J.M. (1993) Estudio de morbilidad psiquiátrica en la población atendida en el centro de salud de Basauri. *Atencion Primaria* 11, 127–132.

Mavreas, V.G., Beis, A. and Mouyias, A. (1986) Prevalence of psychiatric disorders in Athens, A community study. *Social Psychiatry and Psychiatric Epidemiology* 4, 172–181.

Murray, C.J.L. and Lopez, A.D. (1997) Global mortality, disability, and the contribution of risk factors: Global Burden of Disease Study. *Lancet* 349, 1436–1442.

Offord, D.R., Boyle, M.H., Campbell, D., Goering, P., Lin, E., Wong, M. and Racine, Y.A. (1996) One year prevalence of psychiatric disorder in Ontarians 15 to 64 years of age. *Canadian Journal of Psychiatry* 41, 559–563.

Ormel, J., van den Brink, W., Koeter, M.V.J., Giel, R., van der Mee, K.R., van de Willige, G. and Wilmink, F.W. (1990) Recognition, management and outcome of psychological disorders in primary care, a naturalistic follow-up study. *Psychological Medicine* 20, 909–923.

Regier, D.A., Boyd, J.H., Burke, J.D. *et al.* (1988) One-month prevalence of mental disorders in the United States. Based on five epidemiologic catchment area sites. *Archives of General Psychiatry* 45, 977–986.

Robins, L.N., Helzer, J.E. and Croughan, J. (1981) National Institute of Mental Health Diagnostic Interview Schedule. Its history, characteristics, and validity. *Archives of General Psychiatry* 38, 381–388.

Robins, L.N., Wing, J. and Wittchen, H.-U. (1988) The Composite International Diagnostic Interview. *Archives of General Psychiatry* 45, 1069–1077.

Sartorius, N., Üstün, B., Costa e Silva, J.A., Goldberg, D., Lecrubier, Y., Ormel, J., Von Korff, M. and Wittchen, H. (1993) An international study of psychological problems in primary care. *Archives of General Psychiatry* 50, 819–824.

Tiemens, B.G., Ormel, J. (1996) The capricious relationship between recognition and outcome of mental illness in primary care. *Epidemiologia e Psichiatria Sociale* 5, 160–163.

Üstün, T.B. and Sartorius, N. (1995) *Mental Illness in General Health Care. An international study*. Chichester; Wiley.

Vázquez-Barquero, J.L. (1990) Mental health in primary-care settings. In: D. Goldberg and D. Tantam (eds) *The public health impact of mental disorder*. Toronto, Hogrefe and Huber Publishers.

Vázquez-Barquero, J.L., Díez-Manrique, J.F., Peña, C., Aldama, J., Samaniego Rodriguez, C., Menéndez-Arango, J. and Mirapeix, C. (1987) A community mental health survey in Cantabria, A general description of morbidity. *Psychological Medicine* 17, 227–241.

Vázquez-Barquero, J.L., Díez-Manrique, J.F., Peña, C., Arenal, A., Cuesta, M.J. and Artal, J.A. (1989) Patterns of psychotropic drug use in a Spanish rural community. *British Journal of Psychiatry* 155, 633–641.

Vázquez-Barquero, J.L., Herrera Castanedo, S., Artal, J.A., Cuesta, M.J., Nuñez, J., Gaite, L., Goldberg, D. and Sartorius, N. (1993) Pathways to psychiatric care in Cantabria. *Acta Psychiatrica Scandinavica* 88, 229–234.

Vázquez-Barquero, J.L., Gaite, L., Artal, J., Arenal, A., Herrera, S., Díez-Manrique, J.F., Cuesta, M.J. and Higuera, A. (1994) Desarrollo y verificación de la versión Española de la entrevista psiquiátrica 'Sistema SCAN' (cuestionarios para la evaluación clínica en neuropsiquiatría). *Actas Luso-Espanolas de neurología y Psiquiatría* 22, 109–120.

Vázquez-Barquero, J.L., García, J., Artal, J., Iglesias, C., Montejo, J., Herrán, A. and Dunn, G. (1997) Mental health in primary care. An epidemiological study of morbidity and use of health resources. *British Journal of Psychiatry* 170, 529–535.

Von Korff, M., Ormel, K., Katon, W. and Lin, E.H.B. (1992) Disability and depression among high utilizers of health care. *Archives of General Psychiatry* 49, 91–100.

Williams, P., Wilkinson, G. and Arreghini, E. (1990) The determinants of help-seeking for psychological disorders in primary health care settings. In: N. Sartorius, D. Goldberg, G. de Girolamo, J.A. Costa e Silva, Y. Lecrubier and H.U. Wittchen (eds) (1990) *Psychological Disorders in General Medical Settings*. Toronto, Hogrefe and Huber Publishers.

Wing, J.K., Babor, T., Brugha, T., Cooper, J.E., Giel, R., Jablensky, A., Regier, A. and Sartorius, N. (1990) SCAN: Schedules for Clinical Assessment in Neuropsychiatry. *Archives of General Psychiatry* 47, 589–593.

2

MAKING SENSE OF SEROTONIN (5HT) AND ITS ROLE IN COMMON PSYCHOPATHOLOGY

J.F. William Deakin

Introduction

It was a great pleasure to speak at the Institute in September 1998, particularly to see my good friend and collaborator Sir David in his post-Manchester department. Latterly in Manchester, Sir David and I converged from our different starting points in social psychiatry and biological psychiatry to a common interest in brain mechanisms of vulnerability and destabilisation in common psychopathologies (Goldberg and Huxley, 1992; Deakin *et al.* 1990). Sir David initiated our formal collaboration in a study of surreal size and logistical complexity which examined interactions between biological, clinical and psychosocial measures in women in the community. We persuaded the Wellcome Trust to fund us and, amazingly, we completed the study in nearly 500 women. I presented some of the results in the lecture. It was also pleasing to speak at the Institute because I was inspired into biological psychiatry by the speculations of Hans Eysenck and then Jeffrey Gray on the neurobiology of personality (Gray, 1987). Furthermore, someone told me they had seen, in the Institute library, a copy of my PhD thesis on the behavioural functions of 5HT in the rat. This reminded me that the late Ted Marley at the Institute was my London University co-supervisor with Tim Crow. So for many reasons it was meet and right and satisfying to talk about the neurotransmitter that has interested me throughout my research career – 5HT.

An edited and updated version of the lecture – Introduction

Abnormal 5HT function has been implicated in a bewildering array, a veritable alphabet of diseases – alcoholism, anorexia and Alzheimer's disease to mention three that begin with 'A'. It is certainly interesting that abnormal

5HT function has been found in these disorders and that many of them respond to drugs which affect 5HT function. Nevertheless, one yearns for a deeper structure, some simplifying principle which binds all the observations together. This is only going to come from understanding the normal functions of 5HT; what sorts of stimuli normally release 5HT and what psychological processes does it influence? Only when these questions are answered can we understand how symptoms arise when 5HT systems become disturbed. In this talk I am going to argue that 5HT systems are normally activated by aversive stimuli and that this facilitates adaptive coping responses (Deakin and Graeff, 1991; Deakin, 1996). In a nutshell, 5HT systems help prevent us from getting into trouble and if we do get into trouble, 5HT systems help us put up with it. Disturbances in 5HT coping mechanisms are mechanisms of common neurotic psychopathologies.

The right way to think about 5HT is as a diffuse modulatory neurotransmitter which influences information processing in various hardwired circuits in the forebrain. The concept that 5HT has a unitary role as an anxiety or punishment system is no longer compatible with experimental and clinical evidence. There are two main anatomically and pharmacologically distinct 5HT systems which I suggest are also functionally distinct (see Figure 2.1). 5HT neurones in the dorsal raphe nucleus (DRN) give rise to thin fibres with varicosities along them. They innervate 5HT2 receptors in areas of the brain which also receive a parallel dopaminergic innervation – structures involved in locomotor guidance like the basal ganglia, frontal cortex and nucleus accumbens. Dopamine's influence is to direct attention and locomotion to positive incentive stimuli at a distance in the environment (Schulz et al. 1998). My suggestion is that the DRN 5HT2 system has the opposing function of guiding the organism away from danger cues in the environment (Deakin, 1983). Cells of the median raphe nucleus (MRN) send

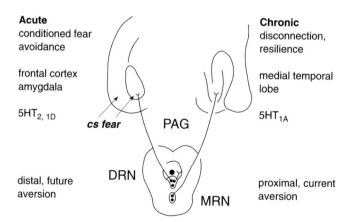

Figure 2.1 Differential role of 5HT pathways in adaptive responses to aversion

thick, non-varicose fibres to cortical structures that receive a noradrenergic innervation. MRN terminals innervate primarily 5HT1A receptors. Noradrenaline has been implicated in the processing of cues currently in the environment – enhancing the signal to noise ratio for example. My suggestion is that the MRN 5HT1A system reduces processing of current aversive stimuli and memories. This promotes resilience in the face of persistent adversity.

There is certainly evidence that 5HT systems are activated by aversive stimuli and most behavioural experiments using, for example, the techniques of in-vivo dialysis, now show that quite mild aversive stimuli substantially increase 5HT release (Bickerdike, Wright and Marsden, 1993). It is likely that this happens mostly by pre-terminal modulation of the amount of 5HT released per nerve-impulse because the rate of firing of 5HT cell bodies is rather steady (Jacobs and Fornal, 1991).

Three types of aversive stimuli and three coping mechanisms

There are many kinds of aversive stimuli (see Figure 2.2) which elicit different kinds of adaptive responses. According to this formulation, 5HT has different actions according to the type of aversive event.

Proximal aversive stimuli – escape reflexes

Proximal aversive stimuli are contact stimuli such as pain or asphyxia. They are unconditioned stimuli that elicit the unconditioned fight–flight reflex – a hardwired emergency response to impending death. This reflex is mediated by the brain aversion system (BAS) which runs from amygdala through

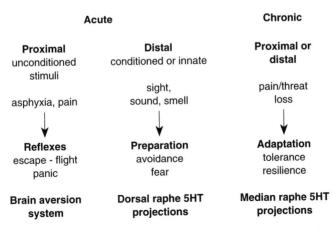

Figure 2.2 Different coping mechanisms for different types of aversive stimuli

19

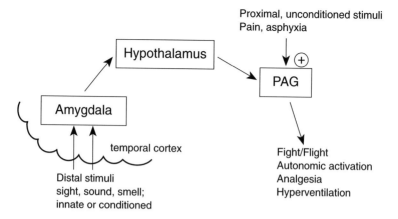

Figure 2.3 Brain Aversion System (BAS)

hypothalamus to the periaqueductal grey matter (PAG; Figure 2.3). It was discovered by the dramatic effects of electrical stimulation of the PAG in freely behaving animals – they run round the cage attempting to escape in a very undirected way. They will attack other animals present. They defecate and urinate and there is autonomic activation and analgesia. Stimulation of the PAG in humans during neurosurgical operations causes dramatic fearful experiences with autonomic activation and an intense desire to escape – a hallmark of a panic attack (see Deakin and Graeff, 1991). A number of people have suggested that panic attacks are due to spontaneous activation of the BAS.

Distal aversive stimuli – anxiety, avoidance and restraint of flight

Distal aversive stimuli are detected by distance receptors – sights, sounds and smells that warn of impending unconditioned stimuli (second column, Figure 2.2). They elicit preparatory responses to prevent contact with noxious stimuli. I suggested that DRN projections are activated during states of anticipatory anxiety (Deakin, 1983) and that this facilitates avoidance behaviour through modulation of dopaminergic guidance mechanisms (Schulz *et al.* 1998). At the same time, 5HT inhibits the PAG fight/flight mechanism until the threat is very proximal. Thus 5HT modulates responses to aversive stimuli according to their proximity and these influences may occur at different levels of the BAS (Figure 2.4; Deakin and Graeff, 1991). I will describe some tests of these ideas in healthy volunteers later.

Excessive neurotransmission through DRN 5HT2 systems would give rise to the symptoms of generalised anxiety disorder (GAD) – a state characterised by worry and apprehension about future possibilities which is strongly asso-

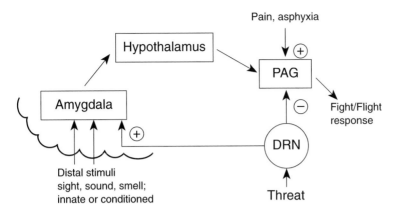

Figure 2.4 5HT modulation of BAS from the dorsal raphe nucleus

ciated with depression (Deakin, 1988). In contrast, deficient anticipatory anxiety mechanisms could underlie elements of antisocial impulsive behaviour so that behaviours are no longer restrained by anxiety. We have carried out a number of investigations of these hypotheses in patients.

This is a highly incomplete and simplified account of anxiety; for example, the hippocampus plays an important role in aversive stimuli such as aversive contexts (dangerous places) and omission of anticipated rewards (frustration, loss). Later, I will discuss anxiety triggered by risky behaviour.

Chronic aversive stimuli – resilience

If avoidance responses to acute aversive events are unsuccessful, aversive stimulation may become chronic or repeated. There is evidence that the brain has mechanisms of adaptation or resilience or tolerance to chronic aversion, which enable the gradual re-emergence of normal behaviour (column 3, Figure 2.2). It is proposed that this adaptation to chronic adversity is mediated by projections of the MRN and when this system breaks down, depression is the result. I will conclude with experimental tests of this hypothesis in depressed patients.

5HT restraint of unconditioned anxiety and panic

To investigate the role of 5HT in an innate form of anxiety, we used the simulated public speaking paradigm (McNair *et al.*, 1982). This involves ratings of subjective anxiety using visual analogue scales and questionnaires at baseline (see Figure 2.5). Subjects are then administered drugs or placebo and after allowing time for drug absorption, ratings are repeated to see whether the drugs affect baseline levels of anxiety. Immediately afterwards the subjects are given the instruction that they have two minutes to prepare a four-

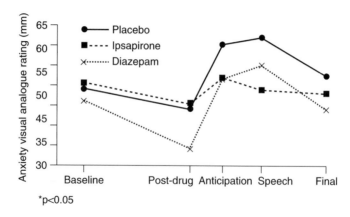

Figure 2.5 Different profiles of anxiolytic drugs in simulated public speaking (Source: Zuardi *et al*. 1993)

minute talk which is going to be assessed by psychologists and which will be video-taped. This elicits a gratifying increase in subjective anxiety accompanied by increased heart rate and sweat gland activity. After two minutes of speaking, the subjects are re-rated and again 15 minutes after cessation of speaking. It is possible to discern different profiles of anxiolytic action using this paradigm. For example, benzodiazepines suppress baseline anxiety upon which quite large increases can occur after the instruction to prepare a speech. However, peak anxiety levels are less because they start from a lower baseline. In contrast, the 5HT1A-agonist ipsapirone had no effect on baseline levels of anxiety but markedly attenuated the increase induced by the instructions (Zuardi *et al*. 1993; Figure 2.5).

We reasoned that if 5HT restrains unconditioned anxiety, then the drug d-fenfluramine which releases 5HT should inhibit anxiety evoked by simulated public speaking. This prediction was directly opposed to prevailing views about 5HT and the influential report that d-fenfluramine enhanced anxiety in patients with panic disorder (Targum and Marshall, 1989). In fact Hetem *et al*. (1993) showed a remarkable dose-dependent anxiolytic effect of d-fenfluramine in simulated public speaking. D-fenfluramine appears to release 5HT primarily onto 5HT2C receptors (Campbell, 1991; Goodall *et al*. 1993), therefore, a directly acting 5HT2C receptor agonist ought to have an anxiolytic effect in the model. This again was a dangerous prediction in view of often-reported anxiogenic effects of mCPP, which has 5HT2C agonism amongst its other properties. We recently tested the compound Organon 12962. This has full and selective agonist activity at the 5HT2C receptor with an affinity of PKI = 8. It has a tenfold lower affinity for the 5HT2A receptor. We found the drug had marked anxiolytic effect on simulated public speaking (Connell *et al*. 1998). These results suggest that 5HT acting through the 5HT2C receptor restrains unconditioned performance anxiety. However, simulated public speaking may have little to do with the morbid state of panic disorder. But we have data in patients too.

Panic attacks in patients can be brought under laboratory control by eliciting them with 7 per cent CO_2 inhalation. In addition, normal subjects breathing 7 per cent CO_2 report increases in subjective anxiety. We tested the hypothesis that 5HT restrains panic by interfering with 5HT function using the technique of tryptophan depletion. This is a dietary manipulation involving drinking a mixture of amino acids except tryptophan. A few hours later, circulating tryptophan levels decline to about 15 per cent of normal. Tryptophan is the dietary precursor of 5HT and tryptophan depletion in animals has been shown to decrease 5HT release in the brain. In a group of patients with panic disorder, Miller, Deakin and Anderson (1995) showed that CO_2 evoked more anxiety and panic attacks after tryptophan depletion than after a control amino-acid drink.

5HT enhancement of anticipatory anxiety

In the CO_2 paradigm, there is an element of anticipatory anxiety prior to inhalation. Ian Anderson in Manchester reasoned that d-fenfluramine should enhance the anticipatory component and suppress the anxiety elicited by CO_2, according to Deakin and Graeff (1991). Mortimore and Anderson (1998) administered placebo on one occasion and d-fenfluramine on another to 13 patients with panic disorder. Ratings of subjective anxiety and of subjective panic sensations were carried out using visual analogue scales. Over the four hours to peak d-fenfluramine concentrations, there were significant increases in anxiety compared to the four-hour placebo session; d-fenfluramine enhanced the anticipatory anxiety component as predicted (Figure 2.6).

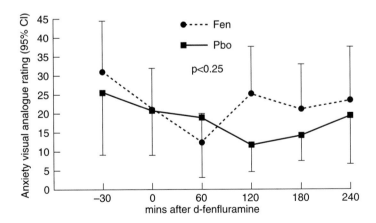

Figure 2.6 d-fenfluramine increased anticipatory anxiety in 13 panic patients (Source: Mortimore and Anderson, 1998)

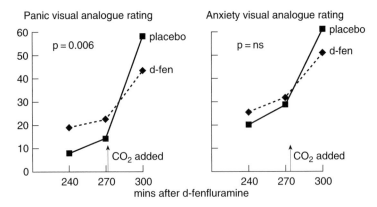

Figure 2.7 d-fenfluramine attenuated CO_2-induced panic ratings in 13 panic patients (Source: Mortimore and Anderson, 1998)

Despite inducing higher levels of anxiety at the onset of 7 per cent CO_2 breathing, d-fenfluramine attenuated the increase in anxiety evoked by CO_2 (Figure 2.7). The results, in a single experiment and in the same subjects, show that increasing 5HT release with d-fenfluramine enhances anticipatory anxiety but suppresses the response to CO_2. The increase in anticipatory anxiety is not attributable to subjective or bodily side-effects because none were detected or spontaneously described by the subjects.

We developed a classical conditioning paradigm to investigate the neuro-pharmacology of conditioned anticipatory anxiety (Guimaraes *et al.* 1991). Subjects listen to a series of neutral tones while skin conductance and heart rate responses are recorded. Responses to the tones rapidly habituate. However, after tone 11, there is a loud white noise. It is 100 decibels in volume but only lasts a second. When the tones are re-presented there is a re-initiation of responses and they do not habituate. The tones have become conditioned fear stimuli. We have shown that the 5HT2C/2A antagonist ritanserin completely antagonises conditioned skin conductance responses (Hensman *et al.* 1991). Conversely, drugs which enhance 5HT2 neurotransmission (fenfluramine, mCPP) enhance conditioning effects. While the conditioning model does not evoke subjective anxiety, nevertheless 5HT clearly has a facilitatory influence on aversive conditioning in contrast with suppressive defects on simulated public speaking and CO_2-evoked panic/anxiety.

Excessive 5HT2 function in depression

A major prediction of the theory is that excessive neurotransmission through DRN synapses gives rise to excessive anxiety and underlies this component of depression. Decisive evidence of this has come from our recent large-scale studies in the community in collaboration with Sir David. Five thousand questionnaires were sent to women on general practitioner lists in a Manchester council estate to identify three groups of women: a group at risk of depression, a depressed group and a control group. Over 460 women gave samples of saliva for cortisol estimations. They were interviewed for life events and difficulties and for measures of self-esteem. Diagnostic interviews were carried out. A subgroup of approximately 150 underwent d-fenfluramine challenges. D-fenfluramine administration is followed by a rise in the secretion of prolactin and this has been used as an index of functional 5HT neurotransmission. As noted earlier this appears to involve 5HT2 receptors and therefore the theory predicts that prolactin responses to d-fenfluramine should be exaggerated in patients with depression. Prolactin responses to d-fenfluramine were compared with responses following administration of placebo carried out within a week of the d-fenfluramine challenge. The order of drug/fenfluramine administration was counterbalanced. Twenty women met ICD-10 criteria for depression and they clearly had exaggerated prolactin responses to d-fenfluramine compared to a group of 63 women who were defined as being psychosocially vulnerable to depression and a group of 61 who were neither vulnerable or depressed (Figure 2.8).

This finding is precisely in line with Deakin and Graeff (1991) but discordant with the few previous studies that have been carried out. Shapira *et al.* (1993) reported blunted responses to d-fenfluramine but the patients were hospitalised with more severe depressive illnesses than our subjects were. More recent studies (Park *et al.* 1996; Kavoussi *et al.* 1998) report no change in responses to d-fenfluramine in outpatient depressives. One recent PET study measuring cerebral blood flow responsiveness to fenfluramine, found blunted responses in various brain areas but another found no difference

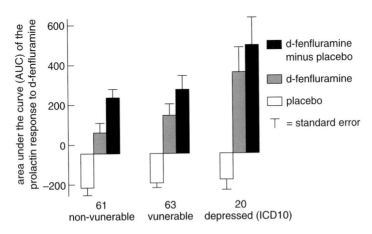

Figure 2.8 Increased 5HT2 prolactin response to d-fenfluramine in depression

(see Meyer *et al.* 1998). The 20 subjects tested in our recent study were for the most part undiagnosed and therefore perhaps both milder and earlier on in the progression of the illness.

Response–anxiety associations

Recently we have been interested in the idea that actions (and plans for actions) which are followed by an aversive outcome may come to elicit anticipatory anxiety (activation of the BAS) in the same way that environmental stimuli acquire aversiveness through Pavlovian conditioning. If so, 5HT should have a facilitatory role and this is depicted highly schematically in Figure 2.9. While environmental stimuli are detected in temporal cortical circuits, it seems likely that actions are constructed in prefrontal circuits. Indeed lesion studies in animals suggest that response-reinforcement learning may involve pathways which are different from those that subserve cuereinforcement learning – the former involving prefrontal mechanisms (Killcross *et al.* 1997). Recent interest in the role of response-aversion learning has also come from Damasio's Somatic Marker Hypothesis. According to Damasio (1994), risky behaviours elicit learned visceral responses (confusingly called somatic markers rather than visceral) which terminate the behaviour. In the social domain the conditioning occurs through the process of socialisation. Orbito frontal cortex (OFC) may have an important role in this form of learning because of its connections with the autonomic nervous system (Figure 2.9). Damasio (1994) suggests that patients with OFC damage develop anti-social traits because somatic markers are not elicited by impulses to anti-social behaviour.

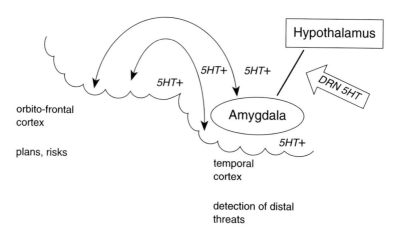

Figure 2.9 Risky behaviour and distal threats elicit anticipatory anxiety: their cortical processors feed into the BAS

We have investigated the role of 5HT in risk evaluation using a gambling paradigm. Ten boxes, some red some blue, appear on a computer screen. The subject has to guess whether a hidden token is under a red box or a blue box. When there are nine red boxes and one blue box, clearly the optimal choice is to choose red. Subjects are able to choose how much of their accumulated points they can gamble on their choice. Normal subjects are more likely to choose the more probable colour. When the odds are 8 to 2 or 9 to 1 they choose the most probable colour on almost 100 per cent of trials. Rogers *et al.* (1999) found that patients with damage to OFC systematically chose the less likely option. Those with lesions to the dorsal lateral prefrontal cortex performed normally on the task. Remarkably, normal subjects after tryptophan depletion were more likely to choose the riskier option – just like the patients with OFC lesions. The results suggest that indeed orbito frontal cortex is involved in risk behaviour. Furthermore, they are compatible with the suggestion that 5HT facilitates anticipatory anxiety elicited by plans for risky behaviour in the same way that environmental cues elicit anticipa-tory anxiety (Figure 2.9). In the absence of an anxiety response, subjects are more likely to choose the riskier option. These data are compatible with Damasio's formulation that risky intentions elicit visceral responses, aware-ness of which inhibit the implementation of the planned but risky behaviour.

Impaired 5HT2 neurotransmission and impulsivity

Impaired acquisition or expression of response–anxiety connections could underlie disorders of impulse control. Mairead Dolan and Ian Anderson have probed 5HT functioning in patients with severe psychopathic disorder using d-fenfluramine challenge tests (Anderson and Dolan, 1996). They carried out tests in over 60 inmates detained in Ashworth Special Hospital with a hospital diagnosis of psychopathy. A few were over-controlled psycho-paths whose violence was calculating rather than impulsive. Measures of impulsiveness, attempts at self-harm and aggressive behaviour were inversely correlated with the prolactin response (Figure 2.10). The lower the prolactin response to d-fenfluramine the greater the scores on impulsivity, aggression and self-harm. These results are compatible with similar findings in less severe antisocial populations (Coccaro *et al.* 1989) suggesting that some indi-viduals with disorders of impulsive control have impaired 5HT neuro-transmission. This may be central to pathogenesis.

Modulation of the BAS by 5HT – summary

The hypothesis that the DRN system mediates effects of anticipatory anxiety has survived a number of experimental tests. Unconditioned anxiety/panic evoked by simulated public speaking and by CO_2 is restrained by 5HT mechanisms (Figures 2.6 and 2.7). In contrast, 5HT enhances anticipatory

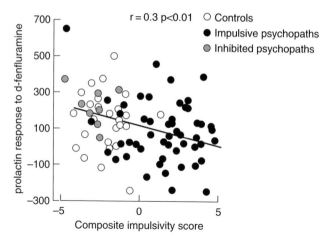

Figure 2.10 Prolactin responses to d-fenfluramine in psychopaths (Source: Anderson and Dolan, 1996)

anxiety elicited by environmental conditioned stimuli. Increased risk-taking in the gambling paradigm in tryptophan-depleted subjects is compatible with the idea that motor plans can also elicit anticipatory anxiety and that these connections are facilitated by 5HT. Overactivity of 5HT2 neurotransmission is associated with depression (we predict the anxiety component: Figure 2.8) and underactivity with impulsive behaviour in psychopathic individuals (Figure 2.10). To complete the picture, let me now turn to the behavioural functions of the MRN – 5HT1A system.

Median raphe projections and adaptation to adversity

MRN terminals innervate 5HT1A receptors in cortical structures in parallel with the distribution of noradrenergic nerve terminals (Figure 2.1). A number of animal behavioural experiments show that as animals become tolerant to repeated stressors so neurotransmission through this pathway progressively increases (e.g. Kennet *et al.* 1985a, 1985b). According to the present theory, failure of 5HT1A neurotransmission causes failure of resilience and so depression is the result. There are a number of interesting interactions between these systems and early and other social experiences (see Checkley, 1996; Fulford and Marsden, 1998) Time does not allow further elaboration of these findings. Nevertheless, they are of obvious relevance to the mechanism by which early and other life experiences give rise to vulnerability to depression in humans.

There is now compelling data that there is an impairment of 5HT1 neurotransmission in depression. The evidence comes from another neuroendocrine challenge paradigm but using tryptophan, the 5HT pre-cursor, instead of

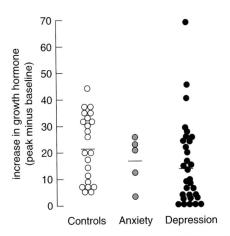

Figure 2.11 Growth hormone responses to tryptophan (5HT1A) (Source: Deakin *et al.*, 1990)

d-fenfluramine. While hormonal responses to d-fenfluramine appear to involve 5HT2 receptors, prolactin and growth hormone response to trypto-phan are antagonised by the 5HT1 antagonist pindolol but not by 5HT2 antagonists. All studies of tryptophan responses in depression find them to be attenuated in depression (Cowan and Charig, 1987; Deakin *et al.* 1990; Figure 2.11) while in our hands 5HT2 mediated fenfluramine responses are enhanced. This seems clear evidence in favour of the idea that depression involves opposite changes in different 5HT systems.

We have argued that there is a direct causal connection between low 5HT1A functioning and depressed mood on the following grounds: first that impaired neuroendocrine tryptophan responses in depression recover with clinical recovery – they are state-dependent (Uphadhyaya *et al.* 1991); and second, that depletion of circulating tryptophan causes a temporary return of symptoms of depression in patients who have recently recovered (Delgado *et al.* 1990). Thus recovery from depression is associated with a return of normal 5HT1A function and experimental impairment of 5HT function reverses recovery. How 5HT1 neurotransmission becomes impaired in depression is not clear.

Studies in Manchester found that depressed subjects with the most blunted prolactin responses were the subjects that had high baseline cortisol concentrations (Figure 2.12). It is well known that there are interactions in animal models in vitro and in vivo between steroid receptors in the brain and 5HT1 neurotransmission (Checkley, 1996). These findings therefore suggested the hypothesis that impaired 5HT1A function occurs in depression because it is undermined by the hypercortisolaemia of depression which in turn might result from life-stresses. However, the idea that life-events increase secretion of cortisol, while plausible and widely assumed, has hardly been

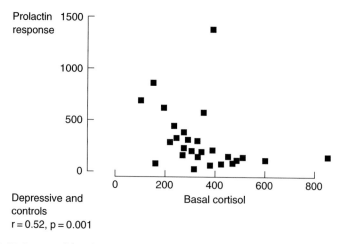

Figure 2.12 Increased basal cortisol and blunted prolactin response to tryptophan

tested (Dolan *et al.* 1985). The relationship was investigated in the Manchester community study. The women were interviewed using the LEDS-SES instruments. Salivary cortisols were collected from over 460 women at 9 a.m. and 11 p.m. on two consecutive days. Cortisol concentrations showed a clear diurnal variation and a sub-group of women with recent severe life events ($n = 46$) had significantly raised 11 p.m. cortisol concentrations. However there was no indication for an increase in cortisols in the 97 women who met ICD-10 criteria for depression. Furthermore, about half the depressed women met the more rigorous DSM-IV criteria and they too showed no evidence of increased cortisol secretion. We conclude that while there is previous evidence of a clear connection between impaired 5HT responsiveness and the state of depression, there is no clear evidence in this large community study that hypercortisolaemia is the mechanism. Indeed we find no evidence that common depression in the community is associated with increased cortisol secretion even though cortisol appears to be responsive to recent psychosocial stresses. Major revision of the role of stress-induced cortisol release in depression is long overdue.

Conclusion

A clear finding from Sir David's work in Manchester is that there is no clear boundary between normal and abnormal states of mood or of anxiety. It seems likely, therefore, that the concept of neurosis as a continuum is correct. Common psychiatric disorders in the community are likely to be extremes of normal physiological responses to adversity. Here I have summarised evidence that understanding normal neurobiological mechanisms involved in adaptation to adversity leads to predictions, some surprising, which fit

	DRN–5HT2	MRN–5HT1A
Genetic variation	Elements of neurotransmission	
Personality dimension	anxiety, venturesomeness, neuroticism?	resilience self-esteem, sociability
Effect of early life vunerability factors	?	impaired resilience, low self-esteem
Effect of life event	increased 5HT2 function; pre or postsynaptic?	breakdown (presynaptic) in compromised MRN– 5HT1A system
Symptom	worry, tension, anxiety	helplessness, depression

Figure 2.13 5HT and mechanisms of common psychopathology

well with experimental tests (Figure 2.13). Undoubtedly, there is much individual variation in responsiveness to adversity but we now have major clues to the relevant neurobiological dimensions affected by early psychosocial factors and genetic variation.

References

Anderson, I. and Dolan, M. (1996). Psychopathy: Neuropsychology, impulse control and serotonin. *Journal of Psychopharmacology* Supplement, 10, A3.

Bickerdike, M.J., Wright, I.K. and Marsden, C.A. (1993). Social isolation attenuates rat forebrain 5–HT release induced by KCl stimulation and exposure to novel environment. *Behavioural Pharmacology* 4/3, 231–236.

Bond, A.J. and Lader, M.H. (1974). The use of analogue scales in rating subjective feelings. *British Journal of Medical Psychology* 47, 211–218.

Campbell, D.B. (1991). Dexfenfluramine: an overview of its mechanisms of action. *Reviews in Contemporary Pharmacotherapy* 2, 93–113.

Checkley, S. (1996). The neuroendocrinology of depression and chronic stress. *British Medical Bulletin* 52, 597–617.

Connell, J., Sennef, C. and Deakin, J.F.W. (1999). The effects of ORG 12962, a 5-HT2C receptor agonist, in two models of experimentally induced anxiety in healthy female volunteers. *International Journal of Neuropsychopharmacology* vol. 2, Supplement 1, S136–137.

Coccaro, E.F., Siever, L.J., Klar, H.M., Maurer, G., Cochrane, K., Cooper, T.B., Mohrs, R.C. and Davis, K.L. (1989). Serotonergic studies in patients with affective and personality disorders; correlates with suicidal and impulsive aggressive behaviour. *Archives of General Psychiatry* 46, 587–599.

Cowen, P.J. and Charig, E.M. (1987). Neuroendocrine responses to tryptophan in major depression. *Archives of General Psychiatry* 44, 958–966.

Damasio, A.R. (1994). *Descartes' Error: Emotion, rationality and the human brain.* New York, Putnam (Grosset Books).

Deakin, J.F.W. (1983). Roles of serotonergic systems in escape, avoidance and other behaviours. In: J.S. Cooper (ed.) *Theory in Psychopharmacology*. Academic Press, New York.

Deakin, J.F.W. (1988). 5HT2 receptors depression and anxiety. *Pharmacology, Biochemistry and Behavior* 29, 819–820.

Deakin, J.F.W. (1996). 5HT, antidepressant drugs and the psychosocial origins of depression. *Journal of Psychopharmacology* 10(1), 31–38.

Deakin, J.W.F. and Graeff, F.G. (1991). 5-HT and mechanisms of defence. *Journal of Psychopharmacology* 5, 305–315.

Deakin, J.F.W., Pennell, I., Upadhyaya, A.K. and Lofthouse, R. (1990). A neuroendocrine study of 5HT function in depression: evidence for biological mechanisms of endogenous and psychosocial causation. *Psychopharmacology* 101, 85–92.

Delgado, P.L., Charney, D.S., Price, L.H., Aghajanian, G.K., Landis, H. and Heninger, G.R. (1990). Serotonin function and the mechanism of antidepressant action. *Archives of General Psychiatry* 47, 411–418.

Dolan, R.J., Calloway, S.P., Fonagy, P., De Souza, F.V.A. and Wakeling, A. (1985). Life events, depression and hypothalamic-pituitary-adrenal axis function. *British Journal of Psychiatry* 147, 429–433.

Fulford, A.J. and Marsden, C.A. (1998). Conditioned release of 5-hydroxytryptamine in vivo in the nucleus accumbens following isolation-rearing in the rat. *Neuroscience* 83, 481–487.

Goldberg, D.P. and Huxley, P. (1992). *Common Mental Disorders. A Bio-social Model.* Routledge, London.

Goodall, E., Cowan, P.J., Franklin, M. and Silverstone, T. (1993). Ritanserin attenuates anorectic, endocrine and thermic responses to *d*-fenfluramine in human volunteers. *Psychopharmacology* 112, 461–466.

Gray, J.A. (1987). *The Psychology of Fear and Stress*. 2nd edn. Cambridge, Cambridge University Press.

Guimaraes, F.S., Hellewell, J.S.E., Hensman, R., Wang, M. and Deakin, J.F.W. (1991). Characterization of a psychophysiological model of classical fear conditioning in healthy volunteers: influence of gender, instruction, personality and placebo. *Psychopharmacology* 104, 231–236.

Hensman, R., Guimaraes, F.S., Wang, M. and Deakin, J.F.W. (1991). Effects of ritanserin on aversive classical conditioning in humans. *Psychopharmacology* 104, 220–224.

Hetem, L.A.B., De Souza, C.J., Guimarães, F.S.G., Zuardi, A.W. and Graeff, F.G. (1993). D-fenfluramine reduces anxiety induced by simulated public speaking. *Brazilian Journal of Medical and Biological Research* 26, 971–974.

Jacobs, B.L. and Fornal, C.A. (1991). Activity of brain serotonergic neurons in the behaving animal. *Pharmacological Review* 43, 563–578.

Kavoussi, R.J., Kramer, J., Hauger, R.L. and Coccaro, E.F. (1998). Prolactin response to D-fenfluramine in outpatients with major depression. *Psychiatry Research* 79, 199–205.

Kennett, G.A., Dickinson, S.L. and Curzon, G. (1985a). Central serotonergic responses and behavioral adaptation to repeated immobilisation: the effect of the corticosterone synthesis inhibitor metyrapone. *European Journal of Pharmacology* 119, 143–152.

Kennett, G.A., Dickinson, S.L. and Curzon, G. (1985b). Enhancement of some 5-HT-dependent behavioral responses following repeated immobilization in rats. *Brain Research* 330, 253–263.

Killcross, S., Robbins, T.W. and Everitt, B.J. (1997). Different types of fear–conditioned behaviour mediated by separate nuclei within amygdala. *Nature* 388, 377–380.

McNair, D.M., Frankenthaler, L.M., Czerlinsky, T., White, T.W., Sasson, S. and Fischer, S. (1982). Simulated public speaking as a model of clinical anxiety. *Psychopharmacology* 77, 7–10.

Meyer, J.H., Kennedy, S. and Brown, G.M. (1998). No effect of depression on [(15)O]H2O PET response to intravenous d-fenfluramine. *American Journal of Psychiatry* 155(9), 1241–1246.

Miller, H., Deakin, J.F.W. and Anderson, I.M. (1995). Acute tryptophan depletion increases panic anxiety in panic disorder patients. *Journal of Psychopharmacology* 9, A18.

Mortimore, C. and Anderson, I.M. (1998). Dexfenfluramine in panic disorder: 5Ht induces anxiety but prevents panic. *Journal of Psychopharmacology* 12 Suppl, A20.

Park, S.B., Williamson, D.J., and Cowen, P.J. (1996). 5-HT neuroendocrine function in major depression: prolactin and cortisol responses to D-fenfluramine. *Psychological Medicine* 26(6), 1191–1196.

Rogers, R.D., Baldacchino, A., Johnson, A.J., Swainson, R., London, M., Deakin, J.F.W., Sahakian, B.J., Robbins, T.W. and Everitt, B.J. (1999). Dissociable deficits in the decision making cognition of chronic amphetamine and opiate abusers, patients with focal damage to prefrontal cortex, and tryptophan-depleted normal volunteers: evidence for monoaminergic mechanisms. *Neuropsychopharmacology* 20, 322–339.

Schulz, W., Dayan, P. and Montague, P.R. (1998). A neural substrate of prediction and reward. *Science* 275, 1593–1599.

Shapira, B., Cohen, J., Newman, N.E. and Lerer, B. (1993). Prolactin response to fenfluramine and placebo. Challenge following maintenance pharmacotherapy withdrawal in remitted depressed. *Biological Psychiatry* 33, 531–535.

Targum, S.D. and Marshall, L. E. (1989). Fenfluramine provocation of anxiety in patients with panic disorder. *Psychiatry Research* 28, 295–306.

Upadhyaya, A.K., Pennell, I., Cowen, P.J. and Deakin, J.F.W. (1991). Blunted growth hormone and prolactin responses to L-tryptophan in depression: a state-dependent abnormality. *Journal of Affective Disorders* 21, 213–218.

Zuardi, A.W., Cosme, R.A., Graeff, F.G. and Guimarães, F.S. (1993). Effects of ipsapirone and cannabidiol on human experimental anxiety, *Journal of Psychopharmacology* 7, 82–88.

3

ON VULNERABILITY TO COMMON MENTAL DISORDERS

An evidence-based plea for a developmental perspective

Johan Ormel and Peter de Jong

Introduction

Current thinking on the aetiology of common mental disorders is saturated with the stress–vulnerability paradigm. However, when critically inspected the definition of vulnerability is less straightforward and the use of the term less informative than its intuitive appeal suggests. The definition raises conceptual concerns, and elicits intriguing substantive questions. Despite its universally recognised significance in the aetiology and course of mental disorders, vulnerability is largely an unexplored area, with some notable exceptions. Much remains to be learned about its nature, origins and plasticity, the determinants of its change over time, and about the distal and proximal mechanisms by which it affects illness risk.

The objectives of this chapter are to look at the current state of theoretical affairs, to propose a dynamic stress–vulnerability model, and to provide a rationale for a developmental perspective on the aetiology of vulnerability. We will conclude by proposing some criteria that determine the effectiveness of study designs to analyse the aetiology of vulnerability: (1) an inter-disciplinary bio-psycho-social developmental stress framework; (2) genetically informative populations such as twins or founder populations; and (3) longitudinal designs including transitions into adolescence and adulthood. Finally, we will argue that the study of the trajectory of vulnerability would benefit from a close collaboration between child, adolescent, and adult psychiatry, and abnormal psychology.

Some remarks are necessary to put this chapter in the right perspective. As used here the term vulnerability refers to the entire continuum from highly vulnerable to highly resilient.[1] In addition, and although the authors acknowledge that some vulnerability factors might predispose to onset and recurrence while others predispose to persistence and chronicity, this distinction will not be made in the following text.

The title of this chapter refers to common mental disorders. These include the three families of anxiety, mood, and addiction disorders. The empirical examples in this chapter are largely from the domain of depression. It is our opinion, however, that the arguments put forward by us also apply to both other domains. On a more general level, it should be noted that some of our arguments are speculative, and cannot be supported by robust evidence yet.

Towards a dynamic variant of the stress–vulnerability model

Central to all stress–vulnerability models is the assertion that stressful agents (negative life events, difficulties, daily hassles) can have pathogenic effects, particularly in vulnerable individuals (Goldberg *et al.* 1990; Rodgers 1991). In the absence of vulnerability, stressful agents will result at most in mild and transient distress, but not in case-level emotional disorders.

Possibly the most influential stress–vulnerability model for depression has been developed by Brown and Harris (1978). Over the past two decades these authors have published a wealth of data showing that life stressors with marked long-term threat are depressogenic in those rated as vulnerable, but have much less impact on risk in the non-vulnerable. Brown and Harris identified several so-called *vulnerability factors;* psychological and social characteristics that strongly modify the effect of the stressors. Examples are negative self-evaluation (similar to low self-esteem), chronic subthreshold anxiety symptoms (similar to neuroticism), lack of emotionally supportive close ties, and lower social class. Others (Rodgers 1991; Goldberg and Huxley 1992; Ormel *et al.* 1988) have added financial hardship, childhood adversity, unemployment, neuroticism, and low control.

While Brown and Harris and their collaborators have constantly refined and elaborated their model (which will here be referred to as the *pure stress–vulnerability model*) over the years, their basic notion of vulnerability as a set of relatively stable characteristics of the individual and her/his social environment has not changed. And although their analyses generally supported their model, the dichotomous and therefore overly simple way in which they have conceptualised, analysed and presented provoking agents and vulnerability factors has hampered the testing of alternative models.

More complex variants can nevertheless be conceived of. There is, for example, the *additive variant.* While the pure model assumes that only the simultaneous presence of vulnerability and severe stress will substantially increase risk, the additive variant asserts that risk is linearly and independently associated with both level of vulnerability and severity of stress. The higher the level of stress the person is exposed to, or the higher the level of

35

his or her vulnerability, the higher the risk. In yet another model, the *additive–interactive variant,* the additive and interaction effects of stress and vulnerability on risk go together. That is, stress and vulnerability have independent linear effects on risk but in addition vulnerability enlarges the effect of stress on risk.

Although conceptually the additive and the additive–interactive variants are improvements on the pure stress–vulnerability models, even in these models the matter of the relationship between stress and vulnerability is still not adequately addressed. In neither model, the growing body of evidence suggesting that vulnerability co-determines people's exposure to life stressors (in particular person-dependent stressors such as interpersonal events) is taken into account. In addition, the evidence that exposure to particular life events may permanently change a person's vulnerability level has not been allowed for.

The dynamic, interactive relationships between vulnerability, person-dependent stressors and life events will be accounted for in the *dynamic stress–vulnerability model* (see Figure 3.1). In this model, vulnerability influences illness risk via at least three mechanisms:

(1) Environmental control, which co-determines exposure to stressors (in addition to other determinants such as chance, bad luck, behaviours of others).

(2) Appraisal processes will modify the pathway from vulnerability to illness risk in several ways. The processes will, for example, influence the personal meaning of the stressor (how a particular event relates to individual needs and values) and the subjective assessment of the capacities for effective coping. Together, the processes determine the (possible) discrepancy between perceived demands of the stressor and capacities to cope with these demands.

(3) The actual coping responses to the discrepancy include affective, cognitive, and behavioural responses. Vulnerabilities may affect the neurophysiological substrates of these responses, and co-determine the nature and severity of perturbations in the affective, cognitive, and behavioural domains of functioning.

Contrary to the traditional image of the individual as the passive recipient of environmental experiences, the dynamic stress–vulnerability model emphasises the active control of the individual by selection, modification and even (re-)creation of (stressful) experiences. The possibly resulting clinical manifestation will be dependent upon disorder-specific sensitivities in neurophysiological subsystems, on features of the coping strategy, and on the personal meaning of the stressor.

Central to the dynamic stress–vulnerability model, then, is the *continuous interplay* between an individual's genetic make-up, the personality he or she

Psychobiological stress–vulnerability paradigm

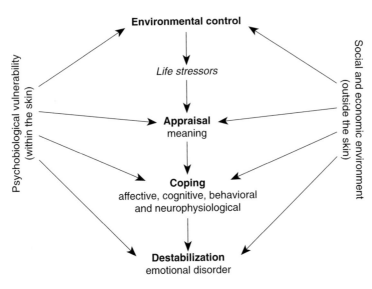

Figure 3.1 The dynamic stress–vulnerability model

develops over time, and the occurrence of life events. The hallmarks of the model can be summarised as follows:

1 Stress exposure increases risk of mental disorder.
2 Certain environments carry an increased risk of occurrence of stressors.
3 Vulnerability factors increase the incidence and duration of stressors (mechanism: environmental control).
4 Vulnerability factors amplify the impact of stressors on risk, by influencing
   (a) the perceived stressfulness and subjective meaning of stressors (mechanism: appraisal styles).
   (b) how people respond to and deal with stressors (mechanism: coping styles).
5 Vulnerability factors co-determine the specific clinical manifestation.
6 Particular experiences can have long-term, even lasting effects on vulnerability, i.e. result in vulnerability accumulation or reduction.

Vulnerability and high permanence of risk

To further clarify the model it is necessary to address the issue of the difference between vulnerability and other risk factors. An individual's vulnerabilities (in whatever shape or form they come) are always risk factors. But not all risk factors (social and economic stressors come to mind) are part of an individual's vulnerability. Exact definitions, however, are difficult to give. The conceptual boundary between vulnerability and other risk factors is dependent on the illness under study. This may be explained, using Rothman's general model of causation.

Rothman (1986) defines a cause as any event, condition, or characteristic which plays an essential part in the onset of the illness. He further distinguishes between component and sufficient causes. A *component cause* is any cause that plays a role in the occurrence of a disease. A *sufficient cause* constitutes a minimal but unique set of conditions and events (component causes) which always produces the illness in question. All component causes in the set must be present, if one is absent, the illness will not occur. A particular illness may have multiple sufficient causes; and component causes in a particular sufficient cause may also be component causes in other sufficient causes.

Rothman's sufficient and component causes may be used to clarify the fleeting boundary between vulnerability and other risk factors. The extent to which a risk factor acts as a disorder-specific vulnerability factor depends on (1) the proportion of sufficient causes of that disorder in which it is a component cause; and (2) the number of times and the degree to which it precedes other component causes in these sufficient causes. The extent to which a risk factor acts as a generic vulnerability factor depends on (1) the proportion of sufficient causes of a defined set of disorders in which it is a component cause; and (2) the number of times and the degree to which it precedes other component causes in these sufficient causes.

In both instances, the second condition referring to the amount of precedence (the *permanence of risk*) is important. Risk factors act more like vulnerability (and less as provoking factors), the higher their permanence of risk and the more sufficient causes in which they are a component cause. Two prototypical risk factors with high permanence of risk are (1) events with lasting effects on the individual personality and neurobiology (which is expressed in, for instance, changed environmental control, appraisal or coping) and (2) stable characteristics of the individual. Examples of the former are physical and psychological trauma and of the latter (social) IQ and response inhibition.

Empirical evidence for the dynamic stress–vulnerability model: the interplay between genes, neuroticism and life events in the onset of emotional disorders

As mentioned before, there is a growing body of evidence supporting the proposed dynamic stress–vulnerability model. The main results will be summarised in the following paragraphs.

Neuroticism increases the risk of depression onset

Various prospective studies have found that neuroticism and related temperaments and traits predict onset of emotional disorders. In the NIMH Collaborative Depression Study (Hirschfeld *et al.* 1983, 1997) it was found that lack of emotional strength and high interpersonal dependence were predictive of depression. Another example is the Dunedin study in which approximately 1,000 children born in Dunedin (New Zealand) in 1972–73 were monitored into young adulthood (Krueger *et al.* 1996). Here it was found that highly restrained behaviour (shyness, timidity and quickness to become upset in new surroundings) at age 3 predicted depression at the age 21. In addition, Caspi *et al.* (1996) found that stress reactivity as measured at age 18 predicted both anxiety and depression at age 21. Similar findings were reported by Kendler *et al.* (1993; Virginia Twin Study) and Clayton *et al.* (1994) in a follow-up study of Swiss military service conscripts. Boyce *et al.* (1991) suggested that the risk of depression is mainly related to interpersonal sensitivity, which they believe has five components: interpersonal awareness, need for approval, separation anxiety, timidity and fragile innerself. Cloninger, finally, in his four-dimensional model of temperament (comprising Harm Avoidance, Reward Dependence, Novelty Seeking, Persistence) has put forward a depressogenic temperament type, comprising high levels of harm avoidance and reward dependence.

Severe life events and long-term difficulties increase risk of depression onset

The link between life events and depression was investigated in a large number of studies. For methodological reasons, however, the validity of most of the conclusions is doubtful. An exception can be made for those studies in which the Life Events and Difficulty Schedule (LEDS) was used. The LEDS (developed by Brown and Harris 1978, 1989) is a semi-structured interview with detailed instructions yielding contextual ratings of a variety of event and difficulty dimensions. Case-control studies have proven that one or more negative life events or long-term difficulties preceded the onset of depression in approximately three-quarters of all cases while only one quarter to a third of all controls had a similar experience in a similar period of time (Brown and Harris 1989; Jenaway and Paykel 1997; Willige *et al.* 1995). In a review by Cooke (1987) Relative Risks (RR) ranged from 3–10, and the Attributional Risk proportions (AR) from 29–69 per cent, with a mean of 40 per cent. RR as well as AR appear to be higher for women, and lower for recurrences than first onsets. In particular, recurrences of melancholic and psychotic depressions seem to be independent of life events (Brown *et al.* 1994).

Based in particular on Beck's research into the *generalisability of hopelessness as the depressogenic mechanism*, Brown, Harris and collaborators have searched for characteristics of experience that might increase the specificity and the predictive power of life events and long-term difficulties (Brown and Harris 1989; Brown *et al.* 1995). Two types of events were found to have considerably increased risks: events which matched an existing difficulty and events which involve loss of primary sources of self-esteem.

Personality and experience mediate genetic effects

Genetic factors may act on risk factors for depression instead of on the disorder itself. There is evidence for genetic influence on dimensional or discrete risk factors which are not part of the pathogenesis of depression, but increase or decrease the risk of onset. Flint *et al.* (1995), for example, identified three loci in the mouse genome associated with emotional reactivity (neuroticism), a risk factor for anxious and depressive disorders in human beings. It has further been shown that practically all major personality traits are partially controlled by genetic factors (Plomin *et al.* 1997). The evidence is particularly strong for neuroticism and extroversion–introversion. Studies of twins and adopted children have estimated that 40-60 per cent of the variations in neuroticism in a given population can be attributed to genetic factors (Loehlin 1992; Heath *et al.* 1992). The fact that genetic effects do not explain 100 per cent of the true score variation shows that environmental factors are also important for neuroticism. This is supported by the evidence that the test–retest correlations of neuroticism get smaller as the interval between the test and retest gets longer (Watson and Clark 1984; Ormel and Rijsdijk in press).

Exposure to stressors is also partly controlled by genetic factors. A range of studies have found that genes consistently influence life experiences (Kendler *et al.* 1993, 1995; Plomin *et al.* 1990; McGuffin *et al.* 1991; Foley *et al.* 1996). Since life events do not have genes, the direct genetic effects on life events and difficulties may be hard to understand. The answer lies in the assumption that the environment is not independent of the individual, but partially selected and created by the individual. This is borne out by the finding that genetic effects seem limited mainly to life events over which the subjects have had some control, i.e. events that resulted from their own behaviour. It is hypothesised that genes influence the environment through their influence on temperament and subsequently on personality.

This hypothesis presupposes that personality influences life-event exposure, which indeed has been upheld by a number of studies. Neuroticism, for example, is associated with the occurrence of unpleasant events and problems. Ormel and Wohlfarth (1991), Fergusson and Horwood (1987), Heady and Wearing (1989), Magnus *et al.* (1993) and Saudino *et al.* (1997) have provided evidence that the exposure to certain events is associated with age,

40

neuroticism, extroversion, openness to new experiences, and position in society. Neuroticism is a predictor mainly of negative events, extroversion of positive events, and openness to experiences predicts both positive and negative. Neuroticism and low social status above all seem to predict the incidence of interpersonal, financial and apolitical and legal stressors.

All of the above implies that genetically sensitive research (quantitative as well as molecular) on continuously distributed vulnerability factors such as neuroticism, interpersonal sensitivity, the tendency to get into stressful situations, and certain socio-cognitive abilities may be very worthwhile. The genetic effects on discrete disorders such as DSM-IV's unipolar major depression may well be the result of the genetic background of such continuously distributed risk factors. Multivariate quantitative genetic studies can clarify the inherited and environmental backgrounds of these risk factors.

Are the same genes involved?

An as yet unresolved question is whether depression, neuroticism and exposure to stressors are influenced by the same genetic factors. Kendler and Karkowski-Shuman (1997), however, found a strong genetic correlation between neuroticism, exposure to stressors under control of the individual, and depression. This suggests that the genes which predispose the individual to depression are *in part* identical to those which control neuroticism and, via neuroticism, influence exposure to certain stressors.

Conclusions: the need for a developmental perspective on vulnerability

The results of the studies summarised in this paragraph clearly fit the proposed dynamic stress–vulnerability model. In particular, the studies are in support of the following aspects of the model:

- Neuroticism increases the probability of the occurrence of depressogenic stressors.
- Neuroticism intensifies the effect of depressogenic stressors on risk of depression onset.
- Part of the genetic influences on risk of depression onset is not mediated by neuroticism and stressors.

In addition to the above and more important with respect to the presumed continuous interplay between the elements in the model, the combined results of these and other studies also suggest that the following may be true:

- Precursors of adult psychopathology can often be found in childhood and/ or adolescence.

41

- Origins of vulnerability can often be traced back to childhood and/or adolescence.
- Most new incidence occurs between ages 14 and 21.
- Continuity of psychopathology across adolescence into adulthood increases with severity.
- Continuity of psychopathology across adolescence into adulthood increases with more generic accounts of psychopathology.
- Even during adulthood vulnerability continues to change.

These (tentative) findings underline the assertion that vulnerability to common mental disorders is continuously developing. During this process vulnerability may accumulate, or reduce, by changes in the nature and rate of particular experiences. This suggests that normal and deviant development may not run parallel but may increasingly diverge as adolescence progresses and exposure to environmental influence accumulates. All this implies that the dynamic stress–vulnerability model can only be fully understood from a developmental perspective.

The developmental perspective: genetic, formative, and instrumental vulnerability

The following three basic assumptions are part of the developmental perspective.

1   Individuals differ in their reactions to the environment. Individual characteristics, such as personality traits, can therefore more fruitfully be defined in terms of individual differences in response tendencies.
2   The environment influences and changes the individual on different levels of functioning, down to and including the level of physiological processes. An individual's personality is not absolutely stable; it does not remain unchanged throughout the adult lifespan. Personality with its underlying neurobiology is malleable. The link between the individual and the environment, however, is a two-way relationship.
3   Essential to this two-way relationship is the notion that people are not the passive recipients of environmental stimuli but are actively involved in changing and choosing them. People actively process environmental information, guided by their personalities (which are determined partly through genes and partly through early experiences). The greater their environmental control, the more they are capable of selecting and creating their experiences. This implies that people's contributions to events are not entirely arbitrary, but partially the result of their personality, their behaviour, and their choices.

To further stimulate discussion and research within the developmental perspective of vulnerability, we propose to distinguish between symptom level, instrumental vulnerability, formative vulnerability, and genetic vulnerability (see Figure 3.2).

Symptom level refers to a person's emotional health status at a particular point in time. People may have no, some, or many symptoms, putting them below or above diagnostic thresholds. Symptom levels are known to differ considerably both within and between persons.

A person's risk to an increase in symptom level (given exposure to a certain amount of stress) is his *instrumental vulnerability*. Instrumental vulnerability is the vulnerability that is active, switched on, at a particular point in time. Its level differs considerably between persons. Within-person changes in instrumental vulnerability, however, are typically slow and gradual compared to changes in symptom levels. Instrumental vulnerability might be defined in terms of between-subject differences in environmental control, appraisal of and coping with stressors. Instrumental vulnerability at a particular point in time is the combined result of the level of instrumental vulnerability at an earlier point in time and all experiences leading to changes in environmental control, appraisal and coping styles occurring in between.

Although instrumental vulnerability may change at any time during adulthood, these changes will generally be incidental and of little consequence. Adult vulnerability, in other words, possesses a high permanence of risk. During childhood and adolescence, however, within-subject changes typically

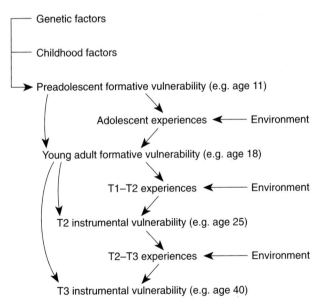

Figure 3.2 Relationships among genetic, formative and instrumental vulnerability

are more frequent and stronger. This and the earlier mentioned incremental character of instrumental vulnerability mean that the changes in this period will determine the (relatively robust and stable) level of instrumental vulnerability in later life to a large extent. Since the developments in this period are of crucial importance to an adult individual's risk on the onset of mental disorders we propose to use a special term for the level of instrumental vulnerability at the time of the transition into adulthood: *formative vulnerability*.

Formative vulnerability, then, is brought about by interactions between experiences (during adolescence, childhood, and perhaps even intra-uterine) and an individual's *genetic vulnerability*. The latter term refers to the vulnerability encoded in the individual's genome. It is therefore an absolutely stable factor, a risk factor with a permanent permanence of risk. It will not change during an individual's lifetime, although its expression likely depends on environmental influences, including age.

Perhaps the critical differences between formative and instrumental vulnerability can best be described as follows:

1   In describing instrumental vulnerability one describes proximal mechanisms through which (particularly external) risk acts. Formative vulnerability, on the other hand, is about the genetic and environmental *roots* of vulnerability, about background vulnerability, developed in interaction between genetic vulnerability and a person's (early) life experiences. In this respect, formative vulnerability will to a large extent determine the boundaries within which instrumental vulnerability will typically fluctuate during adult life.

2   The formative vulnerability component of instrumental vulnerability is comparatively stable (i.e. carried forward with ageing), whereas instrumental vulnerability may change during the life course in response to particular experiences.

3   In terms of the brain, formative vulnerability can be compared to encoding in the hardware, less so than genetic vulnerability, but much more than instrumental vulnerability. The latter type of vulnerability reflects (changeable) dysfunctions in the software. Due to the plasticity of the brain, however, the boundaries between formative and instrumental vulnerability are not absolute and unchangeable.

Experiences that change instrumental vulnerability

Few have addressed the problem of which experiences have lasting effects on instrumental vulnerability and how this is achieved, with some notable exceptions (e.g. Rutter 1996; Brown and Harris 1978; Harris *et al*. 1990; Quinton *et al*. 1993; Andrews *et al*. 1993; and Ormel 1997). Important concepts in this context are turning points (e.g. attachment to the labor force and cohesive marriage; both strengthen social bonds in adulthood), sensitizing and steeling experiences (Rutter 1996; Andrews *et al.* 1993; Caspi and Moffit 1993; Laub and Sampson, 1993). It is easier to imagine intuitively how such experiences can bring about long-term change in exposure to stressors than to grasp how they can influence the organism. For example, a cohesive marriage or cohabitation with a non-deviant partner can reduce exposure to environmental risk factors. But does it act on the psychobiology of the person? And if so, how? Has the biological substrate been altered? Alternatively, are the effects on styles of appraisal and coping? Or do they represent different sides of the same coins?

At least four factors interact to determine the degree to which events have sensitizing and steeling properties respectively (Ormel 1997). First, the event should represent a significant challenge which can turn out as a failure (loss) or a success (gain). Its significance as a challenge depends on its potential for future physical and/or social well-being (Ormel *et al.* in press). What is especially important is not the loss or gain of well-being, but of resources for future production of well-being, such as self-efficacy, a key-relationship, planning capacities, and income. The other three factors that play a role in addition to the outcome of the challenge are attribution of control, social support, and formative vulnerability. Social support, in particular active-emotional support, is important in two respects. In the case of failure, social support that seeks to minimize the generalization of decreased low self-regard to future situations may prevent sensitizing. In the case of success, social support that seeks to maximize the generalization of increased mastery and self-esteem may result in steeling. Formative vulnerability may interact by making the sensitizing effect stronger and the steeling effect weaker in high formative vulnerability subjects as compared to low formative vulnerability subjects (other things equal). This hypothesis implies that, with ageing, individuals steadily tend to grow apart in terms of instrumental vulnerability, until compensatory mechanisms develop, such as treatment and social welfare. Sensitizing and steeling experiences may set the stage for a long-term change in instrumental vulnerability by changing one or more of the proximal etiologic mechanisms: e.g. exposure to stressors, appraisal style, or coping style. The change in exposure to stressors can be brought about by either a change in environment or by a change in environmental control.

The way forward

In 1977, Eisenberg argued that the central, underlying model in psychiatry should be the developmental perspective. His main argument was that this perspective provided the link between genetic and environmental determinants, between psychology, biology and sociology, between physiological (or somatic) and psychogenic causes. Many findings of the last 20 years have lent force to this view (Chicchetti and Cohen 1995; Goldberg and Huxley, 1992; Rutter et al. 1997). Throughout life, man can be seen as the result of the ongoing interaction between his genetic characteristics and experiences to date. The dynamic vulnerability–stress model suggests we shift our research efforts from factors with a low permanence of risk which move a person up or down across rather arbitrary diagnostic thresholds to the components of instrumental vulnerability and how these develop, to the interactive influences between formative vulnerability and the environment in their development, and to how instrumental vulnerability influences risk. More work on risk factors with a high permanence of risk might also help to elucidate the origins of lifetime comorbidity and of concentration of morbidity. Are they the result of generic (shared) instrumental vulnerabilities or is one disorder a risk factor for another one, the consequence model?

As far as environmental effects are concerned, there is a need for theories and research on the ways in which certain events can change vulnerability for a long time, i.e. environmental factors with a high permanence of effect. What do these experiences actually do to the organism? What changes are brought about within and outside the body? It is very important in this context to use methodologies which can distinguish between environmental effects on people, the effects of people on their environment and genetic effects on psychopathology (Rutter et al. 1997). Another question which needs to be answered is whether environmental risks which determine the differences in the prevalence of depression *between* populations are also responsible for *individual* differences in the risk of depression *within* populations (Brown 1998).

Similar work needs to be done on genetic and personality effects. These effects also play a large role in aetiology. But the question of how they function has largely gone unanswered. What makes a certain genotype and personality profile a risk factor? How does this lead to illness? Through which channels is the risk realised? What developmental experiences play a role in this? Are genes directly responsible for somatic deviations which form the basis of emotional disorder? Or do they encode aspects of vulnerability, such as negative affectivity. Similar questions can also be asked about the personality traits involved in depression; how do neuroticism and interpersonal sensitivity work? Through their influence on the environment (environmental control), as several of the presented facts suggest? Or also via effects on the perception of stressors (appraisal)? On the way they cope with stress? Or on the effects of stress on emotions, cognition and physiology?

We strongly believe that genetically sensitive designs within a developmental perspective hold the answers to many of these questions. For epidemiology, this would mean population-based cohort studies in twins, (half-)siblings or founder populations, starting at birth or during pre-adolescence, and following them all the way through adolescence and young adulthood. To enhance their potential, neurobiological and neurocognitive components could be nested in such an epidemiological cohort study by selecting interesting subsamples. Founder populations are an interesting alternative to twins as it is difficult to recruit a large cohort of same-age twins. Founder populations allow highly efficient Identity-by-Descent methodology including candidate gene approaches, fine gene-mapping, and gene-environment analyses.

Why should such cohort studies start in pre-adolescence? Adolescence is a critical period in the development of vulnerability. It is during adolescence that the incidence of emotional disorder begins to rise strongly (Newman *et al.* 1996). First lifetime onsets drop dramatically after age 25. In addition, not only are the causes for continuity and accumulation of vulnerability (via self-selection, cumulative continuity, sensitising experiences and accentuation points) prevalent during adolescence, but also the causes for discontinuity and reduction of vulnerability (via steeling experiences and turning points). The transition from adolescence into adulthood is a critical one because adolescence is a period with important implications for later life. It is at this point that decisions with long-term consequences have to be made. Because the stakes for a successful transition are particularly high, the onset of mental illness in young adulthood may have even more serious and long-lasting consequences than at other stages of the life course. This applies even more to offspring who enter puberty with increased levels of formative vulnerability.

Another requirement for a productive cohort study is assessment of multiple level risk factors and multi-dimensional outcomes. It follows logically from a conception of development as an interactive process that cohort studies which focus on one domain only – such as the individual or, even more narrow, the psychological – can never account for why the development of some adolescents deviates, why some experience temporary problems only and why some, despite apparent high risk, do not. Although it is rare for, for instance, the impact of emotional development on physical health to be reported on, occasionally one gets glimpses of how closely seemingly disparate vulnerability and risk domains are interrelated when it is reported, for instance, that poor *physical* development in childhood and adolescence not only raises risk of natural but even more so of suicidal death (Neeleman *et al.* 1998; Barker *et al.* 1995), when deficient *moral* (social-cognitive) development is quoted as an independent risk factor for future *antisocial* behaviour quite apart from the known link of this outcome with childhood behavioural disinhibition (Miller and Eisenberg 1988), when low intelligence emerges as a risk factor for future affective disorder (Van Os *et al.* 1997), or when exposure to life events or being in possession of an aggressive temperament (Raitakari *et al.* 1995; Hagnell and Rorsman 1980) raises risk not only of suicide and depression but also of cardiovascular death. A comprehensive account of development can emerge only if assessments, at each single stage in a study, are multidisciplinary.

A final reason for a pre-adolescence cohort is that adolescence and young adulthood may be a period where downward and upward spirals of instrumental vulnerability may take off, in particular in those with formative vulnerability. Menarche, one of the best-known stressful events facing girls at the threshold of adolescence, acts as a risk factor for behavioural problems, but especially so in girls who were already predisposed to behavioural problems by virtue of their temperament (Caspi and Moffitt 1991). In other words, a challenging transition, occurring to all, may increase the relative disadvantage of the vulnerable with respect to the non-vulnerable – possibly setting the scene for accumulation of risk much more likely to occur in the vulnerable than the non-vulnerable. This can also be exemplified by the finding that children at risk of substance use by virtue of the family they come from, face additional hazard, because, not only are they exposed to more risk factors such as negative life events but also because they are more vulnerable to them than children of low-risk families (Wills *et al.* 1995). This general principle of *concentration of risk in the vulnerable and dilution of it in the resilient* (Neeleman 1997), implies that exposure to the same risk may be more dangerous for some than others (Maggs *et al.* 1997) – a notion with great public health implications since it suggests that preventive activities may also be most effective when applied to the most vulnerable (Wills *et al.* 1995).

Note

1 Like vulnerability, we consider resilience for the time being as a relatively stable set of characteristics of the individual. While vulnerability and resilience are often opposite ends of the same, bipolar dimensions, low scores on a vulnerability factor do not necessarily reflect resilience, nor is the opposite the case. For some dimensions, the lack of bipolarity is due to lack of discrimination at the lower end of measures of vulnerability or resilience. For instance, the skewed distributions on neuroticism scales with most individuals scoring in the lower ranges suggests that these scales do not differentiate well at the resilience end.

References

Andrews, G., Page, A.G. and Neilson, M.D. (1993) Sending your teenagers away: controlled stress decreases neurotic vulnerability, *Archives of General Psychiatry* 50, 585–589.

Barker, D.J., Osmond, C., Rodin, I., Fall, C.H. and Winter, P.D. (1995) Low weight gain in infancy and suicide in adult life, *British Medical Journal* 312, 510.

Boyce, P., Parker, G., Barnett, B., Cooney, M. and Smith, F. (1991) Personality as a vulnerability factor to depression, *British Journal of Psychiatry* 159, 106–114.

Brown, G.W. (1998) Genetic and population perspectives on life events and depression, *Social Psychiatry and Psychiatric Epidemiology* 33, 363–372.

Brown, G.W. and Harris, T.O. (1978) *Social Origins of Depression,* London: Tavistock.

Brown, G.W. and Harris, T.O. (1989) *Life Events and Illness,* New York: Guilford Press.

Brown, G.W., Harris, T.O. and Hepworth, C. (1994) Life events and endogenous depression. A puzzle re-examined, *Archives of General Psychiatry* 51, 525–534.

Brown, G.W., Harris, T.O. and Hepworth, C. (1995) Loss, humiliation and entrapment among women developing depression: a patient and non-patient comparison, *Psychological Medicine* 25, 7–21.

Caspi, A. and Moffitt, T.E. (1991) Individual differences are accentuated during periods of social change: the sample case of girls at puberty, *Journal of Personality and Social Psychology* 61, 157–168.

Caspi, A. and Moffitt, T.E. (1993) The continuity of maladaptive behavior: from description to understanding in the study of antisocial behavior, in D. Chichetti and D. Cohen (eds) *Manual of Developmental Psychopathology*, New York: Wiley and Sons.

Caspi, A., Moffitt, T.E., Newman, D.L. and Silva, P.A. (1996) Behavioral observations at age 3 years predict adult psychiatric disorders, *Archives of General Psychiatry* 53, 1033–1039.

Chicchetti, D. and Cohen, D.J. (eds) (1995) *Developmental Psychopathology: Vol.1: Theory and Method; Vol. 2: Risk, Disorder, and Adaptation*, New York: J.Wiley and Sons.

Clayton, P.J., Ernst, C. and Angst, J. (1994) Premorbid personality traits of men who develop unipolar or bipolar disorders, *European Archives of Psychiatry and Clinical Neuroscience* 243, 340–346.

Cooke, D.J. (1987) The significance of life events as a cause of psychological and physical disorder, in B.Cooper (ed.) *Psychiatric Epidemiology: Progress and Prospects,* London: Croom Helm.

Eisenberg, L. (1977) Development as a unifying concept in psychiatry, *British Journal of Psychiatry* 131, 225–237.

Fergusson, D.M. and Horwood, L.J. (1987) Vulnerability to life events exposure, *Psychological Medicine*, 17, 739–749.

Flint, J., Corley, R., DeFries, J.C., Fulker, D.W., Gray, J.A., Miller, S. and Collins, A.C. (1995) A simple genetic basis for a complex psychological trait in laboratory mice, *Science* 269, 1432–1435.

Foley, D.L., Neale, M.C. and Kendler, K.S. (1996) A longitudinal study of stressful life events assessed at interview with an epidemiological sample of adult twins: the basis of individual variation in event exposure, *Psychological Medicine* 26, 1239–1252.

Goldberg, D. and Huxley, P. (1992) *Common Mental Disorders. A Bio-Social Model*, London: Routledge.

Goldberg, D., Bridges, K., Cook, D., Evans, B. and Grayson, D. (1990) The influence of social factors on common mental disorders. Destabilisation and restitution, *British Journal of Psychiatry* 156, 704–713.

Hagnell, O. and Rorsman, B. (1980) Suicide in the Lundby study: a controlled prospective investigation of stressful life events, *Neuropsychobiology* 6, 319–332.

Harris, T.O., Brown, G.W. and Bifulco, A.T. (1990) Depression and situational helplessness/mastery in a sample selected to study childhood parental loss, *Journal of Affective Disorders*, 20, 27–41.

Headey, B. and Wearing, A. (1989) Personality, life events, and subjective well-being: Toward a dynamic equilibrium model, *Journal of Personality and Social Psychology* 57, 731–739.

Heath, A.C., Neale, M.C., Kessler, R.C., Eaves, L.J. and Kendler, K.S. (1992) Evidence for genetic influences on personality from self-reports and informant ratings, *Journal of Personality and Social Psychology* 63, 85–96.

Hirschfeld, R.M., Klerman, G.L., Clayton, P.J. and Keller, M.B. (1983) Personality and depression. Empirical findings, *Archives of General Psychiatry* 40, 993–998.

Hirschfeld, R.M., Shea, M.T. and Holzer, C.D. (1997) Personality dysfunction and depression, *Depression: Neurobiological Psychopathological and Therapeutic Advances* 3, 327–341.

Jenaway, A. and Paykel, E.S. (1997) Life events and depression, in A. Honig and H.M. van Praag (eds) *Depression: Neurobiological, Psychopathological and Therapeutic Advances,* New York: Wiley and Sons.

Kendler, K.S. and Karkowski-Shuman, L. (1997) Stressful life events and genetic liability to major depression: genetic control of exposure to the environment? *Psychological Medicine* 27, 539–547.

Kendler, K.S., Neale, M.C., Kessler, R.C., Heath, A. and Eaves, L. (1993) A twin study of recent life events and difficulties, *Archives of General Psychiatry* 50, 789–796.

Kendler, K.S., Kessler, R.C., Walters, E.E., MacLean, C., Neale, M.C., Heath, A.C. and Eaves, L.J. (1995) Stressful life events, genetic liability and onset of an episode of major depression in women, *American Journal of Psychiatry* 152, 833–842.

Krueger, R.F., Caspi, A., Moffit, T.E. and Silva, P.A. (1996) Personality traits are differentially linked to mental disorders; a multitrait–multidiagnosis study of an adolescent birth cohort, *Journal of Abnormal Psychology* 105, 299–312.

Laub, J.H. and Sampson, R.J. (1993) Turning points in the life course: why change matters to the study of crime, *Criminology* 31, 301–325.

Loehlin, J.C. (1992) *Genes and Environment in Personality Development*, Newbury Park: Sage.

McGuffin, P., Katz, R., and Rutherford, J. (1991) Nature, nurture and depression: a twin study, *Psychological Medicine* 21, 329–335.

Maggs, J.L., Frome, P.M., Eccles, J.S. and Barber, B.L. (1997) Psychosocial resources, adolescent risk behaviour and young adult adjustment: is risk taking more danger-ous for some than others? *Journal of Adolescence* 20, 103–119.

Magnus, K., Diener, E., Fujita, F. and Pavot, W. (1993) Extraversion and neuroticism as predictors of objective life events: A longitudinal analysis, *Journal of Personality and Social Psychology* 65, 1046–1053.

Miller, P.A. and Eisenberg, N. (1988) The relation of empathy to aggressive and externalizing/antisocial behaviour, *Psychological Bulletin* 103, 324–344.

Neeleman, J. (1997) *The Social and Epidemiological Context of Suicidal Behaviour*, Ph.D. thesis, University of Groningen.

Neeleman, J., Wessely, S. and Wadsworth, M. (1998) Predictors of suicide, accidental death, and premature natural death in a general-population birth cohort, *Lancet* 351, 93–97.

Newman, D.L., Moffitt, T.E., Caspi, A., Magdol, L. and Silva, P.A. (1996) Psychiatric disorder in a birth cohort of young adults: prevalence, comorbidity, clinical significance, and new case incidence from ages 11 to 21. *Journal of Consulting and Clinical Psychology* 64, 552–562.

Ormel, J. (1997) *Kwetsbare Mensen [Vulnerable People]*, inaugural lecture, University of Groningen, Groningen, The Netherlands.

Ormel, J. and Rijsdijk, F.V. (in press) Continuing within-subject change in neuroti-cism during adulthood: Structural modelling of a 16 year, 5-wave community study.

Ormel, J. and Wohlfarth, T.D. (1991) How neuroticism, long-term difficulties, and changes in quality of life affect psychological distress. A longitudinal approach, *Journal of Personality and Social Psychology* 60, 744–755.

Ormel, J., Sanderman, R. and Stewart, R. (1988) Personality as modifier of the life event-distress relationship: A longitudinal structural equation model, *Personality and Individual Differences* 9, 973–982.

Ormel, J., Lindenberg, S., Steverink, N. and Verbrugge, L.M. (in press) Subjective well-being and social production function, *Social Indicators Research*.

Os, J. van., Jones, P., Lewis, G., Wadsworth, M., and Murray, R. (1997) Developmental precursors of affective illness in a general population birth cohort, *Archives of General Psychiatry* 54, 625–631.

Plomin, R., Lichtenstein, P., Pedersen, N., McClearn, G.E. and Nesselroade, J.R. (1990) Genetic influence on life events during the last half of the life span, *Psychology and Aging* 5, 25–30.

Plomin, R., DeFries, J.C. and McClearn, G.E.(1997) *Behavioural Genetics*, 3rd edn, New York: W.H. Freeman and Co.

Quinton, D., Pickles, A. and Maughan, B. (1993) Partners, peers, and pathways: Assortative pairing and continuities in conduct disorder, *Development and Psychopathology* 5, 763–783.

Raitakari, O.T., Leino, M., Rakkonen, K., Porkka, K.V., Taimela, S., Rasanen, L. and Viikari, J.S. (1995) Clustering of risk habits in young adults. The Cardiovascular Risk in Young Finns Study, *American Journal of Epidemiology* 142, 36–44.

Rodgers, B. (1991) Models of stress, vulnerability and affective disorder, *Journal of Affective Disorders* 21, 1–13.

Rothman, K.J. (1986), *Modern Epidemiology*, Boston/Toronto: Little, Brown and Co.

Rutter, M. (1996), Transitions and turning points in developmental psychopathology: As applied to the age span between childhood and mid-adulthood, *International Journal of Behavior Development* 19, 603–626.

Rutter, M., Dunn, J, Plomin, R., Simonoff, E., Pickles, A., Maughan, B., Ormel, J., Meyer, J. and Eaves, L. (1997) Integrating nature and nurture: implications of person–environment correlations and interactions for developmental psychopathology, *Development and Psychopathology* 9, 335–364.

Saudino, K.J., Pedersen, N.L., Lichtenstein, P., McClearn, G.E. and Plomin, R. (1997) Can personality explain genetic influences on life events? *Journal of Personality and Social Psychology* 72, 196–206.

Watson, D. and Clark, L.A. (1984) Negative affectivity: the disposition to experience aversive emotional states, *Psychological Bulletin* 96, 465–490.

Willige, G. van de, Ormel, J. and Giel, R. (1995) Etiologische betekenis van ingrijpende gebeurtenissen en langdurige moeilijkheden voor het ontstaan van depressie en angststoornissen: een nadere uitwerking, *Tijdschrift voor Psychiatrie* 37, 689–703.

Wills, T.A., McNamara, G. and Vaccaro, D. (1995) Parental education related to adolescent stress-coping and substance use: development of a mediational model, *Health Psychology* 14, 464–478.

4

DISABILITY AND PSYCHOLOGICAL
ILLNESS IN PRIMARY CARE

Michael Von Korff

This chapter reviews recent progress in understanding and ameliorating the impact of psychological illness on disability. This is a fitting topic for a book in honour of Sir David Goldberg. The hallmarks of his work have been devotion to the scientific method, commitment to advancement of the public's health, and conviction that improved recognition and management of mental disorders in the primary care setting will improve the well-being of the population-at-large.

Some of the research reviewed in this chapter has resulted from a productive and enjoyable collaboration between Hans Ormel and myself. This collaborative work was a direct result of David Goldberg's role in the World Health Organisation's Collaborative Study of Psychological Problems in General Health Care. At his behest, Hans and I were asked to serve as Study Advisers. Proving his intuition correct, Hans and I have since enjoyed a long-lasting friendship and collaboration, resulting in several papers reviewed in this chapter.

Impairment, disability and handicap

In 1980, the International Classification of Impairments, Disabilities and Handicaps (ICIDH) codified the Impairment–Disability–Handicap triad (World Health Organization, 1980). *Impairment* was defined as a health-related loss or abnormality of psychological, physiological or anatomical structure or function, including psychological illness and pain. *Disability* was defined as a health-related restriction or lack of ability to perform an activity, within the range considered normal. *Handicap* was defined as a disadvantage resulting from an impairment or disability limiting fulfilment of role expectations for that individual. The triad of impairment, disability and handicap provides a framework for expanding disease concepts to include their impact on social functioning (e.g. Pope and Tarlov, 1991).

Disability concepts and measurement

Disability assessment for geriatric and chronically ill populations initially focused on activities of daily living (self-care and mobility inside the home) and instrumental activities of daily living (household maintenance and mobility outside the home) (Katz and Akpom, 1976; Pope and Tarlov, 1991). Subsequently, reliable and valid self-report disability scales were developed measuring broader dimensions of disability. These measures included the Medical Outcomes Survey SF-36 (Ware *et al.* 1995), the Sickness Impact Profile or SIP (Bergner *et al.* 1981), the Arthritis Impact Measurement Scale (Mason *et al.* 1988), the Dartmouth Co-op Charts (Nelson *et al.* 1987) and others. Research using such scales showed a consistent relationship between psychological illness and disability (Berkman *et al.* 1986; Broadhead *et al.* 1990; Dohrenwend *et al.* 1983; Turner and Noh, 1988; Wohlfarth *et al.* 1993). Across cultures, self-report disability measures were found to be reliable and valid, with a consistent association between disability and psychological illness (Von Korff *et al.* 1996).

Despite growing evidence of a relationship between psychological illness and disability, the meaning and public health significance of this association remained unclear. For some, disability implied marked dependency, such as institutionalisation or total work disability. Or, disability was viewed as resulting largely from physical injury, chronic physical disease, or severe mental disorders such as dementia and schizophrenia. As disability status was assessed in less severely ill populations, and among working age adults, it became necessary to enlarge disability concepts so that they would be relevant to the full spectrum of disability in the population.

An important development was defining disability in terms of social role performance (Wiersma *et al.* 1988). Social role performance in work and family life calls on the highest order capacities of humans: motivation, planning, self-confidence, co-operative action, and sustained effort to achieve a goal in the face of adversity. Physical disease may impair physical abilities including respiratory capacity, muscle strength, fine and gross motor coordination, vision and hearing. But resilience in social role performance in the face of severe physical impairments is not unusual. In contrast, psychological illness impairs the highest order capacities of humans – capacities central to social role performance. Impairments resulting from psychological illness include loss of motivation and energy, reduced ability to engage in planned action, loss of self-confidence, avoidance of important activities due to unrealistic fears, reduced ability to interact effectively, and reduced ability to sustain effort toward achieving goals when difficulties and frustrations arise. Hence, a better understanding of the determinants of social role performance is crucial for understanding the role of psychological illness in disability.

Without a focus on social roles, ability to analyse and understand disability among adults engaged in crucial life activities (e.g. employment and child-rearing) is limited. Development of effective interventions may need to be specific to the form of social disability. Effective interventions for work disability may differ from those targeting disability in family roles. Without grounding in social role theory, disability assessment tends to enumerate long lists of specific disabilities difficult to relate to major life activities. For example, the ICIDH lists 338 disabilities, such as disabilities in awareness, relations, speaking, listening, seeing, personal care, ambulation, transfer, body movement, and dexterity (Thuriaux, 1995). Within each category, more specific forms of disability are identified. For example, disabilities of body movement include retrieval, reaching, arm function, kneeling, and crouching. A more parsimonious and theory-based approach to defining disability is needed.

Epidemiologic data on disability and psychological disorder

In 1988–89, Ken Wells and associates authored seminal papers that brought attention to the magnitude of the problem of disability among persons with psychological disorders. A paper reporting data from the NIMH Epidemiologic Catchment Area surveys found that persons with psychological disorder reported more physical limitations and activity restrictions than persons without psychological illness, after controlling for chronic medical conditions (Wells *et al.* 1988). Results of the Medical Outcomes Study found that depressed persons showed poorer functioning than patients with chronic medical conditions (Wells *et al.* 1989). Only patients with advanced coronary artery disease showed consistently poorer functioning than patients with depressive illness. The WHO Collaborative Study of Psychological Disorders in General Health Care gave cross-national results consistent with these findings (Ormel *et al.* 1994).

Recent studies have examined whether psychological illness is a risk factor for onset of disability. There are now at least five prospective studies reporting that pre-existing depression is a risk factor for the onset of disability (Bruce *et al.*, 1994; Ormel *et al.* forthcoming; Manninen *et al.* 1997; Pennix *et al.* 1998; Armenian *et al.* 1998).

In 1992–93, longitudinal studies of primary care patients showed that disability was reduced among patients whose psychological illness improved (Von Korff *et al.* 1992; Ormel *et al.* 1993). In contrast, patients whose psychological illness ran a chronic course showed elevated disability levels one year to over three years later. These results suggested that chronic psychological disorder was associated with long-lasting disability. However, randomised controlled trials showing the benefits of treatment of psychological illness on disability outcomes were lacking. The lack of experimental studies led us to conclude that: 'At present, there is an urgent need for randomized controlled trials of treatment of depressive illness among medical patients to assess effects of those treatments on functional disability as well as on depressive symptoms. . . . If such results were reliably observed following psychiatric or behavioral intervention with depressed medical patients, current efforts to increase the recognition and effective management of depression by health care providers would be markedly advanced' (Von Korff et al. 1992).

Results of recent randomized controlled trials

The first large randomized controlled trial among depressed primary care patients reporting disability outcomes was carried out at the University of Pittsburgh by Schulberg's research team (Schulberg et al. 1996). They randomly assigned severely depressed primary care patients to pharmaco-therapy, interpersonal therapy or to usual care. In 1997, Coulehan (Coulehan et al. 1997) reported that patients in this study who received active treatment for depression experienced more favourable disability outcomes.

At about the same time, our research group in Seattle was conducting two large randomised controlled trials of Collaborative Care programmes for depression in primary care (Katon et al. 1995; Katon et al. 1996, Von Korff et al. 1998). Collaborative Care strengthens and supports illness self-care while assuring that effective medical, preventive and health maintaining interventions take place (Von Korff et al. 1997). Collaborative Care occurs when patients and providers have shared goals, a sustained working relation-ship, mutual understanding of roles and responsibilities, and requisite skills for carrying out those roles. Collaborative Care is a multi-component inter-vention strategy that includes patient interventions (enhanced patient educa-tion and activation), provider interventions (guidelines and ongoing case consultation) and health care system interventions (e.g. using automated data to monitor medication adherence) (Katon et al. 1997). Patients started on antidepressant medications for depression by the primary care physician were randomly assigned to either a Collaborative Care programme or to Usual Care. In the Collaborative Care programmes, mental health specialists co-managed patients with the primary care physician.

In the first two randomized controlled trials of Collaborative Care, depression symptom outcomes were improved for patients meeting major depression criteria at baseline, but not for patients with minor depression (Katon et al. 1995; Katon et al. 1996). In 1998, Simon and colleagues (Simon et al. 1998) reported combined results of these two trials for disability outcomes for patients with major depression at baseline. The Collaborative Care programme produced more favourable outcomes than Usual Care for somatic distress and for self-rated health status, but not for disability out-comes. Relative to the Schulberg trial, patients in this trial were less severely ill, and Usual Care patients were more likely to receive adequate treatment. In addition, the disability measures employed (measures of physical function and activity limitation days) were probably less sensitive to depression treatment effects than measures of social role disability. Although this study yielded negative results for disability, these circumstances may have reduced our ability to detect intervention effects for disability outcomes.

In our research team's most recent evaluation of Collaborative Care, more severely depressed patients were enrolled and disability measures more sensitive to depression treatment effects were used (Katon *et al.* submitted). We found that disability outcomes were significantly improved among the Collaborative Care relative to Usual Care patients (unpublished data). This randomised trial employed a stepped-care approach in which patients became eligible for the Collaborative Care programme if they continued to have four or more symptoms of major depression 6–8 weeks after starting pharmacotherapy. Disability outcomes were more favourable three and six months after randomisation.

Another recent multi-Center randomised controlled trial of pharmaco-therapy for depressed high utilisers of medical care was led by Katzelnick, Simon and Pearson (Katzelnick *et al.* submitted). This study also used a stepped-care approach using telephone-based case-management to determine when more intensive treatment was needed. Symptom and disability out-comes were improved in this study, relative to Usual Care, over a one year follow-up period.

Taken together, these large randomised controlled trials provide encoura-ging evidence that adequate depression treatment can improve the disability outcomes of primary care patients meeting criteria for major depression. Several more large randomized controlled trials of depression treatments in the primary care setting are nearing completion in the United States. If the combined results of these trials suggest that improved treatment of major depression improves disability outcomes, then the public health imperative for improving care of depressive illness in primary care settings will be immeasurably strengthened.

As evidence of the beneficial effects of treating depressive illness mount for disability outcomes, the research focus will need to shift from effectiveness research to dissemination research. Effectiveness research tests practical models for delivering treatments under real world conditions (Simon *et al.* 1995). Dissemination research evaluates interventions that increase the *reach* of effective interventions on a population basis (Abrams *et al.* 1996). Reach refers to the proportion of the affected population that receives an intervention. The population impact of an intervention is the product of the intervention's efficacy, the quality (or fidelity) of delivery of the inter-vention, and its reach.

In the United States, the AHCPR Depression Practice Outcome Research Team (PORT) led by Ken Wells is now completing a large multi-site randomized controlled trial that will be the first step from effectiveness to dissemination research. In this study, screened patients in large managed care organizations found to have depressive illness were randomly assigned to active treatment or to usual care. Nurse case-managers implemented the care program according to a structured protocol. The results of this study will shed further light on whether depression and disability outcomes can be improved by active treatment under real-world conditions, and whether the new models for organising depression care can be widely disseminated. The results of this study will be of fundamental importance in guiding public health initiatives for depression.

Future directions

What steps need to be taken to improve the functional outcomes of psychological illness on a population basis? In order to improve the effectiveness of care for chronic or recurrent conditions, like major depression and other psychological disorders, health care systems need to fundamentally change the organisation of patient care. Improved clinical and functional outcomes result from productive interactions between a prepared practice team and an informed, activated patient (see Figure 4.1) (Wagner *et al.* 1996). Key elements needed to support such productive interactions include: information systems (e.g. patient registries, reminders, and care monitoring systems); decision support (guidelines, consultation services, expert systems); self-management support systems (e.g. patient education and case management); and delivery systems design (e.g. active follow-up systems). These elements of

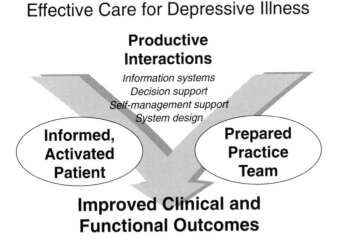

Figure 4.1 A systems approach to improving clinical and functional outcome of depressive illness in organised health care systems

Acute care	MANAGEMENT CONTINUUM	Chronic care
GOALS • Decreasing symptoms • Preventing disability • Preventing chronicity		**GOALS** • Preventing relapse • Minimising disability
STEP 0 • Recognition and diagnosis with screening and diagnostic tools	FOR ALL PATIENTS AT EACH STEP	**STEP 0** • Monitoring patient status to guide long term management
STEP 1 • Treatment by the primary care physician	**Collaborative Management:**	**STEP 1** • Self-management with minimal support
STEP 2 • Consultation with mental health specialist	Shared problem definition and goal setting + Supporting self-management + Active follow-up	**STEP 2** • Continuing support of self-management (Low-intensity case management)
STEP 3 • Referral for brief mental health intervention in primary care		**STEP 3** • Maintenance treatment (High intensity case management)
STEP 4 • Referral to mental health specialist for longer more intensive intervention		

Figure 4.2 An individualised stepped-care model for management of mental disorders in primary care (Source: B. Tiemens (1999) Doctoral dissertation, University of Groningen, The Netherlands)

high quality care for chronic illness are integral to efforts to improve care for major depression (Katon *et al.* 1997), and other common psychological disorders. Thus, efforts to improve functional outcomes require more than *effective treatments,* they also require *effective systems* capable of delivering those treatments on a population basis.

An emerging theme in efforts to improve care of depressive illness is the use of stepped-care strategies. Stepped-care has been used for management of a wide range of medical and behavioral conditions including hypertension (SHEP Cooperative Research Group, 1991), alcohol dependence (Donovan and Marlatt, 1993), nicotine dependence (Hurt, 1993), cholesterol reduction (Oster *et al.* 1995), bulimia (Treasure *et al.* 1996) and back pain (Von Korff, 1999). The essence of a stepped-care approach is that care is modified based on the patient's outcome. For example, a patient whose hypertension is not adequately controlled on a first-line medication, may be stepped up to a second-line medication. Or, patients who do not experience a good outcome after receiving a minimal self-care intervention may be stepped up to more intensive services.

In Chapter 9 of this volume, Lin describes the application of stepped-care to management of depression in the primary care setting, as developed for intervention trials underway in Seattle. In these intervention trials, stepped-care was used to target collaborative care to patients who were unimproved after 6–8 weeks of pharmacotherapy. Patients who were improved, but who were at high risk of relapse, were stepped up to a relapse prevention programme (on a randomised basis). The case-management program developed by Katzelnick, Simon and Pearson in their depressed high utiliser trial also employed a stepped-care approach. The case manager monitored patient outcomes and ensured that patients were stepped up to more intensive treatment if a favourable outcome was not achieved.

Stepped-care may provide a framework for integrating behavioral interventions that directly target disability outcomes into the management of psychological disorders in the primary care setting. Tiemens (1999) has proposed a stepped-care model appropriate for integrating behavioral interventions into management of psychological disorders in the primary care setting (see Figure 4.2). Stepped-care is used to guide acute management of psychological illness (left side of Figure 4.2), with more intensive treatments and increasing specialist involvement being targeted towards patients whose symptoms do not improve with basic primary care treatment. A stepped-care approach is also used to guide chronic care with the objectives of preventing relapse and minimising disability (right side of Figure 4.2). Guided by symptomatic *and* functional outcomes, patients requiring more intensive care are stepped up from self-management with minimal support, to enhanced support by a case manager, and finally to maintenance treatment that may involve more intensive case management often best organised in a speciality setting.

Consistent with an emphasis on patient functioning, this model of stepped care integrates collaborative management strategies (shared problem definition and goal setting, self-management support, and active follow-up) shown to improve functional outcomes for a wide range of chronic conditions (Von Korff *et al.* 1997). This model provides a useful framework for considering how behavioral interventions designed to reduce social role disability might be combined with conventional pharmacotherapeutic or psychotherapeutic treatment of psychological disorders in the primary care setting.

Conclusion

In the late 1980s and early 1990s, epidemiological research showed that common psychological disorders were as or more disabling than common chronic medical diseases. Patients with psychological disorders that did not improve were found to be more likely to experience significant and long-lasting social role disability. This relationship between disability and psychological illness held after controlling for medical co-morbidity. Randomized controlled trials of depression interventions in primary care are now showing significant improvements in disability outcomes relative to care as usual. These effective intervention programs increasingly employ stepped-care strategies and make key system changes in how depressive illness is managed by a team of providers. This team typically includes the primary care physician, a case manager and a consulting mental health specialist.

A promising direction for future research is development and evaluation of stepped-care approaches guided by both disability and symptom outcomes. This new approach to stepped care would target behavioral interventions at those with specific forms of social role disability. Stepped care guided by both symptom and functional outcomes would provide a framework for a truly biopsychosocial approach to patient care. Under this new stepped-care model, conventional pharmacological and psychotherapeutic treatments would be used to manage psychological symptoms, while targeted behavioral interventions would be used to enhance social role performance.

It is heartening that, within one decade, the field has advanced from epidemiological research showing an association between psychological illness and social role disability to randomized controlled trials of interventions that improve clinical and disability outcomes in primary care. The challenge for the coming decade will be to develop intervention programs for primary care patients afflicted by psychological disorders capable of producing substantial and long-lasting improvements in social role functioning, as well as adequate and enduring control of psychological symptoms.

Acknowledgements

This research was supported by NIMH grants MH51338 and MH41739 and by the Improving Chronic Illness Care grant from the Robert Wood Johnson Foundation.

References

Abrams, D.B., Orleans, C.T., Niaura, R.S., Goldstein, M.G., Prochaska, J.O. and Velicer, W. (1996) 'Integrating individual and public health perspectives for treatment of tobacco dependence under managed health care: a combined stepped-care and matching model'. *Annals of Behavioral Medicine* 18, 290–304.

Armenian, H.K., Pratt, L.A., Gallo, J. and Eaton, W.W. (1998) 'Psychopathology as a predictor of disability: a population-based follow-up study in Baltimore, Maryland'. *American Journal of Epidemiology* 148, 269–275.

Bergner, M., Bobbitt, R.A., Carter, W.B. and Gilson, B.S. (1981) 'The Sickness Impact Profile: development and final revision of a health status measure'. *Medical Care* 19, 787–805.

Berkman, L.L.S., Berkman, C.S., Kasl, S., Freeman, D.M., Leo, L., Ostfeld, A.M., Coroni-Huntley, J. and Brody, J.A. (1986) 'Depressive symptoms in relation to physical health and functioning in the elderly'. *American Journal of Epidemiology* 115, 684–694.

Broadhead, W.E., Blazer, D.G., George, L.K. and Tse, C.K. (1990) 'Depression, disability days and days lost from work in a prospective epidemiologic study'. *Journal of the American Medical Association* 264, 2524–2528.

Bruce, M.L., Seeman, T.E., Merrill, S.S. and Blazer, D.G. (1994) 'The impact of depressive symptomatology on physical disability: MacArthur Studies of Successful Aging'. *American Journal of Public Health* 84, 1796–1799.

Coulehan, J.L., Schulberg, H.C., Block, M.R., Madonia, M.J. and Rodriguez, E. (1997) 'Treating depressed primary care patients improves their physical, mental, and social functioning'. *Archives of Internal Medicine* 157, 1113–1120.

Dohrenwend, B.S., Dohrenwend, B.P., Link, B. and Levav, I. (1983) 'Social functioning of psychiatric patients in contrast with community cases in the general population'. *Archives of General Psychiatry* 40, 1174–1182.

Donovan, D.M. and Marlatt, G.A. (1993) 'Recent developments in alcoholism behavioral treatment'. *Recent Developments in Alcoholism* 11, 397–411.

Hurt, R.D. (1993) 'Nicotine dependence – treatment for the 1990s'. *Journal of Internal Medicine* 233, 307–310.

Katon, W., Von Korff, M., Lin, E., Walker, E., Simon, G., Bush, T., Robinson, P. and Russo, J. (1995) 'Collaborative management to achieve treatment guidelines: impact on depression in primary care'. *Journal of the American Medical Association* 273, 1026–1031.

Katon, W., Robinson, P., Von Korff, M., Lin, E., Bush, T., Ludman, E., Simon, G. and Walker, E. (1996) 'A multifaceted intervention to improve treatment of depression in primary care'. *Archives of General Psychiatry* 53, 924–932.

Katon, W., Von Korff, M., Lin, E., Unutzer, J., Simon, G., Walker, E., Ludman, E. and Bush, T. (1997) 'Population-based care of depression: effective disease management strategies to decrease prevalence'. *General Hospital Psychiatry* 19, 169–178.

Katon, W., Von Korff, M., Lin, E.H.B., Simon, G., Walker, E., Bush, T., Ludman, E., Unutzer, J. and Rutter, C. 'A randomized controlled trial of stepped collaborative care for primary care depressive patients with persistent symptoms'. Submitted for publication.

Katz, S. and Akpom, C.A. (1976) 12. Index of ADL. *Medical Care* 14 (Suppl): 116–18.

Katzelnick, D.J., Simon, G.E., Pearson, S.D., Manning, W.G., Helstad, C.P., Henk, H.J., Cole, S.M., Lin, E.H.B., Taylor, L.v.H. and Kobak, K.A. 'Randomized trial of a depression management program in high utilizers of medical care'. Manuscript under review.

Manninen, P., Heliovaara, M., Riihimaki, H. and Makela, P. (1997) 'Does psychological distress predict disability?' *International Journal of Epidemiology* 26, 1063–1070.

Mason, J.H., Anderson, J.J. and Meenan, R.F. (1988) 'A model of health status for rheumatoid arthritis. A factor analysis of the Arthritis Impact Measurement Scales'. *Arthritis Rheum* 31, 714–720.

Nelson, E., Wasson, J., Kirk, J., Keller, A., Clark, D., Dietrich, A., Stewart, A. and Zubkoff, M. (1987) 'Assessment of function in routine clinical practice: description of the COOP Chart method and preliminary findings'. *Journal of Chronic Disease* 40 (Suppl 1), 55S–69S.

Ormel, J., Von Korff, M., Van Den Brink, W., Katon, W., Brilman, E. and Oldehinkel, T. (1993) 'Depression, anxiety and disability show synchrony of change: a $3\frac{1}{2}$ year longitudinal study in primary care'. *American Journal of Public Health* 83, 385–390.

Ormel, J., Von Korff, M., Üstün, T.B., Pini, S., Korten, A. and Oldehinkel, T. (1994) 'Common mental disorders and disability: a strong and cross-culturally consistent relationship. Results from the WHO Collaborative Study'. *Journal of the American Medical Association* 272, 1741–1748.

Ormel, J., Von Korff, M., Simon, G., Tiemens, T.G., Oldehinkel, A.J. and Üstün, T.B. 'Mild depression causes functional disability in medical outpatients: a prospective analysis'. *Psychological Medicine*, in press.

Oster, G., Borok, G.M., Menzin, J., Heys, J.F., Epstein, R.S., Quinn, V., Benson, V.V., Dudl, R.J. and Epstein, A. (1995) 'A randomized trial to assess effectiveness and cost in clinical practice: rationale and design of the Cholesterol Reduction Intervention Study'. *Controlled Clinical Trials* 16, 3–16.

Penninx, B.W., Guralnik, J.M., Ferrucci, L., Simonsick, E.M., Deeg, D.J. and Wallace, R.B. (1998) 'Depressive symptoms and physical decline in community-dwelling older persons'. *Journal of the American Medical Association* 279, 1720–1726.

Pope, A.M. and Tarlov, A.R. (eds) (1991) *Disability in America: Toward a National Agenda for Prevention of Disabilities*. National Academy Press, Washington DC, 362 pp.

Schulberg, H.C., Block, M.R., Madonia, M.J., Scott, C.P., Rodriguez, E., Imber, S.D., Perel, J., Lave, J., Houck, P.R. and Coulehan, J.L. (1996) 'Treating major depression in primary care practice. Eight–month clinical outcomes'. *Archives of General Psychiatry* 53, 913–919.

SHEP Cooperative Research Group (1991) 'Prevention of stroke in antihypertensive drug treatment in older persons with isolated hypertension. Final results of the Systolic Hypertension in the Elderly Program'. *Journal of the American Medical Association* 265, 3255–3264.

Simon, G.E., Wagner, E. and Von Korff, M. (1995) 'Cost-effectiveness comparisons using "real-world" randomized trials: the case of new antidepressant drugs'. *Journal of Clinical Epidemiology* 48, 363–373.

Simon, G., Katon, W., Von Korff, M., Lin, E., Robinson, P., Bush, T., Walker, E., Ludman, E., Russo, J. and Rutter, C. (1998) 'Impact of improved depression treatment in primary care on daily functioning and disability'. *Psychological Medicine* 28, 693–701.

Thuriaux, M.C. (1995) 'The ICIDH: evolution, status, and prospects'. *Disability Rehabilitation* 17, 112–118.

Tiemens, B. (1999) 'Management of mental health problems in primary care. The doctor, the patient, and the medical model'. Doctoral thesis, University of Groningen, Groningen, The Netherlands, 1999.

Treasure, J., Schmidt, U., Troop, N., Tiller, J., Todd, G. and Turnbill, S. (1996) 'Sequential treatment for bulimia nervosa incorporating a self-care manual'. *British Journal of Psychiatry* 168, 94–98.

Turner, R.J. and Noh, S. (1988) 'Physical disability and depression: a longitudinal analysis'. *Journal of Health and Social Behavior* 29: 23–37.

Von Korff, M. (in press) 'Pain management in primary care: an individualized stepped-care approach'. In R. Gatchel and D. Turk (eds) *Psychosocial Factors in Pain: Evolution and Revolutions*, Guilford Press, New York.

Von Korff, M., Ormel, J., Katon, W. and Lin, E.H.B. (1992) 'Disability and depression in medical patients: a longitudinal analysis'. *Archives of General Psychiatry* 49, 91–100.

Von Korff, M., Üstün, T.B., Ormel, J., Kaplan, I. and Simon, G. (1996) 'Self-report disability in an international primary care study of psychological illness'. *Journal of Clinical Epidemiology* 49:,297–303.

Von Korff, M., Gruman, J., Schaefer, J., Curry, S. and Wagner, E.H. (1997) 'Collaborative management of chronic illness'. *Annals of Internal Medicine* 127, 1097–1102.

Von Korff, M., Katon, W., Bush, T., Lin, E., Simon, G.E., Saunders, K., Ludman, E., Walker, E. and Unutzer, J. (1998) 'Treatment costs, cost offset and cost-effectiveness of collaborative management of depression'. *Psychosomatic Medicine* 60, 143–149.

Wagner, E.H., Austin, B.T. and Von Korff, M. (1996) 'Organizing care for patients with chronic illness'. *The Milbank Quarterly* 74, 511–544.

Ware, J.E. Jr, Kosinski, M., Bayliss, M.S., McHorney, C.A., Rogers, W.H. and Raczek, A. (1995) 'Comparison of methods for the scoring and statistical analysis of SF-36 health profile and summary measures: summary of results from the Medical Outcomes Study'. *Medical Care* 33 (Suppl), AS264–79.

Wells, K.B., Golding, J.M. and Burnham, M.A. (1988) 'Psychiatric disorder and limitations in physical functioning in a sample of the Los Angeles general population'. *American Journal of Psychiatry* 145, 712–717.

Wells, K.B., Stewart, A., Hays, R.D., Burnham, A., Rogers, W., Daniels, M., Berry, S., Greenfield, S. and Ware, J. (1989) 'The functioning and well-being of depressed patients'. *Journal of the American Medical Association* 262, 914–919.

Wiersma, D., DeJong, A. and Ormel, J. (1988) 'The Groningen Social Disabilities Schedule: development, relationship with I.C.I.D.H., and psychometric properties'. *International Journal of Rehabilitation Research* 11, 213–224.

Wohlfarth, T.D., van den Brink, W., Ormel, J., Koeter, M.W. and Oldehinkel, A.J. (1993) 'The relationship between social dysfunctioning and psychopathology among primary care attenders'. *British Journal of Psychiatry* 163, 37–44.

World Health Organization (1980) *International Classification of Impairments, Disabilities and Handicaps*. World Health Organization, Geneva.

Part II

TEAMWORK IN PRIMARY CARE

5

MENTAL HEALTH SERVICES IN RURAL PAKISTAN

Malik H. Mubbashar

Introduction

Nearly a hundred million people live in rural areas of Pakistan. Like most developing countries modern medical care facilities are scant and programmes for mental health care abysmal. There is one qualified psychiatrist for one million of the population and each of these too, is based in the urban setting. The allied professionals like trained psychiatric nurses, psychologists and social workers are non-existent. The limited resources are further compartmentalised and jeopardised as the bulk of funding goes to tertiary centres and teaching hospitals and very little is spent on developing facilities in the rural areas. As a result, whatever facilities are available are not within the reach of 66 per cent of the total population of the country so the majority remains unserved, under-served or inappropriately served. Unfortunately the country has failed to provide basic mental health care or to improve the mental health of the people.

In addition, the overwhelming stigmatisation of mental illness, resistance from health administrators and policy makers, ever-growing socio-economic constraints like poverty, illiteracy, over-population, economic and political instability add to the difficulty in establishing mental health services. This is compounded by reliance on folk medicine and pseudo faith healers. In a vulnerable society burdened by a legitimate desire to forge ahead and surrounded by pervasive ignorance, mental disorders are common and widespread.

The health professionals have their own share in being responsible for the prevailing underdeveloped services. They have centralised, institutionalised, mystified and professionalised the field of mental illness. Their emphasis has been on mental illness rather than mental health issues. In doing so they have blindly followed the health care models developed in the West which focus on the curative aspects rather than the preventive strategies which are the need of the hour for a developing country.

To initiate actions to tackle all these difficulties is a daunting and almost Herculean task in the presence of prejudice and poor resources. Under such circumstances, the strengths of the system like motivation of the community and a strong family support system where patients are owned and compliance of treatment ensured can be exploited as natural resources. Therefore, there is a need to evolve innovative and indigenous solutions and doctrine to set up services. This chapter is devoted to the efforts being made to develop mental health care programmes in the rural areas of Pakistan.

Extent of the problem in the rural community

Studies in developed and developing countries have shown that a substantial proportion of patients presenting to primary care physicians may have some degree of psychiatric disorders. The figures range from 15 to 56 per cent (Ormel et al. 1991; Finlay-Jones and Burvill, 1978; Mari and Williams, 1984; Ndeti and Mohangi, 1979). The reason for misdiagnosis by the primary care physicians have been the subject of a number of studies (Goldberg, 1984; Marks et al. 1979; Boardman, 1987; Tyler and Jeeling, 1989).

Community surveys

A few surveys have been carried out in different parts of Pakistan. Mumford et al. (1996), in their survey carried out in Chitral (north-west Pakistan), found that 27 per cent of women and 4 per cent of men had BSI-21 scores in the very high range, 31 per cent of women and 15 per cent of men had scores in the high range and 24 per cent of women and 30 per cent of men had scores in the middle range. The point prevalence of disorders was estimated at 46 per cent for women and 15 per cent for men using very high and high threshold scores for BSI-21. The point prevalence rose to 60 per cent for women and 33 per cent for men when middle range scores on BSI-21 were included.

Another study carried out in rural Punjab (Mumford et al. 1997) showed that 66 per cent of women and 25 per cent of men suffered from anxiety and depressive disorders. Levels of emotional distress increased with age in both genders. Women living in unitary households reported more distress than those living in extended or joint families. With younger men and women, lower levels of education were associated with greater risk of psychiatric disorders. Social disadvantage was associated with more emotional distress.

Iqbal (1994) in his survey used a similar two-stage design at Mandara, Rawalpindi. Point prevalence for the whole population was 13.32 per cent. In the case of women it came to 16.09 per cent and for men 10.65 per cent. The most common diagnosis was depressive illness (11.73 per cent) followed by generalized anxiety disorders (0.9 per cent) and phobic disorders (0.65 per cent).

Psychiatric morbidity among attenders to traditional healers

In Pakistan traditional beliefs and religion play a central role in individual and community life. Native faith healers are not only considered spiritual guides but also serve as a port of call for mental health problems. Hussain *et al.* (1998) conducted a study using a two-stage design, in the Gujarkhan sub-district of Rawalpindi, to assess the psychiatric morbidity among native healer attenders and the classification and its agreement with DSM III R diagnosis. Just over 60 per cent of people attending the native healer were given a research diagnosis of mental disorder according to the research PAS and DSM-IIIR system (see Table 5.1). The most frequent individual diagnosis was major depressive episode (24 per cent), followed by generalised anxiety disorder (5 per cent) and epilepsy (9 per cent). There are marked gender difference in the rates, with women having significantly higher rates than men for major depressive episode and generalised anxiety disorder (gender ratios 1.9 and 3.5 respectively), while there is a trend for men to have higher rates than women for psychosis (gender ratio = 0.4).

Table 5.1 Harnessing traditional wisdom with modern advances: a study of faith healer attenders (*n* = 192)

DSM III-R *Diagnosis*	*Prevalence* *Rate as percentage of attenders* *95% CI*	
Major depressive episode	24	(19–29)
Generalised anxiety disorder	15	(11–19)
Epilepsy	09	(06–13)
Dysthymic disorder	05	(03–09)
Psychosis	04	(02–08)
Panic disorder + agoraphobia	04	(02–07)
Total	**61**	**(56–57)**
Native healer diagnosis	*Prevalence* *Rate as percentage of attenders* *95% CI*	
Saya	27	(22–32)
Jin possession	16	(11–20)
Churail possession	14	(10–18)
Tawiz	09	(06–13)
Medical	**08**	**(05–12)**
Spirit infestation	06	(04–09)
Evil eye	06	(03–09)
Amal	05	(03–09)
Jhalla/Jhally	04	(02–07)
Jadhoo	03	(01–06)

The native healers identified eleven different types of problem among their attenders. The most frequent mystic causes identified were Saya (27 per cent), followed by Jin possession (16 per cent) or Churail (14 per cent) (see Table 5.1). Twenty-five (8 per cent) attenders were identified as suffering from medical problems and advised by the native healers to attend a health facility. Attempts to find a relationship between the type of problem identified by the native healer, and the research assessment in terms of the symptoms, the DMR-IIIR diagnosis or the severity failed to reveal a consistent relationship. However Saya most frequently corresponded with major depressive episode and the anxiety related disorder. The native healer identified possession or Jhalla (madness) for those given a research diagnosis of psychosis. Epilepsy was identified as possession, Saya or a medical problem.

There is a varying degree of belief in the effectiveness of traditional healers. King and Sobal (1988) found that 29 per cent of the 207 psychiatric patients and 23 per cent of the physicians believed that the faith healers can help people whom physicians cannot help.

Hussain et al. (1998) in his study found that 41.2 per cent of the community members in one traditional healer's practice believed that traditional healers can help people whom physicians cannot help. There was an inverse correlation between education and this belief. Similarly females were more inclined towards this belief.

Culture-bound differences in clinical presentation

There are culture-bound differences in the presentation of these psychiatric disorders as well. It is well established that anxious and depressed patients from developing countries present with somatic symptoms. Kleinman (1987) refers to this widespread finding that somatic symptoms in depression and anxiety disorders in non-western societies and ethnic groups are more prevalent than in the West. This phenomenon has been reported in many developing countries, e.g. Sudan, India, Colombia and the Philippines (Harding, 1985); Kenya (Ndeti and Muhangi, 1979); Ethiopia (Giel and Van Lujik, 1969); and Black Africa (German, 1987a, 1987b) and China (Lin, 1989). However Dhadphale et al. (1989) have disputed these findings that Africans do not admit to being depressed.

In the study by Iqbal (1994) it was seen that somatic symptoms (tiredness, easy fatigability, headache and indigestion) and biological symptom (disturbed sleep, decreased appetite) were the most common symptom clusters reported, 35 per cent and 30.6 per cent respectively.

Koriala (1997) found that 75.5 per cent of depressed patients presented to primary care with somatic complaints and 79.3 per cent of these cases were not diagnosed by the primary care physicians. Malik et al. (1990) in their study of general practice attenders found that loss of energy, pains and aches, pain epigastrium, headache and sinking of the heart, difficulty in breathing, fainting fits and paraesthesias were the most common presenting symptoms for the anxiety and dissociative disorders.

Expression of suicidal ideation and intent are determinants of severity of depressive illness in most developed communities. Javed (1993) showed that suicidal ideation and intent were much less common in severely depressed patients (DSM-IIIR) presenting to psychiatric facilities in Pakistan and the major reason cited by the patients was that suicide is expressly forbidden in Islam.

Hysteria, a condition hardly seen in the western countries continues to be a common condition in the developing countries (Okasha, 1996). Although no large-scale studies are available, Malik et al. (1990) found that the diagnosis of hysteria represented about 10 per cent of any form of neurosis. It was mostly seen in young adults (15–20 years old) and most common presentations included fainting fits, difficulty in breathing, and attack of barking sounds from the throat. Hussain et al. (1998) in his study found that dissociative disorders constituted about 15–16 per cent of the attenders at the traditional healer's practice and most common presentations were aphonia, paraplegia and fainting fits.

Methodological limitation of culturally valid diagnostic instruments

Epidemiological studies carried out in developing countries are beset with a number of problems. The first relates to the concept of caseness, which is being tackled by developing standardised interviewing and rating procedures on one hand and operationally defined diagnostic categories on the other. This however raises the question of category fallacy (Kleinman, 1987) which is being tackled by development of indigenous instruments like BSI (Mumford et al. 1991) and validation of instruments like the GHQ (Minhas, 1996).

National mental health programme

It has long been realised that the existing mental health care facilities are both inadequate and inappropriate to meet the mental health needs of the community in Pakistan. The starting point for indigenous and innovative approaches to mental health care was provided by the WHO, Technical Report Series TRS 564, 1975, which recommended the formulation of a national mental health policy, clearly delineating objectives, priorities and appropriate funding for a national mental health programme and finally integration of mental health services with general health services.

The Alma-Ata declaration of 1987 envisaging health for all by the year 2000 with primary health care and inter-sectoral collaboration as its guiding principle, represents a historic point of reference for health services in general and mental health services in particular, to provide universal coverage in an acceptable and affordable manner.

From the viewpoint of developing countries this involves developing an organisational infrastructure, manpower base, priority identification and maintaining harmony with the overall social, political and economic development in the process. Steps taken for actualisation of these goals in developing countries were slow to start, but in the 1980s with the guidance and collaboration of WHO, many of the developing countries developed national mental health policies and programmes. The mental health programme for Pakistan has the following aims and objectives.

Aims of the National Mental Health Programme

1   Prevention and treatment of mental disorders and the subsequent disabilities.
2   Application of mental health technology and behavioral sciences to improve general health services.
3   Use of mental health principles to improve the quality of life.

Objectives of the National Mental Health Programme

1   To make basic care available and accessible for all in the near future, with special emphasis on the vulnerable unserved, under-served and inappropriately served rural populations.
2   To enhance the use of mental health knowledge in general health care, social development and improving the quality of life.
3   To encourage community participation in the development of mental health services and support the non-governmental organisations to generate a spirit of self-help in the common people.
4   To create awareness in the general public and mental health workers regarding the harmful effects of broken homes, juvenile delinquency, drug abuse and impaired performance of roles due to the rapid social changes, e.g. industrialisation and urbanisation affecting the well-being of communities, families and individuals.
5   To devise ways and means of achieving proper mental development of children through parental guidance, school education and social interaction outside home.

To achieve these aims and objectives certain strategies and approaches were also delineated in national mental health programmes.

Strategies for action

1   Integration of basic mental health services in general health services.
2   Decentralisation of mental health care services involving delegation of mental health promotion from specialist to general health.
3   Wide coverage of the population by delivering mental health care services in primary health care.
4   Training in mental health for mental health care personnel at different levels for carrying out appropriate tasks.
5   Multidisciplinary approach and inter-sectoral collaboration and linkage with community development.
6   Integration of mental health promotion with social services and collaboration with non-governmental organisations.

Development of mental health services

Some innovative and indigenous approaches challenging the dogma of western mental health care delivery have been developed in Pakistan over the last decade.

The main thrust of these approaches has been to develop a Community Mental Health Programme incorporating the following principles:

- Community participation in planning and execution
- Geographical continuity
- Informed responsibility
- Inter-sectoral collaboration
- Acknowledgement of indigenous resources
- Emphasis on prevention of mental illnesses and promotion of mental health.

The demonstration project was started in 1985 in the Gujarkhan sub-district of Rawalpindi (Mubbashar *et al.* 1986). This project had four phases.

First phase

In the first phase the thrust was to evaluate the needs and demands for mental health services in the community, to gauge the knowledge, attitude and practices prevalent in the community and to educate the community by mass education programmes using mosques, social congregations, etc.

Second phase

In the next phase, training and teaching materials for primary health care personnel, schoolteachers and community leaders was developed and in this regard manuals for primary health care physicians, school teachers, multi-purpose health care workers and master trainers have so far been developed utilising existing financial allocations. In addition, community education material comprising posters and signboards has also been developed.

This phase involved the training of primary health care personnel and so far more than 840 primary care physicians and more than 3,500 multi-purpose health workers, lady health visitors and trained birth attendants have been trained from all over the country. Furthermore more than 72 middle level health administrators and managers have been sensitised to the needs and methodology of training mental health programmes in their areas of jurisdiction.

Lastly there were development of links with related sectors like education, social welfare and traditional healers. More than 70 social welfare officers from all over the country have been sensitised to the need of incorporating mental health principles in the performance of their duties.

Research and evaluation activities are being carried out side by side with the above mentioned activities particularly in the field of promotion of mental health and prevention of mental illness. The Clear Vision Project, a prospective, matched controlled intervention study of the effects of screening and treatment for refractory errors among 6-year-old schoolchildren in Pakistan. The results showed that the children with refractory errors had more neurotic symptoms, and scored 6–10 per cent lower marks in academic tests than their classmates with clear vision. One year later, after correction of their refractory errors, the neurotic symptoms had fallen to a level similar to their classmates, and academic performance had risen to equal that of their classmates. Thus it was concluded that screening and prescription of glasses for refractory errors is a simple, cost-effective and yet highly effective method to improve academic performance and mental health in school-children (Gater et al. 1999) (see Tables 5.2 and 5.3).

Similarly the Pride Project was carried out at Rawalpindi with the collaboration of the Institute of Child Health, London, for the prevention of iodine deficiency. The results showed significant impact of iodine

Table 5.2 The Clear Vision Project: the effect on school performance after correction of refractory errors

Measure of school performance	Baseline (mean scores)			Follow up (01 year) (mean scores)		
	Cases	Controls	P	Cases	Controls	P
Urdu	54	64	< 0.01	63	65	NS
Mathematics	59	68	< 0.05	69	65	NS
Reading	55	61	< 0.01	67	61	< 0.1

Table 5.3 The Clear Vision Project: the effect on the psychological health of school-children after correction of refractory errors

Measure of psychological health	Baseline (mean scores)			Follow up (01 year) (mean scores)		
	Cases	Controls	P	Cases	Controls	P
Rutter Scale						
Total	14.4	14.5	NS	12.9	14.2	NS
Neurosis sub-scale	3.5	2.8	< 0.05	2.4	2.6	NS
Antisocial sub-scale	0.5	1.0	NS	0.0	1.0	< 0.1

supplementation on intellectual and cognitive development of children in iodine-deficient areas.

Another innovative approach in this regard is collaboration between traditional/faith healers and mental health professionals. The faith healers were provided with colour coded case identification cards, similar to those being used by multipurpose health workers. Faith healers claim that although their results with hysteria are better, they are pleased to have the help of health facilities in the management of epilepsy, drug dependence, etc. and are serving as an important source of referral to health care facilities.

Third phase

The next phase of the programme involved activities in the realm of inter-sectoral collaboration and in this regard, a school mental health programme was developed which is described in detail later.

Fourth phase

The final objective was to develop indicators for evaluating the community mental health programme.

Maqsood (1995), in a study carried out in two areas, one with and the other without the mental health component in primary health care (PHC) has shown that in the index area there was a significant increase in detection of psychiatric cases (62.4 per cent) as compared to the control area (12.7 per cent). In addition to the enhanced detection rates, there was a significant increase in uptake of all services provided at primary care level. There were reduced infant mortality and maternal mortality rates as a result of increased utilisation of the ante-natal care facility and increased rates of immunisation.

Regmi *et al.* (1998) in his study, investigated the prevalence of psychiatric morbidity among primary care attenders in two sub-districts of Rawalpindi, one of which was being covered by the community mental health programme and the other not. Depression and anxiety were the most common diagnosis

(90 per cent), which is comparable with earlier studies (Sartorius and Harding, 1983, Harding *et al.* 1980). An interesting finding was that the recognition rates by PHCPs for psychiatric morbidity in the area with a mental health training programme were significantly higher than in the area without the programme. This finding also replicates the findings in earlier studies (Gask *et al.* 1988). Studies carried out to evaluate the impact of community-based rural mental health programmes have also shown that integration of mental health component in existing PHC systems has resulted in improvement in indicators of general health care.

The School Mental Health Programme and its evaluation

The School Mental Health Programme was initiated in 1987 as a component of the community mental health programme. The programme works directly with schoolchildren and teachers to improve the understanding of mental health in rural communities.

In the first phase, the education administrators were sensitised to the need for incorporating mental health principles in improving the quality of education. This activity has now been completed at the national level.

The second phase involved the development of a training package for schoolteachers, which was carried out in a decentralised manner. The response of schoolteachers and children is overwhelming, with the formation of the All-Pakistan teachers movement for mental health being one example. On the part of schoolchildren it is seen that they are putting an enormous amount of energy in preparing wall charts and posters with mental health slogans and acting as an important source of referral of the mentally ill to health care facilities. Furthermore, the teachers say that they feel closer to schoolchildren, knowing more about them as people. Some claim that absenteeism is down by 50 per cent and that children have started paying more attention to personal hygiene (Goldberg, 1989).

The third phase involved development of indicators for evaluating the impact of the school mental health programme on knowledge, attitudes and superstitions in the community about mental health.

A prospective matched case control study was carried out (Rahman *et al.* 1998). Two secondary schools for boys and two for girls (matched for variables like student strength, staff, dropout rates) were chosen. One hundred children aged 12–16 years (25 girls and 25 boys in each of the study and control groups), 100 friends who did not attend school (one for each child) and 100 neighbours (one for each child) were given a 19-item questionnaire before and after the four-month programme of mental health education. The maximum score for the questionnaire was 16 points (see Tables 5.4 and 5.5).

Before the school mental health programme the awareness of mental health issues was poor in the four groups of participants. There was significant

Table 5.4 Evaluation of the School Mental Health Programme: baseline vs. follow-up

	Baseline			
	Mean score		Mean difference	p
	Study	Control	Study-control	
Schoolchildren	6.4	7.2	−0.8	.217
Parents	6.9	7.0	−0.1	.777
Non-school-going friend	5.7	4.6	1.1	.054
Neighbour	7.6	6.2	1.4	.033
	Follow-up			
	Mean score		Mean difference	p
	Study	Control	Study-control	
Schoolchildren	14	8.7	5.3	<.01
Parents	12.2	7.1	5.1	<.01
Non-school-going friend	10.8	5.4	5.4	<.01
Neighbour	10.9	6.0	4.9	<.01

Table 5.5 Evaluation of the School Mental Health Programme: study group vs. control group

	Study group		Control group	
	Mean difference	p	Mean difference	p
Schoolchildren	7.6	<.01	1.5	.01
Parents	5.3	<.01	0.1	.674
Non-school-going friend	5.1	<.01	0.8	<.01
Neighbour	3.4	<.01	−0.2	.397

improvement in the mean scores after the school programme in the schoolchildren (mean improvement 7.6 [95 per cent CI 6.7–8.5], $p < .01$), their parents (5.3 [4.5–6.1], $p < .01$) friends (5.1 [4.1–6.1]. $p < .01$) and neighbours (3.4 [2.6–4.2], $p < .01$). In the control group the difference in awareness was significant only in school children (1.5 [0.5–2.3], $p = .01$) and their friends (0.8 [0.3–1.3], $p < .01$). This study showed that schoolchildren and teachers are effective agents of social change, and that school mental health programmes can help change the perception of the community of mental health problems.

Conclusion

In the light of our experience in Pakistan, it would be safe to conclude that: mobilising indigenous resources as in the School Mental Health Programme proved to be an effective solution to deal with mental health issues in the community, hence *destigmatising* mental illness. Developing simple preventive strategies for specific targets can be a cost-effective alternative to much more expensive and difficult-to-implement western models of cure. An example is provision of glasses, which are the cheapest mental health aid that money can buy and thus prevent children from dropping out of school into child labour.

Inter-sectoral collaboration, e.g. with native faith healers can be an important resource for providing effective and culture-friendly treatment for the community at large on their doorstep. Integration of a mental health component into primary health care not only provides mental health care at the grass roots but also results in positive utilisation of general health services. Before the above models of community care are accepted for a wider application at the national level, there is obviously the issue of economic evaluation of these projects and analysis of the outcome studies. A pilot project is currently underway to address these issues and those relating to the structure and organisation of delivery of care. Funding of mental health care services in the socio-political/institutional context and cost of outcome measures should also be assessed.

References

Boardman, A.P. (1987) The General Health Questionnaire and the detection of emotional disorder by general practitioners. *British Journal of Psychiatry* 151, 373–381.

Dhadphale, M., Cooper, G. and Cartwright-Taylor, L. (1989) Prevalence and presentation of depressive illness in a primary health care setting in Kenya. *American Journal of Psychiatry* 146, 659–661.

Fernanado, S. (1989) Letter. *Psychiatric Bulletin of the Royal College of Psychiatrists* 13, 250–251.

Finlay-Jones, R.A. and Burvill, P.W. (1978) Contrasting demographic patterns of minor psychiatric morbidity in general practice and the community. *Psychological Medicine* 8, 455–466.

Gask, L., Goldberg, D., Lesser, A. and Millar, T. (1987) Improving the psychiatric skills of the general practice trainee. An evaluation of a group training course. *Medical Education* 21, 362–368.

Gater, R., Saeed, K,. Mubbashar, M., Ali, I., Orley, J., Stevenson, J. and Sartorius, N. (1999) 'Clear Vision': the effects on school attainment and psychological health of screening and treatment of refractory errors among school-children in Pakistan. Submitted for publication.

German, G.A.G. (1987a) Mental health in Africa. I: The extent of mental health problems in Africa today: An update of epidemiological knowledge. *British Journal of Psychiatry* 151, 435–439.

German, G.A.G (1987b) Mental health in Africa. II: the nature of mental disorder in Africa today: Some clinical observations. *British Journal of Psychiatry* 151, 440–446.

Giel, R. and van Lujik, J.N. (1969) Psychiatric morbidity in a small Ethiopian town. *British Journal of Psychiatry* 115, 149–162.

Goldberg, D.P. (1984) The recognition of psychiatric illness by non-psychiatrists. *Australian and New Zealand Journal of Psychiatry* 18, 128–134.

Goldberg, D. (1989) A quantum leap for community psychiatry. *Lancet* ii, 1445–1446.

Harding, T.W. (1985) Mental health services in the developing countries, the issues involved. In T. A. Baasher, G. Carstairs, R. Giel and X. Hassler (eds) *Mental Health Services in Developing Countries*, Geneva: WHO.

Harding, T.W., De Arango, M.V., Baltazar, J., Climent, E.E., Ibrahim, H.H.A., Ladrigo-Ignacio, L., Srinivasa Murthy, R. and Wig, N.N. (1980) Mental disorders in primary health care, a study of their frequency and diagnosis in four developing countries. *Psychological Medicine* 10, 231–241.

Hussain, A., Mubbashar, M., Gater, R. and Saeed, K. (1998) The prevalence, classification and treatment of mental disorders among attenders of native healers in rural Pakistan. Submitted to *Acta Psychiatrica Scandanavica*.

Iqbal, K. (1994) *Prevalence of Psychiatric Disorders in a Rural Population of Rawalpindi District.* Dissertation, College of Physicians and Surgeons Pakistan.

Javed, M.A. (1993) Suicide in schizophrenics. *Pakistan Journal of Clinical Psychiatry* 3.

Kleinman, A. (1987) Anthropology and psychiatry: The role of culture in cross-cultural research illness. *British Journal of Psychiatry* 151, 447–454.

Lin, N. (1989) Measuring depressive symptomatology in China. *Journal of Nervous Mental Disease* 177, 121–131.

Malik, B.A. and Javed, M.A. (1990) Depression and neuroses in general practice. In M.H. Mubbashar and A.R. Syed (eds) *Mental Health for All. All for Mental Health.* Psycho Publication, London.

Mari, J.J. and Williams, P. (1984) Minor psychiatric disorder in primary care in Brazil. A pilot study. *Psychological Medicine* 14, 223–227.

Marks, J., Goldberg, D. and Hiller, V.F. (1979) Determinants of the ability of general practitioners to detect psychiatric illness. *Psychological Medicine* 9, 337–353.

Minhas, F.A. (1996) Validation of GHQ in primary care settings of Pakistan. *Journal of Clinical Psychiatry* 2, 277–281.

Mubbashar, M.H., Malik, S.J. and Wig, N.N. (1986) Community based rural mental health care programme. Report of an experiment in Pakistan. *EMR Health Service Journal* 1, 14–20.

Mumford, D.B., Tareen, I.A., Bhatti, M.R., Bajwa, M.A., Ayub, M. and Pervaiz, T. (1991) An investigation of functional somatic symptoms among patients attending hospital medical clinics in Pakistan-11. Using somatic symptoms to identify patients with psychiatric disorders. *Journal of Psychosomatic Research* 35, 257–264.

Mumford, D.B., Nazir, M. and Jilani, F.M (1996) Stress and psychiatric disorder in the Hindu Kush: a community survey of mountain villages in Chitral, Pakistan. *British Journal of Psychiatry* 168, 299–307.

Mumford, D.B., Saeed, K., Ahmad, I., Latif, S. and Mubbashar, M.H. (1997) Stress and psychiatric disorder in a rural Punjab Community survey. *British Journal of Psychiatry* 170, 473–478.

Ndetei, D.M. and Mohangi, J. (1979) The prevalence and clinical presentation of psychiatric illnesses in a rural setting in Kenya. *British Journal of Psychiatry* 135, 269–272.

Okasha, A. (1996) A cultural psychiatric study of El-Zar in UAR. *British Journal of Psychiatry* 112, 1217–1221.

Ormel, J., Koeter, M.W., van den Brink, W. and van de Willige, G. (1991) Recognition, management, and course of anxiety and depression in general practice. *Archives of General Psychiatry* 48, 700–706.

Rahman, A., Mubbashar, M.H., Gater, R. and Goldberg, D. (1998) Randomised trial of impact of school mental health programme in rural Rawalpindi, Pakistan. *Lancet* 352, 1022–1025.

Regmi, S., Mubbashar, M.H., Saeed, K. and Gater, R. (1998) The impact of a community health service on the prevalence, detection and treatment of psychiatric disorders among primary health care attenders in rural Pakistan. (Submitted to *British Journal of Psychiatry*.)

Sartorius, N. and Harding, T.W. (1983) The WHO collaborative study on strategies for extending mental health care. I: The genesis of the study. *Archives of General Psychiatry* 140, 1470–1473.

6

NEEDS FOR SOCIAL CARE IN PRIMARY CARE

Peter Huxley

Introduction

In this chapter I will attempt to assess the need for social care in primary health care. I make the distinction between primary care and primary health care because, in my view, all services to which the public has direct access should be regarded as 'primary'. The definition of 'primary care' given by Wilkin *et al.* (1997) serves to illustrate the difference. They define primary care as 'the provision of first contact and continuing care in the community for patients undifferentiated by age, sex or disease. It is characterised by generalist health care professionals. It includes general medical, dental, pharmacy, nursing and a range of other community services, as well as their relations with informal (family and community) care, hospitals and social care'.

Implied in the definition are two elements that clearly distinguish this as primary health care. The people who contact services are described as patients implying a health problem of some sort. The community and social care described in the definition are included (and accessed) only because of a relationship with the generalist health professionals. This form of primary care is primary medical care or primary health care (Pietroni, 1996). For my present purpose, defining social care in this way is probably too narrow. People who present a mixture of health, disability and social care problems to community agencies as the first port of call should surely be regarded as contacting primary, but non-medical services. Social services and many non-statutory bodies, such as help-lines, are providing non-medical first points of contact.

The importance of the distinction between medical and non-medical primary care is evident when one considers the way services are organised to meet need. Using a medical definition only implies that the relevant social care is accessed through medicine. This in turn implies a separate existence for social care agents, rather than being an integral or even equal partner in the provision of primary care. These issues have been thoroughly reviewed by Rummery and Glendinning (1997), who make the point that 'people with complex needs do not draw distinctions between the "health" and "social" care elements in seeking help' (p. 7). So long as social services exist in their present form, with a duty to assess social care needs, there will continue to be a separate primary care assessment service. The problems of the organisation of health and social care services in primary care has come to dominate the policy agenda of the late 1990s, much as it has done, in various guises over the past 30 years or more. Before looking at this in greater detail, a brief sojourn into the local circumstances in Manchester is warranted.

Changes in health and social care 1971–1999

When David Goldberg and I came to the University Department in Manchester in 1971 (he as a Senior Lecturer and me as a student of psychiatric social work), the concept of primary and secondary services, and the organisation of health and social care were very different from those of the late 1990s. The old mental welfare departments, located under the jurisdiction of the local authority Medical Officer of Health, and the children's and welfare departments had just been integrated into local authority social services departments. Hospital social work remained out of the new Social Service Departments (SSDs) until 1974. Locally, there had been fairly extensive development of general hospital departments of psychiatry, but a lot of services were still provided from local mental hospitals. In our case, Prestwich Hospital in Salford cared for many of the patients with the most severe disorders who came from our district in central Manchester, and the University department at Gaskell House had only 21 beds at that time.

The new SSDs were clearly providers of social care services. The bulk of provision at that time was residential care for old people and for children. Mental health services included the function of mental welfare officer, replaced by the Approved Social Worker in the 1983 Mental Health Act, and some day services and residential provision. The independent sector made very limited provision, including a Richmond Fellowship house originally for students suffering from mental health problems.

Because health-related social work remained under the auspices of the health service, it was possible to retain the service intact when it transferred to social services after 1974. It was also possible for expansion of the service to take place through the use of joint finance monies. Quite a considerable number of hospital social work posts were created at this time, and at one point the department had the largest staffing in the UK. A development of relevance to this chapter was the provision of six social work attachments to primary health care services in different parts of the city. One of the post-holders remains in post at the time of writing, even though the practice became a fund-holding one in the interim. The bulk of their work was the provision of social care and support for common mental disorder.

There is an intriguing continuity between the local situation in the 1970s and the 1990s. In the late 1980s the University department of psychiatric social work created the Psychiatric Social Work Education Centre (PSWEC) to employ social work practitioners and supervisors for student social workers. In this way, it was able to continue to provide a social work service to psychiatry, long after the rest of the hospital social work service had been relocated into community settings and other aspects of practice. Coincidentally, PSWEC now employs psychiatric social workers in primary care settings (Firth and Ronalds 1997), a service that will be considered in more detail below. Interestingly, June Huntington, who wrote on this topic in 1981 recently described her return to the subject of the relationship between medical and social care as a 'Rip Van Winkle' experience, with 'little change in attitude . . . perceptions of the major problems involved in working more effectively together, and their supposed solutions' (in Meads 1997 p. vii).

Over this period we have seen a shift from the provision of social care by statutory bodies, to the provision of social care by a mixed group of providers. Following the NHS and Community Care Act (DoH 1990) social services have taken on a purchasing and assessment role and reduced dramatically their levels of provision. Their previous provider function has been assumed by not-for-profit organisations (such as PSWEC and Making Space), private care providers (residential, home care and secure accommodation in particular), and voluntary or independent sector bodies.

So, although there have been substantial changes, in practice, philosophy, funding arrangements and the organisation of services, the need for social care provision in primary and secondary health care has remained (see also Henry and Gaskin 1997). I have described some aspects of the local situation in Manchester, and now turn to look at some wider issues, including the development and use of counselling in primary care, the interface between social care and primary care in mental health context.

Counselling in primary care

In the early 1990s, 31 per cent of primary care practices had a counsellor (Sibbald et al 1993) and there was high growth potential among those that did not (Pringle and Laverty 1993). A high proportion of counsellors lacked appropriate qualifications and were referred problems outside their knowledge. Corney (1990) reviewed the evidence for the effectiveness of counselling and concluded that the results of clinical trials were mixed and that there was little or no evidence of the superiority of certain therapies or training over others. Nevertheless, in 1993, Sibbald et al. found that four-fifths of those GPs who did not have counselling services, wanted them.

A few years later, Corney (1995) surveyed local authorities in England and Wales and found over 60 per cent had one or more liaison or attachment schemes with general practice. A social work presence in community mental health centres was even more common (75 per cent). In 1996, Corney surveyed 100 fundholding and 100 non-fundholding practices, and found that the number of professionals employed by, attached to or visiting the practice had increased substantially since 1991, and was particularly marked in fundholding practices. The increase had not reduced referrals to psychiatrists, but had increased the treatment options available for less severely ill patients.

So, in spite of a lack of substantial evidence of effectiveness, counselling services continue to be offered in primary health care. One possible reason is that the counselling services are addressing some of the social care needs of the clientele. Recently, Firth and Ronalds (1997) reported on a service provided by psychiatric social workers (initially styled as 'counselling', but 'a wider approach seemed needed for an inner city clientele'). GPs valued the comprehensiveness of the assessments that were made, and the broad-based nature of the interventions which combined therapeutic and practical help. In order to intervene appropriately, it is essential for the service to be able to mount a reasonably sophisticated social assessment as well as a clinical assessment. Challenger et al. (1998) report that the patients too, welcomed the early assessment of problems, the range of problems addressed, and the fact that this could be achieved in one setting.

Primary care and mental health contacts

In an instructive community survey ($n = 7,974$) in Canada, Lesage and colleagues (1997) found that only 6 per cent of the population surveyed were in contact with any professional mental health provider. However, of those consulting family doctors in Ontario, 25 per cent also had contact with specialist mental health services. This compares with 13 per cent in the USA. Almost 40 per cent of the patients in contact with both primary care and specialist mental health services were in contact with a social worker. For patients in contact with specialist services only, 44 per cent were receiving social work services. These figures reflect the different status of social work in North America, where social workers are the largest professional group working in the specialist mental health field.

In a series of papers in the 1980s we established that a substantial proportion of people who consulted social services had recognisable mental health problems, whether in inner city or more socially heterogeneous areas. The rate determined by research interviews using standardised psychiatric assessments (Huxley et al. 1988) was, on average, about 50 per cent of cases ($n = 141$). These findings were confirmed recently by Roughton (1997) who, when reviewing care management assessments, also found 50 per cent of applicants had mental health problems (total $n = 163$).

Looking at the reasons behind consultations in primary health care one finds a very familiar list of social problems and major life events. These factors are associated with the continuation of symptoms over long periods of time; Kedward (1969) in a three-year follow-up study in primary care found that chronic housing problems, chronic physical illness and the adverse financial consequences of caring for a disabled relative were all associated with the failure to get better. The resolution of social problems was associated with symptomatic recovery. Similar results were obtained by Johnstone and Shepley (1986) and David Goldberg and colleagues (1990) in primary care and by our research projects in social services (Huxley et al. 1989).

Ford and Sathyamoorthy (1996) showed that fundholding increased the number of patients with less severe illness referred to the local community mental health team, and one quarter had no definite clinical symptoms. The patients seen by psychiatrists were likely to be psychotic, but stable, while social workers were seeing the most disabled patients. Huxley (1996) also reported that social services cases had longer periods of care, and were more likely to be compulsorily treated. They also had more self-neglect, and higher rates of aggression and suicidal behaviours. The psychotic cases in contact with social services had the worst (lowest) global assessment scores, and social services support workers were working with some of the most poorly functioning patients. Table 6.1 shows a more detailed analysis of findings from the same pilot study. Community psychiatric nurses

Table 6.1 Problems of people with non-psychotic illness on community mental health workers' caseloads

Variable	Non-psychotic group % (n)		Psychotic group % (n)		Total n[1]
In contact with 2 or more agencies	48.3	(396)	95.3	(1,122)	1,997
Interpersonal problems	17.4	(140)	31.5	(350)	1,914
Financial problems	12.3	(99)	34.2	(381)	1,919
Difficult to engage	11.9	(95)	22.4	(259)	1,954
Housing problems	8.9	(72)	30.2	(337)	1,922
Suicide risk	5.2	(42)	8.2	(94)	1,963
Medication non-compliance	4.8	(36)	9.6	(111)	1,898
At risk of institutional care	3.1	(24)	12.4	(137)	1,873
Serious self-neglect	2.1	(17)	10.3	(119)	1,966
Severe behavioural problems[2]	1.6	(13)	4.0	(47)	1,997
Statutory care used[3]	0.4	(3)	8.6	(101)	1,997

Notes
[1] Varies because of missing data
[2] Includes self-neglect, suicidal and aggressive behaviour
[3] Includes Mental Health Act Sections 2, 3, 4 and 117

(CPNs) were more likely than social workers to have non-psychotic patients on their caseloads (an average of 43 per cent compared to 34 per cent).

Almost all the people with psychotic illness were in touch with two or more agencies, and so were almost half of the people with non-psychotic disorders. Although there is always a lower percentage of problems than among people with psychosis, this sample of 820 people with non-psychotic and non-organic disorders have substantial problems. Most notable are 100 who are difficult to engage, 99 with serious financial problems, 72 with serious housing problems and 140 with severe interpersonal problems. Suicidal risk is present in 42 cases, compared to 94 in those with psychosis, and non-compliance with medication is not confined to the psychotic group.

Clearly at this level of care, there are many people who do not have a psychotic illness, who are in touch with social workers, and who have complex needs. Gask (1997) confirms that most morbidity in primary care falls into the categories of anxiety and depression, and argues that this diagnostic over-simplicity diminishes the complexity of the social problems that lie behind the morbidity, such as bereavement, separation, terminal illness, and family problems. The very characterisation of the problem in these clinical terms 'promotes over-dependence on medical models of assessment and treatment' (p. 41). The issue here is that the factors creating demand are not medical, on the whole. The true picture of need for social care at the primary care level may differ very little from that portrayed in Table 6.1.

A key variable in meeting these social needs, must be the extent to which the social problems that cause mental disorders, are themselves transient or long-term. In instances where restitution is likely within 9 months or so, the need for social care may be less. Speeding up restitution might be considered important and worthwhile in some cases, for instance where there is suicide risk. However, long-standing or intractable social difficulties will prevent restitution (Goldberg and Huxley 1992) and so could be considered to be a legitimate priority for social care. Similarly, people with chronic physical conditions will also restitute slowly, and they too could be regarded as a priority. Where there are long-term social problems plus physical ill health or disability, then multidisciplinary primary health and social care may be the best option.

The integration of social care in primary care settings

The presumed advantages of integration of social care at the primary care level have been described by Jones (1997). These are a single point of access (see also Murray 1997); removal of cost shunting; improved strategic planning; enhanced skill mix; greater efficiency in care management arrangements; pooled budgets; reduced delays; and the elimination of some duplication especially in assessments. Jones suggests a model involving larger primary care teams with increased budgetary responsibility and increased numbers of managerial and personnel support posts. The GP becomes primarily a provider of clinical care, and not of managerial functions. This model sounds very like the development of some community mental health services in the USA, and in parts of the UK. The doctor becomes a team player, not the team owner.

The aim of the introduction of primary care groups in the UK is intended to improve both health and social care. They are said to have the potential to bring GPs into the centre of health service planning (May 1998). The current government proposes to introduce legislation that will allow primary health care to provide some social care services (DoH 1998b). The remit of primary care groups is much wider than clinical care provision alone. The three main functions of primary care groups are improving health and cutting health inequalities, commissioning services and developing primary and community services. One-stop care centres as envisaged by Jones, are included in the NHS national priorities guidance 1999-2002 (DoH 1998a). According to this guidance, social services and health will share the lead responsibility for cutting health inequalities and for mental health. Paradoxically, social services will have the lead responsibility for inter-agency working, which one might have thought of as naturally 'joint', and health the lead for primary care.

Wiltshire is often held to be the leading example of primary care integration in the UK (Meads 1997). By the end of 1996, 26 social care link-workers covered 53 per cent of GPs in Wiltshire. They are employed by the local authority and their role combines care management with a development function. They aim to promote better coordinated care for service users. A practice-based joint commissioning arrangement began in 1993 in Trowbridge and Malmesbury, but primarily for older people and their carers. This can include the provision of joint needs assessment, joint care plans, and shared information systems.

There may be a critical mass problem, related to the severity of illness and social care needs. It has been suggested that unless practices are of sufficient size they cannot produce enough severe cases to occupy a social worker. Four partners or fewer do not generate a sufficient number of high priority cases (Stannard 1997).

The service arrangements described above and in the literature (Rummery and Glendinning 1997) are based predominantly on the integration of social care for older people and not for those with mental health problems. There are a number of obstacles to the achievement of genuinely integrated care for people with mental health problems. Firstly, the SSD is no longer the main provider of social care for people with mental health problems. Link-workers in this context could expect themselves to be working with a wide range of community and voluntary groups making the actual provision. Whether this brokerage model of care management would work is debatable. There is conflicting evidence about the value of the brokerage model of care management. Brokerage appears to be unpopular with people with a severe mental illness (Huxley and Warner 1992) for whom only assertive community treatment appears to offer significant gains (Lafave *et al.* 1996; Marshall and Lockwood 1998).

Second, local authority expenditure on purchasing social care for people with mental health is small by comparison to that for older people. Even the growth in joint finance and the mental illness specific grant monies have not increased the availability of SSD provision but rather added to the modest growth of independent providers. Third, the response from GPs to people with mental health problems is very mixed, so that in some places there is little interest in keeping mental health care, let alone social care, within the primary setting. Fourth, referring these cases to community mental health teams reduces the latter's capacity to provide for those with more severe disorders. Fifth, it has only recently become clear which interface models between primary and secondary care actually work best (Gask *et al.* 1997b), and in none of these studies has improved social care been considered as one of the objectives. Goldberg *et al.* (1992) have shown that GPs were significantly more satisfied with social work care, when provided from a mental health team based in primary care, than when it was provided in the traditional secondary services.

The care management role in social services appears to be confined to purchasing services for priority groups, and it is not entirely clear how social care priorities and clinical priorities can become aligned in primary care. Ignoring the priority group of severely ill psychotic patients with long histories of care (and for whom combined care programme approach and care management might provide a suitable solution), are there other groups with social care needs that would be better met by integrated health and social care? Possibly some of those currently considered suitable for counselling may have serious and long-term social problems. Possibly some cases currently being seen in secondary care services might be suitable. As indicated earlier a substantial number of non-psychotic cases are being seen by community psychiatric nurses and social workers. On the basis of the research evidence cited earlier, people with mental and physical illness in the context of enduring social difficulties seem the group most likely to profit from an integrated approach in primary health care.

The future organisation of social care in primary settings

The findings emerging from the total purchasing pilot study (Gask *et al.* 1997a) with respect to mental health provision, confirm that mental health services in primary care are difficult to configure, and expensive. The study includes 27 total purchasing sites and 13 extended fundholding sites. Most sites (17) were using a detailed assessment of practice populations, though these appear to have been confined to health needs. Only five had adopted specific liaison or attachment schemes, aimed principally at improving primary–secondary care links rather than improving social care links. Eight of the sites that had an expressed interest in mental health were attempting to increase their role with people suffering from severe mental illness. Most sites (13) saw a distinct separation with primary care focused on the care of 'more moderate problems' and specialist services on severe cases. There was no indication that improvements in the social care of either the moderate or the severe group was a specific focus, and social care was not one of the common emerging themes.

Gask *et al.* (1997b) suggest that studies of the outcomes of different patterns of care should focus on disability rather than clinical outcome. However, until we have a better understanding of the social care needs of people in contact with primary care groups we are unlikely to be able to organise services to meet them. Given that the social care needs of patients are likely to be determinants of length of contact, and probably cost as well, studies of social care needs in primary care mental health cases are urgently needed. As Butler *et al.* (1997) argued 'local mental health commissioned purchasing should focus on outcomes not structures and follow local assessments of need'. They could have gone on to add 'including social care needs and social care outcomes'.

References

Butler, T., Glendenning, C., Gask, L., Rummery, K., Rogers, A., Lee, J. and Bower, P. (1997) Mental health and primary care: An alternative policy agenda. *Journal of Mental Health* 6, 331–334.

Challenger, A., Dyer, M. and Marsden, H. (1998) Open heart surgery. *Community Care* 2–8 July, 22.

Corney, R. (1990) Counselling in general practice – does it work? Discussion Paper. *Journal of the Royal Society of Medicine* 83, 253–257.

Corney, R. (1995) Social work involvement in primary care settings and mental health centres: A survey in England and Wales. *Journal of Mental Health* 4, 275–280.

Corney, R. (1996) Links between mental health care professionals and general practices in England and Wales: the impact of GP fundholding. *British Journal of General Practice* 46, 221–224.

DoH (1990) *The NHS and Community Care Act.* HMSO, London.

DoH (1998a) *Modernising Health and Social Services: National Priorities Guidance 1990/0 – 2001/02.* NHS Executive, Leeds.

DoH (1998b) *Partnership in Action: New Opportunities for Joint Working between Health and Social Services. A discussion document.* HMSO, London.

Firth, M.T. and Ronalds, C.M. (1997) Psychiatric social work in primary care: a pilot scheme in one inner-city practice. *Journal of Interprofessional Care* 11, 295–302.

Ford, R. and Sathyamoorthy, G. (1996) Team games. *Health Service Journal*, 27 June, 32–33.

Gask, L. (1997) Mental health perspectives on a primary care led NHS. In *What is the Future for a Primary Care Led NHS?* Radcliffe Medical Press, Oxford.

Gask, L., Lee, J., Donnan, S. and Roland, M. (1997a) *Evaluation of the Effect of Total Purchasing and Extended Fundholding on Services for Mentally Ill People.* National Primary Care Research and Development Centre, University of Manchester.

Gask, L., Sibbald, B. and Creed, F. (1997b) Evaluating models of working at the interface between mental health services and primary care. *British Journal of Psychiatry* 170, 6–11.

Goldberg, D. and Huxley, P. (1992) *Common Mental Disorders: A Bio-Social Model.* Routledge, London.

Goldberg, D., Bridges, K., Cook, D., Evans, B. and Grayson, D. (1990) The influence of social factors on common mental disorders: destabilisation and restitution. *British Journal of Psychiatry* 156, 704–713.

Goldberg, D., Tantam, D., Gater, R., Jackson, G., Jennet, N. and Lowson, K. (1992) *The Interface between Primary Care and Specialist Mental Health Services in the Community.* Final report on the evaluation of a multidisciplinary community mental health team based in primary care. Mental Illness Research Unit, University of Manchester.

Henry, S. and Gaskin, L. (1997) The Trowbridge Experience: Care in the community for elderly people. In G. Meads (ed.) *Health and Social Services in Primary Care: An Effective Combination?* Financial Times Healthcare, London.

Huntington, J. (1997) Foreword in Meads, G. (ed.) *Health and Social Services in Primary Care: An Effective Combination?* Financial Times Healthcare, London.

Huxley, P. (1996) Describing mental health services: the development of a mental health census in the North West of England. In M. Tansella (ed.) *Making Rational Mental Health Services.* Il Pensiero Scientifico Editore, Roma.

Huxley, P. and Warner, R. (1992) Case management, quality of life and satisfaction with services of long-term psychiatric patients. *Psychiatric Services* 43, 799–802.

Huxley, P., Korer, J. and Tolley, S. (1988) Psychiatric morbidity in the clients of social workers. *Journal of Psychiatric Research* 22, 57–67.

Huxley, P.J., Raval, H., Korer, J. and Jacob, C. (1989) Psychiatric morbidity in the clients of social workers: social outcome. *Social Psychiatry and Psychiatric Epidemiology* 19, 189–197.

Johnstone, A. and Shepley, M. (1986) The outcome of hidden neurotic illness treated in general practice. *Journal of the Royal College of General Practitioners* 36, 413–415.

Jones, R. (1997) Realising the potential. In G. Meads (ed.) *Health and Social Services in Primary Care: An Effective Combination?* Financial Times Healthcare, London.

Kedward, H.B. (1969) The outcome of neurotic illness in the community. *Social Psychiatry and Psychiatric Epidemiology* 4, 1–4.

Lafave, H.G., de Souza, H.R. and Gerber, G.J. (1996) Assertive community treatment of severe mental illness: A Canadian experience. *Psychiatric Services* 47, 757–759.

Lesage, A.D., Goering, P. and Lin, E. (1997) Family physicians and the mental health system. *Canadian Family Physician* 43, 251–256.

Marshall, M. and Lockwood, A. (1998) Assertive Community Treatment for People with Severe Mental Disorders. *Cochrane Review*, Cochrane Library, Oxford.

May, N. (1998) Total Purchasing: A step towards Primary Care Groups. Kings Fund, London.

Meads, G. (ed.) (1997) *Health and Social Services in Primary Care: An Effective Combination?* Financial Times Healthcare, London.

Murray, P. (1997) The County Durham experience: From primary health services to primary care teams. In G. Meads (ed.) *Health and Social Services in Primary Care: An Effective Combination?* Financial Times Healthcare, London.

Pietroni, P. (1996) A Primary Care-led NHS. Trick or treat? *Purchasing in Practice* 9,1.

Pringle, M. and Laverty, J. (1993) A counsellor in every practice? *British Medical Journal* 306, 2–3.

Roughton, H. (1997) Professional effectiveness: The Somerset example. In G. Meads (ed.) *Health and Social Services in Primary Care: An Effective Combination?* Financial Times Healthcare, London.

Rummery, K. and Glendinning, C. (1997) *Working Together: Primary Care Involvement in Commissioning Social Care Services.* National Primary Care Research and Development Centre. Debates in Primary Care 2, Manchester.

Sibbald, B., Addington-Hall, J., Brenneman, D. and Freeling, P. (1993) Counsellors in English and Welsh general practices: their nature and distribution. *British Medical Journal* 306, 29–33.

Stannard, J. (1997) Organisational effectiveness: The Southampton example. In G. Meads (ed.) *Health and Social Services in Primary Care: An Effective Combination?* Financial Times Healthcare, London.

Wilkin, D., Butler, T. and Coulter, A. (1997) *New Models of Primary Care: A Development and Research Programme.* NPCRDC Discussion Paper No. 2, Manchester.

7

FUTURE ROLE OF THE NURSE IN PRIMARY MENTAL HEALTH CARE

Kevin Gournay

Introduction

While the focus of this chapter is on nursing in primary care, it is important to view this area in the more general context of developments in nursing and mental health care. In the specific setting of this book, it is also important to note that David Goldberg has been a very influential figure, (although somewhat uncharacteristically, a background one), in the development of British mental health nursing. Goldberg and his supervisee Kate Wooff in their research in Salford (Wooff and Goldberg 1988), showed that, in the latter part of the 1980s, community psychiatric nursing practice was drifting away from its previous focus on people with serious mental illnesses such as schizophrenia, towards patients with neurotic problems in primary care. Wooff and Goldberg were particularly concerned that people with schizophrenia in the community would be left without any skilled nursing input. At the same time they were concerned with an apparent lack of appropriate training for nurses working in the primary care arena. This work in Salford stimulated others, including myself, to carry out further research into these changing roles of community psychiatric nurses (CPNs) (Gournay and Brooking 1994, 1995). Subsequently, David Goldberg was one of a small group in Manchester who planned the research and development on training for nurses in family interventions in schizophrenia carried out by Charlie Brooker and others (Brooker *et al*. 1994). Following David Goldberg's move to the Institute of Psychiatry, he continued to support these training initiatives for community psychiatric nurses, and provided invaluable assistance in disseminating such training (now known as the Thorn Programme) more widely across the UK and now internationally. One of David Goldberg's first tasks at the Institute of Psychiatry was to establish a significant nursing section and to support initiatives in both research and training. This led to the inauguration of a Chair in Psychiatric Nursing in 1995. His continuing support has led to the Section at the Institute now having

92

the largest portfolio of mental health nursing research in Europe, and to the section of nursing now developing a range of training innovations for nurses, including forensic care, neuropsychiatry and cognitive behaviour therapy. It should also be said that throughout the 1990s, David Goldberg has supported nursing behind the scenes and in his various roles in the Department of Health and other policy fora has promoted mental health nursing wherever possible.

Mention of David Goldberg's contribution to nursing would not be complete without saying something of his position with regard to nurse behaviour therapy. In the mid 1970s he was one of the fiercest opponents of the development of training for nurses in behaviour therapy. This initiative commenced at the Maudsley Hospital in 1972, and has, from that time until the present, been led by Professor Isaac Marks. David commented that training nurses as therapists was analogous to training lorry drivers as airline pilots! However, as is also characteristic of the man, David changed his views when evidence of efficacy emerged. It has to be said that in the last three or four years David has not only supported this form of training, but has ensured that in a new Master's Programme in Cognitive Behaviour Therapy at the Institute, nurses have become equal partners with psychiatrists and psychologists.

Background

As noted above, it is necessary first to understand the more general psychiatric nursing context and to see that the current developments in primary care are an extension of more traditional community psychiatric nursing roles. At the present time, there are 637,000 nurses registered in the UK; of these, approximately 57,000 are registered mental nurses. Although it is difficult to be precise, it is probable that 20,000 of these nurses are employed in hospital-based practice. Furthermore, data from the latest Census of Community Psychiatric Nursing (Brooker and White 1998) shows that there are approximately 8,000 nurses in the United Kingdom who are designated community psychiatric nurses. It is also worth noting by way of background that, in primary care, there may be up to 30,000 individuals employed as practice nurses, although in whole-time equivalents this number may be closer to 20,000. These practice nurses do not generally have a mental health nursing qualification, although some recent research (Gray et al. 1999) suggests that many practice nurses carry out a significant number and range of mental health nursing roles.

The first community psychiatric nursing services were developed at Warlingham Park Hospital, Croydon, in 1954 (Greene 1968). Nurses were sent out to follow up patients, following their discharge from hospital. In the next 25 years, community psychiatric nursing services gradually expanded across the UK, with nurses following up patients after their discharge from hospital, giving general support, liaising with the GP and other agencies, and giving and supervising medication. Although training for CPNs was variable, and in many cases largely theoretical in its content, the outcome of their work was largely positive. Indeed, Paykel *et al.* (1982) in a randomised controlled trial at Springfield Hospital in South London, showed that CPNs providing aftercare for patients who had suffered an acute episode which required admission, were as good as psychiatrists in terms of clinical, social and economic outcomes.

The numbers of CPNs in the UK grew significantly from 1,000 in 1980 to 5,000 in 1990 (White 1990). However, during this decade, community psychiatric nurses began to relinquish their roles with people with schizophrenia and other long-term mental illnesses and based themselves in GP surgeries or health centres. By 1990, CPNs were taking almost as many referrals from GPs as from psychiatrists (White 1990), and the patient population had also changed. Various research studies (e.g. Barratt 1989) showed that CPNs were increasingly adopting the role of counsellor with people with depression, anxiety and adjustment disorders. Gournay and Brooking (1994, 1995) carried out a randomised controlled trial involving CPNs working in six primary care settings in two North London health authorities. Of patients whom the GP would normally have referred to CPNs, 177 were randomised to either routine continuing care from the GP, or to CPN intervention. The vast majority of patients referred had adjustment disorders and various states of general depression and anxiety. Video-taped interviews revealed that the CPN intervention was, by and large, best described as non-directive counselling. Patients in both groups showed significant improvement on a range of measures of clinical status and social functioning over time. However there was no difference in outcome at post treatment and follow up between patients receiving CPN intervention and those receiving GP care. The study also showed that there were high levels of drop out by patients from the CPN intervention (50 per cent), and patient satisfaction ratings did not correlate with outcome measures. The study also revealed that CPNs who had received a one-year full-time training in community psychiatric nursing did no better with their patients than did CPNs who had not received training. This finding was of course understandable, given that the CPN training programmes at that time lacked any content concerned with evidence-based skills in methods such as behaviour therapy. The economic analysis (Gournay and Brooking 1995) showed that per unit of health gain, CPN intervention was very expensive (with a cost per Quality Adjusted Life Year (QALY) for people in the study at approximately £28,000 – while other work had revealed that the cost per QALY of CPNs working with people with schizophrenia was £6,000 and £10,000 for those with affective disorders (Wilkinson *et al.* 1990). This study was completed at a time when there was widespread concern concerning the increasing focus of CPNs on these primary care populations. For this and several other reasons, various policy initiatives in the mid 1990s made strong recom-mendations for a refocus of CPNs on people with serious and enduring mental illness. Perhaps the most notable example of the problems this CPN work caused was best seen in the data from the 1990 census of CPNs (White 1990) which showed that approximately 80 per cent of people with schizophrenia in the community did not have the services of a CPN. Unfortunately, for various reasons, there has been a continuation of CPNs' work in primary care with neurotic populations using interventions with no evidence base, counselling being the prime example. On a more positive note, CPNs have now been availed of training in evidence-based approaches. Since 1992, a training programme has been run at the Institute of Psychiatry and the University of Manchester to train nurses, and now other mental health professionals, with skills in assertive community treatment. This programme, known as the Thorn Initiative, was developed with the assistance of a large donation from the Sir Jules Thorn Charitable Trust, and the work has been spearheaded by Dr Jim Birley, one time Dean of the Institute of Psychiatry. Jim Birley's view was that there was a need to develop a model of nursing in schizophrenia analogous to that of the Macmillan Cancer care nurses. Originally, Thorn training focused on family interventions in schizophrenia, relying heavily on work carried out in London by Julian Leff and Christine Vaughn (Leff and Vaughn 1985) and in Manchester by Nick Tarrier, Christine Barrowclough and others (Tarrier et al. 1988). (It was at this early point that David Goldberg was involved.) The programme has developed considerably in its scope, and now mental health professionals receive training in cognitive behavioural methods, medication management and various aspects of the clinical case manager role, in addition to the research-based approaches with families (Mari et al. 1996). There is some uncontrolled evaluation of this work including skill and knowledge outcomes of the CPNs and on the clinical and social status of patients. The results of this study, which involved a cohort of nearly 100 nurses, is strongly suggestive of positive effects of training (Lancashire et al. 1997). However, there is still a need to test the training within the context of a properly designed randomised controlled trial. At the present time, some 400 mental health professionals (about 95 per cent of whom are nurses) have been trained, and the Thorn Programme has now been set up in various cities across the UK and recently in Australia. Therefore, although it may be some time before the effects of such training programmes filter through to all CPNs, there is no doubt that this initiative will lead to an improvement in the quality of services received by people with schizophrenia, and their families and carers. At the present time, most of these trained workers are located within com-munity mental health teams. However, in a discussion paper, Goldberg and Gournay (1997) have proposed that such nurses could be located at the interface between primary and secondary care, and provide the GP directly

95

with a resource, both liaising with specialist mental health team and as a training and consultation facility.

Nurse behaviour therapists in primary care

In 1972, Isaac Marks set up a three-year experimental programme at the Maudsley Hospital to test his notion that nurses could be trained as behaviour therapists for a well-defined group of conditions, which at that time were shown to be responsive to behavioural treatment. Marks recognised that behaviour therapy had great potential. At that time he suggested that 10 per cent of outpatients might benefit from this approach (Marks *et al.* 1977). He also recognised that there was a great shortage of suitably trained psychiatrists and psychologists and that we would need to look to other potential workforces to disseminate this form of treatment. Marks believed that nurses were a logical choice for this role, as they had the necessary background experience and training with mental illness. In turn, he argued that suitably selected individuals could acquire the necessary therapeutic skills without knowledge of psychological theory. On this latter point, Marks encountered fierce opposition from psychologists who (e.g. Wilson 1981) believed that in order to practise behaviour therapy, one needed a detailed knowledge of learning and other psychological theory. Marks' approach was pragmatic, rather than atheoretical. He held the view that neurotic phenomena such as phobias and obsessions had a complex aetiology, which included evolutionary influences, as well as various biological, psychological, and social factors. He posited that the central component of effective treatment was prolonged, repeated exposure which simply entailed keeping the patient in contact with the phobic stimulus until they habituated to anxiety (Marks 1987).

The original three-year training programme was very intensive, and involved considerable use of interview training with video feedback, teaching the nurses the value of repeated measurement, training in various case management skills, and finally, the acquisition of therapeutic skills. At first, this training was conducted under intensive supervision, and then gradually, the nurses were allowed more and more independence. The main categories of patients originally targeted were people with:

- specific phobias
- agoraphobia
- obsessive compulsive disorder (OCD)
- sexual problems
- social phobias and social skills deficit
- habit disorders, such as enuresis, tics, stammering.

By 1975, Marks had collected a great deal of outcome data on the patients targeted by these five nurses, and this was sufficient to convince government, and the then nurse education bodies, to establish the course as a bona fide method of training (Marks *et al.* 1977). By the end of the three years, many of the early opponents of the programme (who included many nurses) had begun to see that Marks was correct in his earlier assertions, and as noted above, David Goldberg became a convert. This programme, which was reduced in length to an 18-month full-time course, has been running at the Maudsley Hospital continuously since 1972. Other training sites have been set up, run for a few years, and then discontinued. One of the problems of setting up new courses has been that training requires intensive input from psychiatrists and nurse tutors, and is thus very expensive. To date, about 300 nurses have received this training, and it is pleasing to note that the majority have stayed in clinical practice using the methods with which they were trained, and have continued in practice for many years after qualification (Newell and Gournay 1994, Gournay *et al.* 1999). The work of nurse therapists has been tested in a randomised controlled trial in primary care (Marks 1985). The results of the study were convincing, showing that nurse therapist intervention produced substantial clinical, social and economic benefits over routine GP care. On the basis of the results of this study, Marks made convincing arguments that nurse therapists located in primary care would be a substantial resource for dealing with patients with often very handicapping problems, such as obsessive compulsive disorder, and severe agoraphobia (Marks 1985). Marks suggested that one nurse therapist might serve a population of 20,000, i.e. a large health centre, and could be kept fully occupied treating the target groups described above. However, because of the funding difficulties regarding setting up of training programmes, the numbers of nurse therapists trained are relatively small. Another important factor which explains why this training has not been disseminated more widely is the recent focus on people with severe mental illnesses, such as schizophrenia. As a consequence, patients with neurotic disorders, even those with very great handicaps which one often sees with conditions such as OCD, have been neglected despite a range of evidence that relatively brief treatment produces, significant gains in clinical, social and economic outcomes (Gournay 1995).

Since the original development of nurse therapists, behaviour therapy has grown in its scope to embrace cognitive techniques, and now cognitive behaviour therapy is certainly the treatment of choice for a great deal more than the 10 per cent of conditions for which behaviour therapy was the ideal treatment some 25 years ago. There is of course now an array of evidence which suggests that cognitive behaviour therapy is an effective treatment for many other conditions, including Chronic Fatigue Syndrome (Deale *et al.* 1997), Body Dysmorphic Disorder (Gournay *et al.* 1997), Post Traumatic Stress Disorder (Lovell 1997) and also more general states of depression and anxiety.

Practice nurses

Practice nurses are an increasingly important workforce in primary care. Nowadays, most general practices have one or more practice nurses. These individuals are usually general trained nurses who take responsibilities for a wide range of activities, undertaking electrocardiography, ear syringing, giving injections, carrying out surgical dressings and undertaking specialist roles in asthma, diabetes and health promotion. It is difficult to be certain how many practice nurses there are in the UK as the majority of them are currently employed directly by GPs, and central information is not available. One estimate is there may be 20,000 such individuals in practice (Gray *et al.* 1999). What has become clear, with regard to mental health, is that practice nurses are increasingly engaged in a range of tasks with a variety of mental health problems. Recently a research team at the Institute, including David Goldberg, conducted a survey (Gray *et al.* 1999) that showed that practice nurses are now frequently involved in the administration of depot injections of antipsychotic agents, have considerable contact with people with mental health problems, and often give information and advice to patients and their families regarding depression and anti-depressant medication. However, the survey also showed that practice nurses have very little education and training for this role. There is of course some work which suggests that practice nurses with appropriate training may potentially have a very positive role in the detection and management of depression (Wilkinson *et al.* 1993). However, until the present time, there have been no large-scale trials of training practice nurses in this role. Currently a research team from the Institute of Psychiatry is running a trial across Southern England, whose central aim is to assess the efficacy of training of practice nurses in this role. The study includes 36 practice nurses and 1,700 patients. Data from the first part of the study confirm that practice nurses' ability (prior to training) to detect depression, is very poor, with rates of only 17 per cent of cases being detected. Whilst this programme seems to show that the training has a benefit, the question remains of how valuable practice nurse time can be used. It is certainly true to say that practice nurses already have a great deal of pressure to perform a number of roles across physical health care, and thus the amount of time and attention given to a new role with mental health tasks is limited. There are several options for the way that practice nurses may be used. First, they may provide a supportive role for the GP, following up depressed patients, monitoring their mood, medication side-effects, and providing education to the patient and family. However, another possibility for using practice nurses would be to provide them with brief focused training in the management of specific conditions. Thus, for example, they may be taught some simple behavioural and cognitive strategies for managing panic disorder, or, alternatively, brief problem-solving counselling approaches for adjustment disorders. If one accepts that these methods of working are a reasonable use of practice nurse time, there are still problems connected with further support, clinical supervision and how practice nurses may link with the community mental health team. At the present time, practice nurses are relatively isolated in primary care, and if use of this growing workforce is to be increased, there is a need to ensure that linkages with community psychiatric nurses and others are strengthened. In general, however there is a clear need to embark on further research and development with this workforce.

Nurses and computer-assisted treatment

Self-help has been increasingly recognised as a valuable method for dealing with mental health problems. In anxiety disorders, various self-help organisations including Triumph over Phobia and No Panic have mushroomed across the country, mainly as a result of poor, or non-existent, service provision. At the same time, there has been an enormous growth in self-help material published in the form of books, audio tapes and videos. The material published has been very variable in its content and quality, although increasingly books are providing structured behavioural advice for a range of common psychological problems. 'Living with Fear' (Marks 1978) was probably the first structured, systematic attempt to help patients help themselves, using the exposure principle for the treatment of phobic and obsessional problems. During the 1980s a team from the Institute of Psychiatry developed the first computer program for delivering self-help based on this book. Eventually, this program was tested within the context of a randomised controlled trial, comparing the book, the computer program, and standard therapist-aided exposure (Ghosh et al. 1988). The results showed convincing evidence that both book and computer methods were helpful for a significant number of patients. Since that time, and particularly in the last three or four years, when computers have become much cheaper and more powerful, a number of other computer programs for various disorders including OCD and depression have been developed (Greist et al. 1998). Obviously, such automated treatment has the potential for making a great impact on the ubiquitous mental health problems in primary care. However, if it is to be applied most effectively, there will still be a need for professional personnel to co-ordinate treatment sites, introduce patients to the system, and give assistance when patients either have specific difficulty or fail to respond. Nurse therapists are an obvious and logical choice for fulfilling such roles, but obviously, in this area alone, there is probably a need for several hundred nurse therapists working across the country.

Conclusion

There is clear evidence that nurses can provide a major contribution to the delivery of mental health care. The future will require that a number of levels of nursing skill are available to the public, the GP and to community mental health teams, including generic practice nurses, community psychiatric nurses, and nurse therapists. In addition, we will also need to recognise that other nurses, such as health visitors, may have an important role with specific populations. For example, the work of Holden *et al.* (1989) pointed to the potential contribution of health visitors in the management of post-natal depression.

Perhaps what is paramount in primary care, is that all members of the team are both aware of, and competent with, the management of mental health problems. Obviously, nursing has a potentially enormous contribution to this area, but education and training initiatives should include all members of the team, and we are now beginning to realise that unidisciplinary, rather than multidisciplinary education has great limitations.

In summary, therefore, the last three decades have seen major developments in the training of the nursing workforce. However, it is only recently that the implications for primary care have been properly explored. There is obviously a need for developments which affect, not just education and training, but a broad strategic use of the nursing workforce.

References

Barratt, E. (1989) Community psychiatric nurses: their self-perceived roles, *Journal of Advanced Nursing* 14, 42–48.

Brooker, C. and White, E. (1998) *The Fourth Quinnenial Survey of CPNs*, Department of Nursing Monograph: University of Manchester.

Brooker, C., Falloon, I., Butterworth, A., Goldberg, D., Graham-Hole, V. and Hillier, V. (1994) The outcome of training community psychiatric nurses to deliver psychosocial interventions, *British Journal of Psychiatry* 165, 222–230.

Deale, A., Chalder, T., Marks, I. and Wessley, S. (1997) Cognitive behaviour therapy for chronic fatigue syndrome: a randomised controlled trial, *American Journal of Psychiatry* 154, 408–414.

Ghosh, A., Marks, I. and Carr, A. (1988) Therapist contact and outcome of self exposure treatment for phobias: a controlled study, *British Journal of Psychiatry* 152, 234–238.

Goldberg, D. and Gournay, K. (1997) The GP, the psychiatrist and the burden of mental health care. *Maudsley Discussion Paper No. 1*, Institute of Psychiatry: London.

Gournay, K. (1995) The treatment of obsessive compulsive disorder using behavioural psychotherapy, alone or in combination with other approaches, *Journal of Seratonin Research* suppl. 1, 37–47.

Gournay, K. and Brooking, J. (1994) The CPN in primary care: an outcome study, *British Journal of Psychiatry* 165, 231–238.

—— (1995) The CPN in primary care: an economic analysis, *Journal of Advanced Nursing* 22, 769–778.

Gournay, K., Veale, D. and Walburn, J. (1997) Body dysmorphic disorder: pilot randomised controlled trial of treatment implications for nurse therapy, research and practice, *Clinical Effectiveness in Nursing* 1, 38–46.

Gournay, K., Denford, L., Newell, R. and Parr, A.M. (1999) Nurse therapists in behavioural psychotherapy in the UK: a 25 year follow up, *Journal of Advanced Nursing* (submitted).

Gray, R., Parr, A.M., Plummer, S., Sandford, T., Ritter, S., Leach, R., Goldberg, D. and Gournay, K. (1999) A national survey of practice nurse involvement in mental health interventions, *Journal of Advanced Nursing* (in press).

Greene, J. (1968) The psychiatric nurse in the community nursing service, *International Journal of Nursing Studies* 5, 175–184.

Greist, J., Marks, I., Baer, L. *et al.* (1998) Self treatment for obsessive compulsive disorder using a manual and the computerised telephone interview: a US/UK study, *MD Computing* 15, 3, 149–157.

Holden, J., Sagovsky, R. and Cox, J. (1989) Counselling in general practice settings: controlled study of health visitor intervention in treatment of post natal depression, *British Medical Journal* 298, 223–226.

Lancashire, S., Haddock, G. and Tarrier, N. (1997) Effects of training in psychological interventions for community psychiatric nurses in England, *Psychiatric Services* 48, 1, 39–41.

Leff, J. and Vaughn, C. (1985) *Expressed Emotion in Families: Its Significance for Mental Illness*, New York: Guildford.

Lovell, K. (1997) The Treatment of Post Traumatic Stress Disorder, unpublished PhD thesis: University of London.

Mari, J., Adams, C. and Streiner, D. (1996) *Family Interventions for those with Schizophrenia*, Cochrane Library BMJ Publications: London.

Marks, I.M. (1978) *Living with Fear*, McGraw-Hill: New York.

—— (1985) *The Nurse Therapist in Primary Care*, RCN Publications: London.

—— (1987) *Fears, Phobias, and Rituals*, Oxford University Press: Oxford.

Marks, I., Connolly, J., Hallam, R. and Philpot, R. (1977) *Nursing in Behavioural Psychotherapy*, Royal College of Nursing Publications: London.

Newell, R. and Gournay, K. (1994) British nurses in behavioural psychotherapy: a 20 year follow up, *Journal of Advanced Nursing* 20, 53–60.

Paykel, E., Mangen, S., Griffiths, J. and Burns, T. (1982) Community psychiatric nursing for neurotic patients: a controlled trial, *British Journal of Psychiatry* 140, 573–581.

Tarrier, N., Barrowclough, C. and Vaughn, C. (1988) The community management of schizophrenia: a controlled trial of behavioural intervention with families to reduce relapse, *British Journal of Psychiatry* 153, 532–542.

White, E. (1990) The work of the Community Psychiatric Nurses Association: a survey of the membership, *Community Psychiatric Nursing Journal* 10, 30–35.

Wilkinson, G., Croft-Jeffreys, C., Krekorian, H., McLees, S. and Falloon, I. (1990) QALYS in psychiatric care, *Psychiatric Bulletin* 14, 582–585.

Wilkinson, G., Allan, P. and Marshall, G. (1993) The role of the practice nurse in the management of depression in general practice, *Psychological Medicine* 23, 229–239.

Wilson, G. (1981) Behavioural concepts and treatment of neurosis: comments on Marks, *Behavioural Psychotherapy* 9, 155–166.

Wooff, K. and Goldberg, D. (1988) Further observations on the practice of community care in Salford: differences between community psychiatric nurses and mental health social workers, *British Journal of Psychiatry* 153, 30–37.

Part III

IMPROVING MANAGEMENT

8

THE CONTRIBUTION OF PSYCHIATRISTS TO MANAGEMENT IN PRIMARY CARE

Gregory E. Simon

Over 25 years ago, Goldberg and colleagues first described the high prevalence of common mental disorders among patients presenting to general practitioners (Goldberg and Blackwell, 1970). A subsequent quarter-century of research has led to dramatic shifts in our understanding of mental disorders and mental health services. We now understand that patients presenting to psychiatric hospitals or speciality clinics represent only the conspicuous tip of the iceberg of psychiatric morbidity (Regier *et al.* 1978; Regier *et al.* 1993; Goldberg *et al.* 1976). Over the last decade, new models of mental health care have been developed to address the major portion of psychiatric morbidity which never appears in the speciality clinic. These new treatment models have led to a fundamental re-definition of the role of the psychiatrist in the management of psychiatric morbidity. This review will describe recent research which has contributed to the development of these new models of treatment and will discuss the implications of this research for the roles of psychiatrist.

The epidemiology of common mental disorders

Abundant research over the last 25 years demonstrates that primary care is the most important source of care for common mental disorders (Regier *et al.* 1978; Regier *et al.* 1993; Goldberg *et al.* 1976). Community surveys have consistently found that fewer than 25 per cent of those with well-defined anxiety or depressive disorders seek care from speciality mental health providers (Regier *et al.* 1978). Most community residents who receive treatment for anxiety and depressive disorders are treated exclusively in primary care (Regier *et al.* 1978; Regier *et al.* 1993; Goldberg *et al.* 1976). An even larger number are seen by primary care providers, but anxiety or depressive disorders are neither recognized nor treated (Goldberg and Blackwell, 1970; Bridges and Goldberg, 1985).

GREGORY E. SIMON

Drawing on epidemiological studies in community and primary care samples, Goldberg and Huxley developed a model for understanding the prevalence of and sources of care for common mental disorders (Goldberg and Huxley, 1980). This model describes various levels of treatment for common mental disorders ranging from self-help and community resources to psychiatric hospital care. The transition into each of these levels (e.g. presenting in primary care, recognition/treatment in primary care, referral to speciality care) depends on various factors which together constitute what Goldberg and Huxley call a 'filter'. These filters are typically influenced by characteristics of the patient (both clinical and non-clinical characteristics), the individual health care providers involved, and the health care system. For example, the probability of receiving speciality care for management of anxiety or depression is influenced by age, race, severity of illness, level of disability, the individual physician's beliefs and attitudes, and level of insurance coverage. In general, these different levels of care form a pyramid – with each higher level including a smaller number of individuals than the level below.

The 'filter' model described by Goldberg and Huxley (Goldberg and Huxley, 1980) has two important implications for the distribution of common mental disorders between the primary care and speciality sectors. First, the vast majority of those with common mental disorders do not receive speciality care. In the traditional model of speciality practice, most morbidity is 'out of sight and out of mind'. Second, patients presenting in primary care (or those receiving no care at all) are likely to differ in important ways from those seen in speciality clinics. Important areas of difference include presenting symptoms or complaints, medical comorbidity, explanatory model, and attitudes toward mental health care. Each of these factors is likely to influence selection of treatment and treatment adherence.

Gaps in current management

Of primary care patients with anxiety and depressive disorders, half or more go unrecognized by the treating physician. In the language of Goldberg and Huxley (Goldberg and Huxley, 1980), these patients fail to (or are not allowed to) pass through the filter between hidden morbidity and conspicuous morbidity in primary care. As discussed above, this failure is typically multiply determined. Research by Goldberg and Bridges has demonstrated that primary care patients suffering from anxiety or depressive disorders often present with somatic symptoms or medical concerns (Bridges and Goldberg, 1985; Goldberg and Bridges, 1988). Likelihood of recognising emotional distress is also influenced by the physician's skill at detecting patient cues and willingness to pursue psychological issues (Millar and Goldberg, 1991; Goldberg et al. 1993).

Of patients whose anxiety or depressive disorder is recognized, fewer than half receive an appropriate level of treatment (Eisenberg 1992). Of patients treated with antidepressant medications in primary care, nearly half discontinue medication after only a few weeks and a similar number never receive doses considered therapeutic. Consequently, only 25 per cent of those initiating antidepressant treatment receive appropriate acute-phase pharmacotherapy. When counselling is provided in primary care, it is typically minimal in intensity and duration.

New models for collaborative care

The significant gaps in treatment described above have prompted the development of several innovative models of collaboration between primary care physicians and psychiatrists (or other speciality mental health providers). These collaborative programmes attempt to address several of the specific difficulties described above: failure to recognise anxiety or depressive disorders, deficiencies in pharmacotherapy, limited access to appropriate psychotherapeutic treatment.

Goldberg and colleagues have developed and tested several training programmes intended to improve primary care physicians' recognition of mental disorders (Goldberg et al. 1980; Goldberg et al. 1989; Gask et al. 1989; Kaaya et al. 1992; Goldberg et al. 1995). These programmes are all built around the assumption that traditional didactic education is not sufficient to improve the recognition and management of mental disorders in primary care. Each of these programmes involves ongoing collaboration between primary care physicians and a liaison psychiatrist. These programmes assume that improved mental health treatment in primary care must consider the experience and perspectives of both the psychiatrist and the primary care physician. While the psychiatrist may have specialised knowledge regarding the diagnosis and management of mental disorders, this knowledge is often based on patients presenting to the speciality clinic. The primary care physician contributes expertise in different areas, including the clinical presentation of mental disorder in primary care and the need to balance competing priorities in the clinical encounter (i.e. simultaneous consideration of mental disorders and comorbid medical disorders). Effective training requires an ongoing collaborative relationship between the liaison psychiatrist and the primary care team (Bowman et al. 1992; Warner et al. 1993). One example of this collaborative training approach is the programme developed by Goldberg and Gask to improve primary care physicians' management of somatising patients (Goldberg et al. 1989; Gask et al. 1989). This programme has been shown to significantly improve the performance of primary care physicians in the care of psychologically-distressed patients who present with somatic symptoms. Another example is the World Health Organization's Primary Care adaptation of the ICD-10 classification of mental and behavioral disorders (Goldberg et al. 1995). Use of this training programme was shown to increase primary care physicians' confidence regarding management of depression as well as improve physicians' reported treatment practices.

During the last decade, several research teams have developed and tested treatment programmes built around collaboration between primary care physicians and liaison psychiatrists. Goldberg and colleagues were among the first to develop and formally evaluate these collaborative practice models (Jackson et al. 1993; Warner et al. 1993). Building on this work, several research groups have developed primary-care programmes for treatment of depression (the most common well-defined mental disorder in primary care). Large randomised trials have consistently confirmed the effectiveness of these models. Katon and colleagues have described two different models of collaborative care intended to improve the treatment of depression in primary care (Katon et al. 1995, 1996). In the first of these, a liaison psychiatrist was located in the primary care clinic to improve the management of patients beginning antidepressant treatment for depression (Katon et al. 1995). The psychiatrist's role in this collaborative care model included several tasks. First, psychiatrists provided didactic education to physicians and nurses about recognition and management of depression. Second, psychiatrists were directly involved in the early stages of treatment, typically sharing responsibility for management for a period of six to ten weeks (including a programme of alternating follow-up visits between the psychiatrist and the primary care physician). The duration of direct involvement by the consulting psychiatrist was allowed to vary according to clinical need, ranging from two visits up to five or more. Finally, the psychiatrist was responsible for ongoing monitoring of patients' progress as well as ongoing education and consultation to the treating primary care physician. In a randomised trial of this programme, primary care patients beginning antidepressant treatment for depression were assigned to the collaborative care programme or usual primary care. The psychiatrist collaborative care model significantly improved treatment adherence, patient satisfaction, and clinical outcomes. In a subsequent programme, a liaison psychologist provided education and support to the primary care practice as well as sharing responsibility for management during the initial weeks of treatment (Katon et al. 1996). The treatment programme included four to six in-person sessions with the consulting psychologist focused on behavioral activation, problem-solving, and improving adherence to antidepressant pharmacotherapy. As with the psychiatrist-liaison programme, the consulting psychologist was responsible for ongoing monitoring of treatment adherence and ongoing support of treating primary care physicians. In a randomised comparison with care as usual, this programme showed benefits quite similar to those of the psychiatrist-liaison programme: improved treatment adherence, improved patient satisfaction, and improved clinical outcomes.

Schulberg and colleagues have described the effectiveness of two models of treatment for depression in primary care (Schulberg et al. 1996). A structured pharmacotherapy programme was designed to provide antidepressant treatment consistent with expert guidelines. Pharmacotherapy was provided by a selected group of primary care physicians. These 'specialised' primary care physicians were extensively trained and closely supervised by consulting psychiatrists. Interpersonal psychotherapy was provided by speciality therapists (psychiatrists and psychologists) working in the primary care clinic. Both programmes were considerably more structured and more intensive than those developed by Katon and colleagues. In a randomised trial, primary care patients with major depression detected by a multi-stage screening programme were assigned to one of the two intervention programmes or to usual primary care. Both programmes resulted in robust improvements in clinical outcomes and daily functioning (Schulberg et al. 1996; Coulehan et al. 1997).

Mynors-Wallis and colleagues have also developed and evaluated primary-care based programs of pharmacotherapy and Problem-Solving psychotherapy (Mynors-Wallis et al. 1995). In these programmes, treatments were provided by both consulting psychiatrists and specially trained general practitioners – a strategy similar to that used by Schulberg and colleagues. In contrast with the Schulberg models (Schulberg et al. 1996), the programmes described by Mynors-Wallis and colleagues were considerably less structured and less intensive (i.e. three to four hours of psychotherapy contact time compared to more than 12 hours in the Schulberg programme). In a randomised trial, patients with depression detected by the treating general practitioner were assigned one of the treatment programmes or to a pill-placebo control group. The psychotherapy programme resulted in significant improvements in clinical outcomes and social functioning. The pharmacotherapy programme resulted in improvements which were roughly similar in magnitude, but not statistically significant.

Katzelnick and colleagues developed a 'Depression Management Program' specifically designed for 'high utilisers' of general medical care (Katzelnick et al. 1997b; Katzelnick et al. 1997a). The programme was built around patient education, monitoring and support by a telephone case manager, and (if indicated) antidepressant pharmacotherapy provided by the patient's own primary care physician. Treating physicians received initial training and ongoing supervision by a consulting psychiatrist. The case manager monitored treatment adherence and treatment response by telephone. Patients with persistent depression after 12 to 18 weeks of primary care management were referred for in-person assessment by the consulting psychiatrist. In a randomised trial, 'high utilisers' of general medical care with major depression (detected by a two-stage screening process) were randomly assigned to the Depression Management Program or usual primary care. The programme resulted in significant improvements in quality of depression treatment, clinical outcomes, and daily functioning.

The specific programs described above can be placed along a continuum of direct involvement by psychiatrists or other speciality providers. In programmes developed by Katon and colleagues (Katon *et al.* 1995; Katon *et al.* 1996), all patients had direct treatment contact with consulting psychiatrists or psychologists. While the number of visits to the consulting specialist was typically less than five, the specialist maintained some ongoing responsibility for quality of treatment and treatment adherence. In the models developed by Schulberg (Schulberg *et al.* 1996), and Mynors-Wallis (Mynors-Wallis *et al.* 1995), treatment was provided either by specialists or 'specialised' primary care providers. This group of selected and specially trained physicians might be considered as intermediate between specialists (psychiatrists or psychologists) and 'real world' primary care physicians. The programme described by Katzelnick (Katzelnick *et al.* 1997b) relied on antidepressant pharmacotherapy initiated by the patient's own primary care physician. The consulting psychiatrist, however, was responsible for training primary care physicians, providing ongoing supervision, and providing direct treatment to patients whose depression persisted following three to four months of primary care management.

In contrast with the above efforts, attempts to improve depression treatment that have not involved direct collaboration between primary care physicians and consulting specialists have generally proven ineffective. In an earlier study of depression treatment among 'high utilisers', Katon and colleagues evaluated the impact of a one-time psychiatric consultation visit followed by feedback of diagnosis and treatment recommendations to the treating primary care physicians (Katon *et al.* 1992). Consulting psychiatrists had no involvement in or responsibility for ongoing management. The intervention programme had minimal impact on treatment provided and no significant impact on patient outcomes compared to care as usual. Callahan and colleagues evaluated a similar intervention in a sample of depressed elderly primary care patients (Callahan *et al.* 1994). In that randomised trial, feedback of depression diagnoses and treatment recommendations had no significant impact on clinical outcomes. In a third example of this type of intervention, Mathias and colleagues found that feedback of diagnoses and management advice had no impact on the clinical outcomes of primary care patients with anxiety disorders (Mathias *et al.* 1994). Harold Goldberg and colleagues have recently reported the results of an attempt to implement the US Agency for Health Care Policy and Research guidelines for management of depression in primary care using Academic Detailing and Continuous Quality Improvement methods (Goldberg *et al.* 1998). Both methods attempted to engage the primary care physician in sustained efforts to improve practice, but neither included any involvement by psychiatrists or other specialists in treatment (either directly or via consultation). Neither programme had any significant impact on quality of treatment or clinical outcomes. Finally, Lin and colleagues have described a follow-up study of the Katon collaborative care models described above (Lin *et al.* 1997). Surveys of patients treated before, during, and after the study period indicated no sustained improvement in care following the intervention. After withdrawal of consulting specialists from the treatment team, practice returned to 'care as usual'.

Taken together, the last decade of intervention studies suggests a minimal effective 'dose' of psychiatric involvement in order to provide effective treatment in primary care. While the successful interventions varied in the intensity of specialist involvement, all included at least the following elements: training by consulting specialists (including practice of specific treatment skills), ongoing specialist responsibility for supervision and quality of care, and some direct involvement in treatment by specialists or 'specialised' primary care physicians (even if this direct involvement was reserved for those with more severe depression). Attempts to provide effective primary-care based treatment using a lower 'dose' of psychiatrist and/or psychologist involvement have yielded disappointing results.

Implications for the role of psychiatrists

The research evidence described above indicates the need for a fundamental shift in the role of psychiatrists. Traditional psychiatric practice has focused on the needs of patients presenting for speciality care – and paid little attention to the needs of those who do not pass through the speciality filter. Concerns about privacy and confidentiality have often limited communication and collaboration with colleagues in primary care or other medical specialities. A tradition of segregating the financial and/or administrative responsibility for mental health care has also contributed to the isolation of psychiatric practice.

This important shift in the professional role of psychiatrists begins with accepting responsibility for mental health needs of an entire population. Goldberg and Huxley's understanding of the prevalence of common mental disorders (Goldberg and Huxley, 1980) was a first step in shifting our attention from the tip of the iceberg to the larger portion which is hidden from traditional speciality practice. The subsequent research described above suggests new models for improving mental health care for patients outside the speciality sector. These models for training and collaborative treatment recognise that a population-based approach to mental health care requires more than the export of traditional speciality practice to new locations.

In this new model of psychiatric practice, education should be a significant responsibility. Psychiatrists responsible for populations of patients (and populations of primary care physicians) must be concerned with improving recognition and treatment of common mental disorders among patients who will never cross the filter into the speciality sector (Goldberg and Gater, 1996). As discussed above, accomplishing real improvement in clinical practice requires more than traditional didactic education. Effective education should focus on specific skills and include practice, role-playing, and ongoing feedback (Goldberg *et al.* 1980; Goldberg *et al.* 1995). Education is similar to clinical practice in one important respect: technical exactness and good intentions are probably less important than persistent follow-up in the setting of an ongoing relationship (Bowman *et al.* 1992). Long-term education includes formal consultation and informal or 'kerbside' consultation as well as formal training sessions.

Suggesting that psychiatrists assume responsibility for an entire population does not imply that psychiatrists' clinical efforts should be distributed evenly without respect to clinical need. Psychiatrists' level of direct involvement would vary between patients and over time. For many primary care patients with anxiety and depressive disorders, the consulting psychiatrist's influence will occur solely through education and training of primary care physicians. For patients with slightly greater need, the primary care physician may rely on periodic consultation with the liaison psychiatrist. A significant minority of patients with anxiety and depressive disorders will not respond to appropriate initial management in primary care. For many of these patients, a brief period of direct speciality treatment (either exclusive speciality treatment or shared speciality/primary care treatment) will be sufficient. Finally, for patients with more complex or treatment-resistant illness, transfer to speciality care is necessary and appropriate. While some patients may eventually be transferred back to the primary care physician, long-term speciality management will sometimes be necessary. This overall scheme of graded speciality involvement recognises that the supply of specialists is far from sufficient to provide direct treatment to all with common mental disorders – even in relatively affluent urban and suburban areas of the United States. A rational matching of treatment intensity with clinical need requires that each of the filters described by Goldberg and Huxley (Goldberg and Huxley, 1980) help to sort patients according to need for treatment. Any 'filtering' based on non-clinical factors (such as race, education, income, or health insurance coverage) will only interfere with effective use of speciality care.

'De-constructing' the role of the specialist

The new models of collaborative practice described above also offer a framework for considering the various contributions of psychiatrists to improving management of common mental disorders in primary care.

The most obvious attribute of the consulting specialist is expertise in a particular clinical area. This clinical expertise is a product of both speciality training and concentrated clinical experience. One goal of training programmes is to transfer this expertise to practising primary care physicians. Effective training programmes must concentrate on the specific expertise which is relevant to primary care practice. For example, training to improve depression management might consider the following: clues to recognising emotional distress, focused diagnostic assessment, basic pharmacotherapy, and brief supportive counselling (e.g. scheduling pleasant activities, problem-solving techniques). While primary care physicians could certainly master the intricacies of exotic antidepressants used in combination, the time and effort required would be better spent on clinical issues encountered frequently in general practice.

Specialists can also contribute a more organised approach to clinical practice. The narrower scope of speciality practice allows greater attention to the routine tasks of monitoring medication adherence and frequency of follow-up visits. Implementation of organised treatment 'pathways' is much less daunting when the number of clinical conditions to be considered is five rather than 500. Fortunately, computers can remember and remind much more accurately than brains of busy physicians. Technological advances such as computerised records and appointment systems can allow primary care practice teams to 'pay attention' to the numerous clinical problems which compete for attention.

Among the contributions of psychiatrists to the management of common mental disorders, motivation and persistence may be as important as any specialised knowledge. Psychiatrists' perseverance in the treatment of depression and anxiety represents a number of beliefs and attitudes: mental disorders are important causes of suffering; depressive and anxiety disorders are important health conditions rather than moral weaknesses; effective treatment of common mental disorders can produce dramatic benefits. These attitudes and beliefs grow out of speciality training and clinical experience. Transferring these attitudes and beliefs to primary care physicians requires much more than traditional didactic education. Training must include practice of specific skills as well as ongoing liaison and support. Most important, any psychiatrist-educator who hopes to motivate primary care physicians effectively must enter the world of primary care with enthusiasm, a healthy sense of scepticism about speciality-based knowledge, and a spirit of true partnership with practitioners 'in the trenches'. For psychiatrists hoping to carry out this work in the coming decades, the work of Sir David Goldberg provides excellent examples of each of these virtues.

References

Bowman, F.M., Goldberg, D.P., Millar, T., Gask, L. and McGrath, G. (1992), 'Improving the skills of established general practitioners: the long-term benefits of group teaching', *Medical Education* 26, 63–68.

Bridges, K.W. and Goldberg, D.P. (1985), 'Somatic presentations of DSM-III psychiatric disorders in primary care', *Journal of Psychosomatic Research* 29, 563–569.

Callahan, C.M., Hendrie, H.C., Dittus, R.S., Brater, D.C., Hui, S.L. and Tierney, W.M. (1994), 'Improving treatment of late life depression in primary care: A randomized clinical trial', *Journal of the American Geriatric Society* 42, 839–846.

Coulehan, J.L., Schulberg, H.C., Block, M.R., Madonia, M.J. and Rodriguez, E. (1997), 'Treating depressed primary care patients improves their physical, mental, and social functioning', *Archives of Internal Medicine* 157, 1113–1120.

Eisenberg, L. (1992), 'Treating depression and anxiety in primary care: Closing the gap between knowledge and practice', *New England Journal of Medicine* 326, 1080–1084.

Gask, L., Goldberg, D., Porter, R. and Creed, F. (1989), 'The treatment of somatization: Evaluation of a teaching package with general practice trainees', *Journal of Psychosomatic Research* 33, 697–703.

Goldberg, D.P. and Blackwell, B. (1970), 'Psychiatric illness in general practice: A detailed study using a new method of case identification', *British Medical Journal* 2, 439–443.

Goldberg, D.P. and Bridges, K. (1988), 'Somatic presentations of psychiatric illness in primary care', *Journal of Psychosomatic Research* 32, 137–144.

Goldberg, D. and Gater, R. (1996), 'Implications of the World Health Organization study of mental illness in general health care for training primary care staff', *British Journal of General Practice* 46, 483–485.

Goldberg, D.P. and Huxley, P. (1980), *Mental Illness in the Community: the pathways to psychiatric care*. Tavistock, New York.

Goldberg, D., Kay, C. and Thompson, L. (1976), 'Psychiatric morbidity in general practice and the community', *Psychological Medicine* 6, 565–569.

Goldberg, D.P., Steele, J.J., Smith, C. and Spivey, L. (1980), 'Training family doctors to recognise psychiatric illness with increased accuracy', *Lancet* 2, 8193, 521–523.

Goldberg, D., Gask, L. and O'Dowd, T. (1989), 'The treatment of somatization: Teaching techniques of reattribution', *Journal of Psychosomatic Research* 33, 689–695.

Goldberg, D.P., Jenkins, L., Millar, T. and Faragher, E.B. (1993), 'The ability of trainee general practitioners to identify psychological distress among their patients', *Psychological Medicine* 23, 185–193.

Goldberg, D., Sharp, D. and Nanayakkara, K. (1995), 'The field trial of the mental disorders section of ICD-10 designed for primary care (ICD10-PHC) in England', *Family Practice* 12, 466–473.

Goldberg, H.I., Wagner, E.H., Fihn, S.D., Martin, D.P., Horowitz, C.P., Christensen, D.B., Cheadle, A.D., Diehr, P. and Simon, G. (1998), 'A randomized controlled trial of CQI teams and Academic Detailing: Can they alter compliance with guidelines?', *Joint Commission Journal on Quality Improvement* 24, 130–142.

Jackson, G., Gater, R., Goldberg, D., Tantam, D., Loftus, L. and Taylor, H. (1993), 'A new community mental health team based in primary care. A description of the service and its effect on service use in the first year', *British Journal of Psychiatry* 162, 375–384.

Kaaya, S., Goldberg, D. and Gask, L. (1992), 'Management of somatic presentations of psychiatric illness in general medical settings: evaluation of a new training course for general practitioners', *Medical Education* 26, 138–144.

Katon, W., Von Korff, M., Lin, E., Bush, T., Lipscomb, P. and Russo, J. (1992), 'A randomized trial of psychiatric consultation with distressed high utilizers'. *General Hospital Psychiatry* 14, 86–98.

Katon, W., Von Korff, M., Lin, E., Walker, E., Simon, G., Bush, T., Robinson, P. and Russo, J. (1995), 'Collaborative management to achieve treatment guidelines: Impact on depression in primary care', *JAMA* 273, 1026–1031.

Katon, W., Robinson, P., Von Korff, M., Lin, E., Bush, T., Ludman, E., Simon, G. and Walker, E. (1996), 'A multifaceted intervention to improve treatment of depression in primary care', *Archives of General Psychiatry* 53, 924–932.

Katzelnick, D.J., Kobak, K.A., Greist, J.H., Jefferson, J.W. and Henk, H.J. (1997), 'Effect of primary care treatment of depression on service use by patients with high medical expenditures', *Psychiatric Services* 48, 59–64.

Katzelnick, D.J., Simon, G.E., Pearson, S.D., Manning, W.G., Helstad, C.P., Henk, H.J. and Kobak, K.A. (1997a), Randomized trial of a depression management program in high utilizers of medical care. Presented at 12th International NIMH Conference on Mental Health Problems in the General Heatlh Care Sector.

Lin, E., Katon, W., Simon, G., Von Korff, M., Bush, T., Rutter, C., Saunders, K. and Walker, E. (1997), 'Achieving guidelines for treatment of depression in primary care: Is physician education enough?', *Medical Care* 35, 831–842.

Mathias, S.D., Fifer, S.K., Mazonson, P.D., Lubeck, D.P., Buesching, D.P. and Patrick, D.L. (1994) 'Necessary but not sufficient: The effect of screening and feedback on outcomes of primary care patients with untreated anxiety', *Journal of General Internal Medicine* 9, 606–615.

Millar, T. and Goldberg, D.P. (1991), 'Link between the ability to detect and manage emotional disorder: a study of general practitioner trainees', *British Journal of General Practice* 41, 357–359.

Mynors-Wallis, L.M., Gath, D.H., LLoyd-Thomas, A.R. and Tomlinson, D. (1995), 'Randomised controlled trial comparing problem solving treatment with amitriptyline and placebo for major depression in primary care', *British Medical Journal* 310, 441–445.

Regier, D.A., Goldberg, I.D. and Taube, C.A. (1978), 'The de facto US mental health services system: A public health perspective', *Archives of General Psychiatry* 35, 685–693.

Regier, D.A., Narrow, W.E., Rae, D.S., Mandersheid, R.W., Locke, B.Z. and Goodwin, F.K. (1993), 'The de facto US mental and addictive disorders service system: Epidemiologic catchment area prospective 1-year prevalence rates of disorders and services', *Archives of General Psychiatry* 50, 85–94.

Schulberg, H.C., Block, M.R., Madonia, M.J., Scott, C.P., Rodriguez, E., Imber, S.D., Perel, J., Lave, J., Houck, P.R. and Coulehan, J.L. (1996) 'Treating major depression in primary care practice: Eight-month clinical outcomes', *Archives of General Psychiatry* 53, 913–919.

Warner, R.W., Gater, R., Jackson, M.G. and Goldberg, D.P. (1993), 'Effects of a community mental health service on the practice and attitudes of general practitioners', *British Journal of General Practice* 43, 507–511.

9

IMPROVING MANAGEMENT OF DEPRESSION BY PRIMARY CARE PHYSICIANS

Elizabeth H.B. Lin

Introduction

Treatment of depression has traditionally been assumed as a responsibility primarily of psychiatrists. This view has changed over the last three decades. Primary care physicians are recognized as primary providers of depression treatment. Sir David Goldberg's initial research on the epidemiology of mental disorders provided impetus for this trend (Goldberg and Blackwell, 1970). The finding that general health care setting was an important point of service for patients with psychiatric disorders continues to be validated by recent epidemiological surveys (Spitzer, *et al.* 1994). Over the last two decades, the field of mental health research in primary care has flourished worldwide and is yielding advances to lessen the burden of psychological disorders.

Depression is a case in point. This chapter will propose a model for improving the management of depression by primary care physicians. Based on a series of randomized controlled trials, our research team identified an individualized stepped care strategy to translate efficacious speciality psychiatric interventions into the general health care setting. Speciality interventions are difficult and potentially costly to implement in a primary care practice. Unless carefully adapted, these speciality models would not fully meet the needs of primary care patients and providers. In order to succeed in improving management of depression in the general health sector, these interventions need to be adjusted to reflect: (1) the time pressures and the many competing responsibilities facing primary care physicians; (2) the distinctive characteristics of primary care depressed patients; and (3) effective strategies for changing the treatment by primary care physicians. This chapter will: (1) describe the unique challenges of primary care practice through the eyes of a primary care physician, (2) contrast the epidemiology of depression

116

in primary care with speciality care, (3) review educational interventions used for changing physician practice, and (4) highlight successful primary care interventions for depressed patients.

Over the last decade, research has consistently shown that primary care treatment of depression is not optimal (Schulberg, *et al.* 1997, Eisenberg, 1992). Primary care providers recognize about half of their depressed patients (Wells, *et al.* 1989, Higgins, 1994). An even smaller proportion of patients receives adequate treatment (Katon, *et al.* 1992a). There is a growing consensus that improving usual care for depressed patients is a priority for primary care. (Public Health Service Agency for Health Care Policy and Research, 1993) A better understanding of primary care patients, and the reality of primary care practices will help us understand forces that detract from optimal management and guide future efforts.

Primary care physicians and their practice responsibilities

Why should primary care physicians treat depression? The Epidemiologic Catchment Area data showed that the majority of depressed patients first seek help from their primary care physicians (Regier, *et al.* 1978). Even when these patients were subsequently referred to mental health specialists, many did not complete the referral (Callahan, *et al.* 1996). This help-seeking behavior provides a rationale for designating primary care physicians as the essential providers of mental health services for their depressed patients. Family physicians and internists can provide care for depression as part of a long-standing patient–physician relationship. By integrating mental health treatment into general health services, these treatments can be more accessible and less stigmatized.

However primary care practice also presents competing demands for primary care physicians (Klinkman, 1997). These front-line clinicians are counted on to meet the acute and urgent needs of patients as well as providing comprehensive medical care to persons of all ages. Their mission spans the prevention of illness to treatment of complications for problems as diverse as heart attacks, fractures, child abuse and the common headache. Primary care physicians must be proficient in handling a wide spectrum of emergencies as well as the common chronic illnesses affecting populations.

Mental health research in primary care has consistently identified depression as a very common disorder affecting 5–10 per cent of primary care patients (Public Health Service Agency for Health Care Policy and Research, 1993). Although its prevalence equals hypertension, depression is often not recognized. Most primary care physicians do not dispute the public health significance of depression. However, the total burden of illness and preventive care often overwhelms the available resources. In the face of these competing demands, acute crises usually overshadow the less acute but equally important health problems of chronic illness.

117

The under-detection of depression is better grasped by understanding the setting and priorities of primary care. In general, primary care physicians detect and treat more severe cases of depression. Patients who are mildly depressed and less impaired functionally are often unrecognized or untreated (Simon and Von Korff, 1995; Coyne, et al. 1995). These mildly depressed patients have been shown to have good outcomes in primary care setting (Katon, et al. 1995). These findings add an important dimension to the frequent criticism that primary care physicians diagnose one half of primary care patients suffering from depression. Lack of time is a critical consideration for primary care providers. S/he must prioritize their time to generate the most benefit. In the face of competing demands, primary care clinicians tend to focus their time and treatment for the more severely ill and functionally impaired patients. These sicker patients may have accepted more readily diagnosis and treatment for their depression. Since benefits of treating milder depression are still uncertain, we need to question the rationale behind screening primary care patients to increase depression detection (Lin and Katon, 1998). Is it wise to create additional responsibilities for primary care physicians when the more severe and less functional patients they have recognized are receiving sub-optimal treatment?

The primary care patients who have been accurately diagnosed and have appropriately started treatment do not, however, receive therapy as recommended by Agency for Health Care Policy and Research (AHCPR) guidelines (Public Health Service Agency for Health Care Policy and Procedure, 1993). In general, they receive inadequate pharmacotherapy. Monitoring of patient adherence and response to treatment is infrequent and unorganized (Simon, 1998). Both patients and providers contribute to this sub-optimal care. Patients do not adhere to recommended treatment and follow-up (Lin, et al. 1995). Clinicians do not systematically monitor treatment response and adjust therapy accordingly. Support for educating and activating patients to carry out treatment plans is often unavailable. Organizing depression care within the broader framework of efforts to improve care of other chronic conditions can provide practical solutions for primary care (Wagner, et al. 1996; Von Korff, et al. 1997). Alternatively, Goldberg and Gournay proposed organizing community health teams in Britain to be more in line with primary care teams (Goldberg and Gournay, 1997). A 'link worker' would facilitate, co-ordinate and support the care of patients, as well as educating primary care teams in mental health skills. Either of these approaches may help deliver effective depression treatment to the greatest number of patients.

Are depressed primary care patients different?

Until the last two decades, psychiatric studies based on tertiary care populations provided most of the data on depression. Findings regarding patient characteristics, efficacious treatment, predictors of depression relapse and suicide risk were extrapolated to primary care populations. Recent research conducted in primary care settings has shown that depressed primary care patients differ from their psychiatric counterparts. The contrasts include help seeking, expression of distress, treatment expectations, symptom severity, functional impairment and natural history (Klinkman, *et al.* 1997; Katon, 1985). Patients who choose to obtain primary care service are likely to have a somatic explanation for their problems. Bridges and Goldberg described that even in western cultures, primary care patients with psychiatric disorders often presented initially with physical complaints (Bridges and Goldberg, 1985). Not only can somatization contribute to underdiagnosis of depression, it can foster a dissonant and frustrating patient and physician relationship (Lin, *et al.* 1991).

Primary care patients also experience more physical co-morbidity such as diabetes, chronic obstructive pulmonary disease, and heart disease (Coulehan, *et al.* 1990; Kiseley and Goldberg, 1996). Both somatization and physical co-morbidity influence patient expectations of treatment. Patients expect their physicians to find physical causes and cures for their problems. They are often disappointed to receive a diagnosis of depression ('My doc told me it was all in my head!') when they present physical symptoms such as aches and tiredness. In general, primary care patients experience milder depression severity as compared with their psychiatric counterparts. Moreover, primary care depressives usually have more favourable prognosis, and less co-existing severe psychiatric disorders (Coyne, *et al.* 1994).

Educating primary care physicians in practice

How does one help physicians improve their practice? There is no single universally effective strategy to change clinician behavior. In a recent symposium devoted to the application of successful continuing medical educational techniques to mental health in primary care, Oxman and colleagues proposed a comprehensive (tripartite) model for improving physician practices (Oxman, 1998). The various modalities used to change provider behavior can be viewed as acting on one of three phases: predisposition, enablement and reinforcement. Examples of predisposing activities are formal continuing medical education programs, and small group discussions aimed at increasing provider knowledge, and improving attitudes toward depression treatment. Academic detailing can be effective (Soumerai, 1998). It is a brief face-to-face educational outreach program aimed at enabling physicians to make sound clinical decisions. Patient education is another example of enabling activities. Practice-based techniques such as chart audits and peer comparisons reinforce behavior change. In general, traditional continuing medical education lectures and printed educational materials have little impact on physician practice. Timely audits and feedback of physician behavior such as use of the diagnostic lab or drug prescription can improve the practice of health care providers (Davis, 1998).

Whatever method or combination one chooses, it is essential to start with a needs assessment of the receiving physicians. Determine, from their perspective, what are the daunting impediments and what solutions they think would work best. The more the intervention is tailored to their specific practice, the more likely the success. Roter and colleagues have addressed specific needs of busy primary care physicians by teaching interviewing skills that reduce patient emotional distress without increasing the length of the visit (Roter, *et al*. 1995).

One successful method of training general practitioners was developed by Gask and Goldberg (Gask, 1998). They taught interviewing skills by using videotaped feedback of general practitioners conducting real and role-played patient consultations. Further refinement with problem-based interviewing and group teaching showed that this method can help a larger number of practitioners to improve psychological skills and management strategies.

In a review of 99 randomized controlled trials using 160 educational interventions, Davis found that one third failed to change either physician performance or patient outcomes, and about 62 per cent showed improvement in a measure of practice (Davis, 1998). Among the 46 interventions aimed at improving patient outcomes, less than half of the interventions succeeded. The more specific and simpler the behaviors, the easier and more successful they were to implement. In contrast, improving the management of depression requires a series of changes in practice, some of which may be difficult to achieve (e.g. adequate dosage and duration of pharmacotherapy, increased patient education, supportive counselling and more intensive follow-up of patients).

Efforts to implement depression guidelines through physician education alone, unfortunately have not achieved improvement in physician practice or patient outcomes. A continuous quality improvement (CQI) program with academic detailing was not able to enhance the treatment or outcomes of hypertension or depression (Goldberg, *et al*. 1998). For the Collaborative Care interventions our research team evaluated, we found better outcomes in treatment adequacy, patient satisfaction and depression severity for major depressives at the four- and seven-month follow-up (Katon, *et al*. 1995; Katon, *et al*. 1996). However, these improvements did not generalize to other patients after the intervention even though the physicians received multifaceted training including case-by-case consultations, didactics, academic detailing and role play of optimal treatment (Lin, *et al*. 1997). These training efforts mainly focused on the predisposition phase of the tripartite model described above. The subsequent section will describe ways that the Collaborative Care interventions included additional key components of the tripartite model by integrating enablement and reinforcement tools into the primary care practice.

Wagner, Von Korff and colleagues proposed a framework for re-organizing primary care practices to improve care of chronic illness management (Wagner, *et al.* 1996). Depression is a relapsing or chronic condition for most primary care patients (Lin, *et al.* 1998). Bolstering acute phase treatment did not produce long-term benefits (Lin, *et al.* 1998). The needs of depressed patients would be better served by using a chronic illness management framework. Physician training is only a component of this practice redesign (Katon, *et al.* 1997). Other key components are: decision support (i.e. evidence-based guidelines, speciality consultants), information systems (e.g. a registry of depressed patients receiving treatment, reminders, and automated pharmacy and diagnostic data), self-management support (e.g. patient education outreach) and practice and team re-organization (e.g. active monitoring systems for patient progress). From this systems' perspective, if physician training stands alone and is not woven into the system of care, it will be unlikely to succeed.

Effective primary care interventions

In the last decade, excellent randomized controlled studies tested programs to enhance depression management by primary care physicians (McGruder-Habib, *et al.* 1990; Katon, *et al.* 1992b; Callahan, *et al.* 1994; Katon, *et al.* 1995; Katon, *et al.* 1996; Mynor-Wallis, *et al.* 1995; Schulberg, *et al.* 1996; Scott, *et al.* 1997; Katzelnick, *et al.* under review). These interventions shared common emphasis including: (1) tailoring treatment to meet the needs of busy primary care practices and (2) adapting therapy to the distinctive needs of primary care populations. Table 9.1 summarizes salient features and findings of these studies. The earlier three studies were able to enhance physician processes of care such as improved diagnoses, and increased prescription of antidepressant medicine (Mcgruder-Habib, *et al.* 1990; Katon, *et al.* 1992b; Callahan, *et al.* 1994). However, patient outcome either did not change significantly or was not measured (Table 9.1). These earlier interventions consisted mainly of in-depth diagnostic assessments followed by treatment recommendations. They did not further enable the primary care physicians to deliver the recommended treatments. Nor was there a systematic follow-up of patient progress to ensure symptom resolution. In contrast, the subsequent clinical trials in Table 9.1 resulted in better patient outcomes for the intervention groups, in addition to enhancing process of care.

What did these latter randomized controlled trials have in common that enabled the primary care physician to provide quality treatment and improve patient well-being? The key was re-organizing the system of care to help primary care physicians to achieve better practice. I will use the Collaborative Care programs for illustration (Katon, *et al.* 1995; Katon, *et al.* 1996). In this

Table 9.1 Intervention trials to enable primary care physicians' treatment of depression

Randomized controlled trials	Pertinent primary care interventions	Intervention vs. control outcomes
Mcgruder-Habib, Zung et al. (1990)	Veteran Administration patients screened ($n = 100$ randomized)	⇑ Recognition and treatment. Patient outcomes not assessed
Katon et al.: High Users Study (1992)	High-users screened ($n = 251$ randomized) Brief physician training In depth psychiatric interview with $\frac{1}{2}$ hour joint interview with PCP Written recommendation	⇑ Antidepressant prescription. No change in psychological outcomes
Callahan et al.: Senior Study (1994)	> 60 yrs ($n = 175$) In depth diagnostic assessment Physician training + algorithm Patient education Written treatment recommendation letters specific to patient	⇑ Diagnoses ⇑ Start of antidepressant medicine No increased referral to psychiatry No change in symptoms
Katon et al.: Collaborative Care Programs (1995 and 1996)	PCP recognized and referred depressives More intensive physician training Onsite mental health consultants PCP + psychiatrist co-management 1995 ($n = 217$) PCP + psychologist co-management 1996 ($n = 153$) Patient education and reminders Pro-active follow-up of adherence and symptoms	*Patients with major depression* ⇑ Adequate pharmacotherapy ⇑ Satisfaction ⇓ Depressive symptoms *Patients with minor depression* ⇑ Adequate pharmacotherapy ⇑ Satisfaction. No change in depressive symptoms

Study	Intervention	Results
Schulberg et al. (1995)	Screening (n = 276 randomized) to usual care, or pharmacotherapy or psychotherapy (IPT) Physician training and pharmacotherapy protocol (nortriptyline) PCP managed patient + onsite psychotherapist/ psychiatrist consultants	⇓ (Better) Ham-D scores for nortriptyline ⇓ (Better) Ham-D scores for psychotherapy (IPT)
Mynor Wallis et al. (1995)	Problem-solving or amitriptyline or placebo Referred (n = 91 randomized) GP trained in problem solving and Rx protocol: 6 weeks of problem solving (about $3\frac{1}{2}$ hrs total)	Problem-solving better than placebo Problem solving about equivalent to amitriptyline
Scott et al. (1997)	GP recognized and referred depressives (n = 48, randomized) Acute phase BCT + routine GP care	BCT earlier ⇓ Depressive symptoms ⇑ Sustained improvement
Katzelnick et al.: Care	Screening of high users (n = 407 randomized) Physician training PCP + case manager: reminders, appointment making Psychiatric referrals only Proactive follow-up of adherence and symptoms	⇑ Medication adherence ⇓ (Better) Ham-D scores.

Notes
PCP = primary care physician; IPT = interpersonal therapy; Rx = Prescription; BCT = brief cognitive therapy. ⇑ = increased; ⇓ = decreased.

effective care model, *collaboration* takes place on three fronts: primary care clinicians working together with speciality mental health consultants, patients allying with care providers, and primary care team members co-operating and coordinating service delivery. Collaborative Care is a systematic and multifaceted approach that addresses patient, provider and health system factors to provide best evidence-based treatment for a depressed population. Physician training, a short didactic, role-play, and academic detailing, was only the first step. We further enabled and reinforced better treatment practices by reorganizing primary care service delivery.

Collaborative Care bolstered routine primary care services by structuring family physicians to co-manage depressed patients with on-site mental health consultants. This program began with careful diagnosis of depression and coexisting problems such as panic or chronic social stresses, followed by proactive monitoring of patient progress. We ensured the frequency of follow-up visits by using telephone contacts between in-person visits and patient reminders of appointments. Primary care team members such as the nurse or pharmacist cooperated with the proactive monitoring of patient adherence to medication and treatment response. Patients were provided written and video educational materials and encouraged to be active participants in their care. This systematic restructuring of primary care services is essential to achieving better patient outcomes beyond improving physician process of care. Without this systematic support, chaotic demands compete for the primary care physician's attention and he or she often responds by treating whatever problem is most pressing.

Individualised stepped care management of depression

Based on lessons learned from these successful primary care interventions, and evidence gathered by Coyne and Klinkman on the distinguishing character-istics of primary care depressed patients, our research team refined the initial collaborative care model. We conducted a needs assessment for depressed primary care patients receiving treatment (Lin, *et al.* under review). A signi-ficant proportion of depressed patients did well while receiving routine primary care during the initial six weeks of treatment. Approximately three-quarters of depressed patients had substantial symptom resolution; while the remaining quarter of depressed patients reported more than four depressive symptoms and were thereby at increased risk of chronic depression (Katon, *et al.* 1994). Among the patients with significant resolution of depres-sion, a little over half had increased risk factors for relapse such dysthymia or two or more prior episodes of major depression. This needs assessment led our research group to develop an individualized stepped care approach for primary care management of depression.

The essence of stepped care is matching patient outcomes to different levels of treatment. Patients initially receive routine primary care services. Those who do not respond adequately are provided more intensive management in a step-wise manner to achieve good patient outcomes, if possible. Those patients (about one-third of total) who experienced substantial symptom reduction and had no increased risk of depression relapse may benefit from continued monitoring and routine management. They probably would not need additional treatment beyond usual care (Level 1). A recently completed randomized study shows that patients with substantial persistent depressive symptom six weeks after starting treatment experienced better depression outcomes when they received additional services (Level 2) to prevent depression chronicity (Katon *et al.* under review). Lastly, patients whose prior history placed them at increased risk of depression relapse may also benefit from additional services such as relapse prevention (Level 3). A randomized trial is currently underway to assess whether such an intervention would decrease relapse in this primary care population. Appropriate levels of care can thus be matched to treatment needs according to individual patient outcomes and prior history.

This chapter summarizes efforts over the last three decades for improving care of depressed primary care patients. Research conducted in primary care settings was selected to highlight the need for adapting efficacious psychiatric speciality interventions to the challenges of primary care practice and patients. Practical approaches aimed at delivering efficacious depression treatment to the greatest number of primary care patients were also described.

Acknowledgements

This chapter would not have been possible without the long-lasting collaboration of our research team: Drs Wayne Katon, Michael Von Korff, Gregory Simon, Edward Walker, Terry Bush, Joan Russo, Evette Ludman, Carolyn Rutter and Katherine Saunders. Last, but very important, I would also like to thank my father: Dr. Tsung-yi Lin for his enduring encouragement.

References

Bridges, K.W. and Goldberg, D.P. (1985) 'Somatic presentation of DSM III psychiatric disorders in primary care', *Journal of Psychosomatic Research*, 29, 563–569.

Callahan, C.M., Hendrie, H.C., Dittus, R.S., Brater, D.C., Hui, S.L. and Tierney, W.M. (1994) 'Improving treatment of late life depression in primary care: A randomized clinical trial', *Journal of American Geriatric Society*, 42, 839–846.

Callahan, C.M., Hendrie, H.C. and Tierney, W.M. (1996) 'The recognition and treatment of late-life depression: a view from primary care', *International Journal of Psychiatry in Medicine*, 26, 155–171.

Coulehan, J.L., Schulberg, H.C., Block, M.R., Janosky, J.E. and Arena, V.C. (1990) 'Depressive symptomatology and medical co-morbidity in a primary care clinic', *International Journal of Psychiatry in Medicine*, 20, 335–347.

Coyne, J.C., Fechner-Bates, S. and Schwenk, T.L. (1994) 'Prevalence, nature and comorbidity of depressive disorders in primary care', *General Hospital Psychiatry*, 16, 267–276.

Coyne, J.C., Schwenk, T.L. and Fechner-Bates, S. (1995) 'Non-detection of depression by primary care physicians reconsidered', *General Hospital Psychiatry*, 17, 3–12.

Davis, D. (1998) 'Does CME work? An analysis of the effect of educational activities on physician performance or health care outcome', *International Journal of Psychiatry in Medicine*, 28, 21–39.

Eisenberg, L. (1992) 'Treating depression and anxiety in primary care. Closing the gap between knowledge and practice', *New England Journal of Medicine,* 326, 1080–1084.

Gask, L. (1998) 'Small group interactive techniques utilizing video feedback', *International Journal of Psychiatry in Medicine*, 28, 97–113.

Goldberg, D.P. and Blackwell, B. (1970) 'Psychiatric illness in general practice. A detailed study using a new method of case identification', *British Medical Journal*, 2, 439–443.

Goldberg, D.P. and Gournay, K. (1997) 'The general practitioner, the psychiatrist, and the burden of mental health care', *Maudsley Discussion Paper*, No. 1, 1–30.

Goldberg, H.I., Wagner, E.H., Fihn, S.D., Martin, D.P., Horowitz, C.R., Christensen, D.B., Cheadle, A.D., Diehr, P. and Simon, G. (1998) 'A randomized controlled trial of CQI teams and academic detailing: Can they alter compliance with guidelines?' *Journal of Quality Improvement*, 24, 130–142.

Higgins, E.S. (1994) 'A review of unrecognized mental illness in primary care: prevalence, natural history and efforts to change the course', *Archives of Family Medicine*, 3, 908–917.

Katon, W. (1985) 'Somatization in primary care', *Journal of Family Practice*, 21, 257–258.

Katon, W., Von Korff, M., Lin, E.H.B., Bush, T. and Ormel, J. (1992a) 'Adequacy and duration of antidepressant treatment in primary care', *Medical Care*, 67–76.

Katon, W., Von Korff, M., Lin, E.H.B., Bush, T., Russo, J., Lipscomb, P. and Wagner, E. (1992b) 'A randomized trial of psychiatric consultation with distressed high-utilizers', *General Hospital Psychiatry*, 14, 86–98.

Katon, W., Lin, E.H.B., Von Korff, M., Bush, T., Walker, E., Simon, G.E. and Robinson, P. (1994) 'The predictors of persistence of depression in primary care', *Journal of Affective Disorder*, 31, 81–90.

Katon, W., Von Korff, M., Lin, E.H.B., Walker, E., Simon, G.E., Bush, T., Robinson, P. and Russo, J. (1995) 'Collaborative management to achieve treatment guidelines: impact on depression in primary care', *Journal of the American Medical Association*, 273, 1026–1031.

Katon, W., Robinson, P., Von Korff, M., Lin, E.H.B., Bush, T.M., Ludman, E., Simon, G. and Walker, E. (1996) 'A multifaceted intervention to improve treatment of depression in primary care', *Archives of General Psychiatry*, 53, 924–932.

Katon, W., Von Korff, M., Lin, E.H.B., Unutzer, J., Simon, G.E., Walker, E., Ludman, E. and Bush, T.M. (1997) 'Population-based care of depression: effective disease management strategies to decrease prevalence', *General Hospital Psychiatry*, 19, 169–177.

Katon, W., Von Korff, M., Lin, E.H.B., Simon, G.E., Walker, E., Unutzer, J., Bush, T., Russo, J., Ludman, E. and Rutter, C. (under review) 'A randomized trial of stepped collaborative care for primary care depressed patients with persistent symptoms'.

Katzelnick, D., Simon, G.E., Pearson, S., Manning, W.G., Helstad, C., Henk, H.J., Cole, S., Lin, E.H.B., Taylor, L. and Kobak, K.A. (under review) 'Randomized trial of a depression management program in high utilizers of medical care'.

Kiseley, S.R. and Goldberg, D.P. (1996) 'Physical and psychiatric comorbidity in general practice', British Journal of Psychiatry, 6, 169, 236–242.

Klinkman, M.S. (1997) 'Competing demands in psychosocial care: A model for the identification and treatment of depressive disorders in primary care', General Hospital Psychiatry, 19, 98–111.

Klinkman, M.S., Schwenk, T.L. and Coyne, J.C. (1997) 'Depression in primary care – more like asthma than appendicitis: the Michigan Depression Project', Canadian Journal of Psychiatry, 42, 966–973.

Lin, E.H.B. and Katon, W. (1998) 'Beyond the diagnosis of depression', General Hospital Psychiatry, 20, 207–208.

Lin, E.H.B., Katon, W., Von Korff, M., Bush, T., Lipscomb, P., Russo, J. and Wagner, E. (1991) 'Frustrating patients: physician and patient perspectives among distressed high users', Journal of General Internal Medicine, 6, 241–246.

Lin, E.H.B., Von Korff, M., Katon, W., Bush, T., Simon, G.E., Walker, E. and Robinson, P. (1995) 'The role of the primary care physician in patients' adherence to antidepressant therapy', Medical Care, 33, 67–74.

Lin, E.H.B., Katon, W., Simon, G.E., Von Korff, M., Bush, T.M., Rutter, C.M., Saunders, K.W. and Walker, E.A. (1997) 'Achieving guidelines for the treatment of depression in primary care: is physician training enough?', Medical Care, 35, 831–842.

Lin, E.H.B., Katon, W., Von Korff, M., Russo, J., Simon, G., Bush, T., Rutter, C., Walker, E. and Ludman, E. (1998) 'Relapse and recurrence of depression in primary care: rate and clinical predictors', Archives of Family Medicine, 7, 443–449.

Lin, E.H.B., Simon, G., Katon, W., Russo, J., Von Korff, M., Bush, T., Walker, E. and Ludman, E. (in press) 'Can enhanced acute phase treatment of depression improve long-term outcomes? A report of randomized trials in primary care', American Journal of Psychiatry.

Lin, E.H.B., Von Korff, M., Katon, W., Walker, E., Bush, T.M., Simon, G.E., Ludman, E.J. and Saunders, K. (under review) 'Outcomes and service use of depressed primary care patients: A needs assessment for individualized stepped care.'

McGruder-Habib, K., Zung, W.W. and Feussner, J.R. (1990) 'Improving physicians' recognition and treatment of depression in general medical care. Results from a randomized clinical trial', Medical Care, 28, 239–250.

Mynor-Wallis, L.M., Gath, D.H., Lloyd-Thomas, A.R. and Tomlinson, A.R. (1995) 'Randomized controlled trial comparing problem solving treatment with amitriptyline and placebo for major depression in primary care', British Medical Journal, 310, 441–445.

Oxman, T.E. (1998) 'Effective educational techniques for primary care providers: Application to the management of psychiatric disorders', International Journal of Psychiatry in Medicine, 28, 3–9.

Public Health Service Agency for Health Care Policy and Research (1993) Depression in Primary Care: Vol. 1 Detection and Diagnosis and Vol. 2. Treatment of Major Depression. US Dept. Health and Human Services (AHCPR Publication no. 93–0550 and 51), Rockville, MD.

Regier, D.A., Goldberg, I.D. and Taube, C.A. (1978) 'The de facto US mental health service system: A public health perspective', Archives of General Psychiatry, 85, 685–693.

Roter, D.L., Hall, J.A., Kern, D.E., Barker, L.R., Cole, K.A. and Roca, R.P. (1995) 'Improving physicians' interviewing skills and reducing patients' emotional distress. A randomized clinical trial', *Archives of Internal Medicine*, 155, 1877–1884.

Schulberg, H.C., Block, M.R., Madonia, M.J., Scott, C.P., Rodriguez, E., Imber, S.D., Perel, J., Lave, J., Houch, P.R. and Coulehan, J.L. (1996) 'Treating major depression in primary care practice. Eight-month clinical outcomes', *Archives of General Psychiatry*, 53, 913–919.

Schulberg, H.C., Block, M.R., Madonia, M.J., Scott, C.P., Lave, J.R., Rodriguez, E. and Coulehan, J.L. (1997) 'The usual care of major depression in primary care practice', *Archives of Family Medicine*, 6, 334–339.

Scott, C., Tacchi, M.J., Jones, R. and Scott, J. (1997) 'Acute and one-year outcome of a randomized controlled trial of brief cognitive therapy for major depressive disorder in primary care', *British Journal of Psychiatry*, 171, 131–134.

Simon, G.E. (1998) 'Can depression be appropriately managed in primary care?', *Journal of Clinical Psychiatry*, 59 Supplement 2, 3–8.

Simon, G.E. and Von Korff, M. (1995) 'Recognition, management, and outcomes of depression in primary care', *Archives of Family Medicine*, 4, 99–105.

Soumerai, S.B. (1998) 'Principles and uses of academic detailing to improve the management of psychiatric disorders', *International Journal of Psychiatry in Medicine*, 28, 81–96.

Spitzer, R.L., Williams, J.B., Kroenke, K., Linzer, M., deGruy, F., Hahn, S.R., Brody, D. and Johnson, J.G. (1994) 'Utility of a new procedure for diagnosing mental disorders in primary care. The PRIME-MD 1000 Study', *Journal of the American Medical Association*, 272, 1749–1756.

Von Korff, M., Gruman, J., Schaefer, J., Curry, S.J. and Wagner, E.H. (1997) 'Collaborative management of chronic illness', *Annals of Internal Medicine*, 127, 1097–1102.

Wagner, E.H., Austin, B.T. and Von Korff, M. (1996) 'Organizing care for patients with chronic illness', *Milbank Memorial Quarterly*, 74, 511–544.

Wells, K.B., Hays, R.D., Burnam, A., Rogers, W., Greenfield, S. and Ware, J.E. (1989) 'Detection of depressive disorder for patients receiving prepaid or fee-for-service care: results from the Medical Outcomes Study', *Journal of the American Medical Association* 262, 3298–3392.

10

OLD AGE MENTAL DISORDERS IN PRIMARY CARE

Anthony Mann

Introduction

The 'Cinderella' of primary care research?

The highest rates of consultation are at the extremes of life for both males and females. The rates of doctor contact rises sharply in men from 3.3 per 10,000 years at risk in middle-life to 4.2 (65–74) and 5.6 (over 75) compared to the equivalent for women, being 4.5, 4.6 and 6.3. After the age of 75, the proportion of consultations in the United Kingdom that require home visits by a general practitioner exceeds those in the surgery (OPCS, 1995). The rates of consultation for severe physical illness and severe mental illness is also seen to rise with age. The consultation rates for what are perceived as disorders of intermediate severity (presumably anxiety and depression) remain stable from middle-age onwards. Physicians in primary care are, therefore, likely to see large numbers of older patients consulting with complaints in which physical and psychiatric illness coexist. The doctors are faced with a complex, clinical problem to disentangle in brief contact(s). Comments by specialist colleagues from secondary care services that primary care physicians could do better in their detection of psychiatric disorders are unhelpful unless this context is taken into account.

Psychiatrists, who have researched primary care, have not contributed much to help the general practitioner with their older subjects with mental illness. The substantial research into the nature of mental disorders – their outcome, detection and management – have almost entirely concerned patients under the age of 65. The reason for this age restriction is never made clear, particularly as the levels of disability due to physical illness or intellectual deterioration do not show marked increases until the age of 75. Those between 65 and 74 are no more than older adults and probably subject to more adverse experiences – the onset of physical disease, the loss of occupational role, fall in income, or bereavement – that are deemed important for the onset and maintenance of common mental disorders in their younger counterparts. Their exclusion from research is not logical and the lumping of those over 65 into one group of old people might suggest ageism in the minds of researchers. The primary care research that has been published on older age subjects has been the result of forays by old age psychiatrists mainly interested in the detection and management of a specific disorder. As a result of their work, screening questionnaires are available and some manuals or training packages for practice staff have been developed, but their use has not been documented or evaluated.

Prevalence and nature of psychiatric disorders in old age

Depression

Depression is the commonest disorder that affects those over 65. Prevalence figures vary, depending on the criteria used for diagnosis. A strict application of DSMIV criteria for major depression requires depressed mood or loss of interest and 4 out of 8 characteristic accompanying symptoms of depression. Attribution of any of these symptoms to an accompanying physical illness by the interviewer or patient, militates against the diagnosis, as will the reduced frequency with which older patients report sadness or low mood (Georgotas et al. 1983). For these reasons, depression has been claimed to be rare in old age (Weismann et al. 1985; Henderson et al. 1993). However, if other depressive diagnostic terms are included – 'minor depression', 'subthreshold syndrome' or 'depressive symptoms' – then the total rate of depression is, in fact, higher than in younger age groups. This categorical juggling is obviated by an approach to diagnosis based upon a symptom screening scale which has a cut point validated against the clinician's judgement that an intervention would be indicated. The Geriatric Mental State (Copeland et al. 1986) and its related community-screen interview (the SHORT-CARE) (Gurland et al. 1984) have been widely used for the detection of depression in community studies. A pooled data rate of 12.3 per cent is reported from the United Kingdom and eight other European countries (Copeland et al. 1999). This rate is the relevant one for primary care physicians. Blanchard et al. (1994) provided a DSMIII-R diagnostic breakdown of 90 patients reaching SHORT-CARE case criteria, who were identified by a community screening in North London. He showed that the depressions identified were a mixed bag: 23 per cent with major depression; 57 per cent with dysthymia or other depressions not meeting major depression threshold; 15 per cent with a depression secondary to other psychiatric diagnoses. The importance of accepting all forms of depression as important in older people was emphasised by Kennedy et al. (1989) who had studied loss of function associated with depression symptoms. These authors concluded 'Any health policy based upon the prevalence of major depressive disorders will be ineffective if loss of social, emotional, psychological and cognitive function is associated with depressive symptoms that are substantial and widespread, but not congruent with a diagnosis of major disorder'.

Studies of consecutive attenders over 65 with depression are rare. Macdonald (1986) reported that 30 per cent of those over 65 met case criteria and 41 per cent of those consecutive attenders who agreed to participate in a validation study for a rating scale for depression were diagnosed as depressed by a brief psychiatric interview (Bird *et al.* 1987). These figures from the United Kingdom might suggest that the first filter in the Goldberg/ Huxley model may be selectively permeable to this diagnosis in older people, as depression seems to be twice as prevalent amongst elderly attenders than in the community. This increase may reflect the association between physical illness and, in particular, handicap, with the onset and maintenance of depression in older people (Prince *et al.* 1997a, 1997b).

Anxiety and depression

Anxiety disorders *per se* are said to be less prevalent in older people than their younger counterparts. The Epidemiological Catchment Area studies suggested a six-month prevalence rate of 4.8 per cent for phobic disorders, but very low rates of 1.4 per cent for panic and 0.6 per cent for social phobias (Robins and Regier, 1988). The reasons for these low rates have been examined by Krasucki *et al.* (1998). Diagnostic shift is put forward as an explanation. In clinical practice, which is mirrored in the standard instruments devised to research psychiatric disorders, there is a diagnostic hierarchy in which anxiety is placed at the bottom, i.e. anxiety disorders can only be the primary diagnosis once the superordinate diagnoses of depression, psychosis or cognitive impairment have been excluded. Thus studies which suspend the hierarchical rule in applying anxiety screening scales in the community, find much higher rates of anxiety disorder: 10 per cent phobic disorder; 3 per cent generalised anxiety disorder (Lindesey *et al.* 1989); 15 per cent for any anxiety diagnosis (Manela *et al.* 1996). The most common comorbid condition under these circumstances is depression; most of those with GAD and a substantial proportion of those with phobic disorder also meet case criteria for depression (Lindesay *et al.* 1989). Another complicating factor is in the diagnosis of anxiety disorders. There are circumstances, such as crime in the neighbourhood or falling out of doors, that may lead to avoidance and, thus, an apparent phobia. Studies of anxiety in primary care in older attenders are few. Krasucki *et al.* (1999) found that 16 per cent met anxiety case-level criteria for generalised anxiety disorder.

Cognitive impairment and dementia

Around 10 per cent of those over 65 will have an impaired score on a standard screening test of cognitive impairment and about half these (5 per cent) will meet a diagnosis of clinical dementia. Cognitive impairment and dementia are age-related; the rate of the latter rising from 1 per cent around the age of 65 to 25 per cent around the age of 85. These figures are based upon pooled prevalence rates across Europe (Hoffman *et al.* 1991). A survey of those over 75, registered in North London general practices, found cognitive impairment in 2.6 per cent of those between 75 and 79, rising to 12.5 per cent for those between 85 and 89 and 29 per cent for those over 90 (Iliffe *et al.* 1990). These figures appear somewhat lower than might be predicted from community samples, but could reflect the different response rates between two studies.

Late-life psychoses

Ideas of reference and paranoid ideation are reported to affect 4 per cent of the older population (Christensen and Blazer, 1984). However, late-life psychosis is rare, with an estimated prevalence rate 1 per cent, with frequency increasing with age. Elderly patients with late-life psychoses, although few in number, are likely to be drawn to the general practitioner's attention through other agencies. The majority suffer from circumscribed persecutory delusions. Because personality remains intact, these patients may well act appropriately for their own protection – by calling the police or through litigation against neighbours. An overlapping group are those who come to the attention of a general practitioner because they live in squalor – the Diogenes Syndrome. Surveys of these older people indicate that they are a mixed diagnostic group: dementia, alcoholism, psychosis and personality disorder (Post, 1982).

Detection

As with the younger age groups, the primary care team could be key agents in the detection of the psychiatric disorders. The elderly patient does, however, present obstacles to easy diagnosis. The presentation of a psychiatric illness may be part of a chronic, disabling, medical condition or occur alongside long-term social difficulties. Therefore, the psychiatric morbidity may well be subsumed under the other diagnosis or may be seen as an understandable reaction. Therefore, on neither occasion would it be assessed in its own right for contribution to the presenting picture or to the level of disability. Second, some older patients can be reluctant to admit to symptoms of distress because of the stigma of mental illness, as many will still recall the local asylums. While others with cognitive impairment, and some with depression, may not reveal the core diagnostic symptom and focus the interview on other areas. Third, the doctor (him/herself) may well hold attitudes that counter proper enquiry. Butler (1969) wrote of an ageism of health care professionals as 'An attitude implying that old people are in state of decline'. Some may have mixed feelings about their older patients based upon anxieties for their own old age or ambivalent feelings about their parents. Finally, uncertainty over effectiveness of treatments of psychiatric disorders in the elderly, particularly over the side-effects of antidepressant medication or a belief that there is nothing to be done e.g. for dementia, may be additional disincentives to making a diagnosis.

In fact, the older patient does deserve proper diagnosis. Certainly for depression, the commonest diagnosis, effective treatments do exist. But research into the diagnostic accuracy and process of detection of psychiatric disorders in the older patient is sparse.

Depression

Williamson *et al.* (1964) reported that general practitioners were aware of depression in only one quarter of those who were so suffering. A similar figure reported from Australia (Bowers, 1990). In contrast, Macdonald *et al.* (1986) found that general practitioners missed 18 per cent of those depressed, but suggested that the problem was being overdiagnosed, as 34 per cent per cent of those who were not depressed were also so labelled. This increased diagnostic frequency may have been associated with the general practitioners' knowledge that a depression study was underway in the surgery. Reality probably lies between the two sets of figures. After interviewing all those over 65 screened as depressed in a North London community, Blanchard *et al.* (1994) reported that only 38 per cent claimed they had discussed depression with their general practitioner. Crawford *et al.* (1998) in a later study in the same population, showed that the general practitioners identified 52 per cent of those known to be depressed at a community survey as suffering from depression or being depression-prone, but also 32 per cent of the non-depressed. The level of agreement was relatively low (kappa 0.19). The last three studies considered the case criteria as clinical depression needing treatment, rather than a major depressive episode.

Better detection of depression should follow a greater awareness amongst practice staff about the high prevalence rate of depression and its associations in older people. Second, specific training of general practitioners to be sensitive to emotional cues emitted by the patient is now available (Gask, 1992), but, so far, such exercises have not focused on older people. The same principles should apply. Another important step might be to ensure that practice and district nurses are trained to introduce some questions about depression during their contacts with older people for physical health reasons. Many such older people are at high risk for depression. Finally, there are two screening questionnaires validated and used in general practice: the Geriatric Depression Scale (Yesavage *et al.* 1983) and SELF-CARE(D) (Bird *et al.* 1987).

Cognitive impairment and dementia

The ability of general practitioners to detect dementia has been studied in the United Kingdom and Germany. O'Connor *et al.* (1988) found that general practitioners could identify only half of the cases of dementia in those over 75, discovered through community screening. In contrast, in Mannheim, a stratified sample of consecutive general practitioner attenders was assessed using a standard measure for cognitive impairment (Cooper *et al.* 1992). The general practitioners recognised many, with a positive, predictive value of 61 per cent and a negative predictive value of 96 per cent. However, the authors commented that in an unstratified population sample, where the levels of mild dementia would be higher and severe dementia lower, than in the study sample, the positive predictive value would fall to 53 per cent. Illife *et al.* (1990) reported that in only 18 per cent of those with cognitive impairment, identified by the Mini-Mental State Examination, had any mention suggestive of impaired function been recorded in the case notes.

Detection of cognitive impairment can be aided by screening tests, of which the Abbreviated Mental Test Score (AMTS) (Hodkinson, 1972) is recommended in the United Kingdom. The encouragement in the United Kingdom for general practitioners to review the health of those over 75 in their practices on a regular basis, provides an opportunity to carry out this screen at an age when the onset rates of cognitive impairment and/or dementia start to increase.

Management in primary care

Introduction

Management of psychiatric disorder in older age requires an assessment not only of the psychiatric symptomatology itself, but of accompanying physical health and social state; the three interact to affect clinical presentation and prognosis. Therefore, a treatment approach should be capable of addressing factors in any or all these three areas; it being rare for a prescription for medication alone to be sufficient. The primary care physician may need to involve others in the practice team and seek help from outside agencies. The relationship with old age psychiatry and secondary care services will be discussed later.

Depression

Depression is the most common disorder to be addressed. There is now a consensus statement on management (Katona *et al.* 1995). Antidepressant medication is effective in older subjects with major depression (Gerson, 1985). However, there are difficulties in successful prescriptions, particularly for tricyclic compounds. Donoghue and Tylee (1996) showed that, all for all age groups, 88 per cent of the prescriptions for tricyclic antidepressants in primary care were at doses below the therapeutic range recommended by the United Kingdom 'Defeat Depression Campaign'. This was in contrast to the Selective Serotonin Reuptake Inhibitor (SSRI), where 99 per cent were at adequate dosage. In a paper considering those over 65, Donoghue *et al.* (1998) showed that 43.5 per cent of patients received adequate doses of tricyclics, but that older people were still more likely be prescribed a tricyclic than an SSRI in a proportion of two to one. This is unfortunate, as there are particular difficulties with tricyclic medication in older people; somatic side-effects and delayed onset of action make it a difficult proposition in a group already reluctant to accept depression. Therefore, a shift to a newer antidepressant – with lower side-effect profile, standard dosage and more rapid onset – is desirable. However, the symptoms of many of the elderly patients with depression, as indicated earlier, will not meet criteria for a major depression. Here, psychological and social interventions should be beneficial. However, there have been no primary care studies of cognitive behaviour therapy or problem-solving as interventions in older subjects. Schonfield *et al.* (1985) did report benefit (based upon the Beck Depression score) from resocialisation – measured by making new friends – in a case-controlled study of subjects over 55.

The range of interventions needed for older people with depression and evidence of effectiveness if these interventions are coordinated, was demonstrated in a random control trial based in North London (Blanchard *et al.* 1994). Ninety-six residents in Gospel Oak, North London, 83 per cent female and a mean age of 76, were identified through screening as suffering from clinical depression. Only 12 subjects were being prescribed antidepressant medication and three receiving any form of psychological intervention. The prescription rate for the subgroup with DSMIII major depression was 18 per cent. Each subject was then discussed with the local multidisciplinary old age psychiatry team and suitable interventions recommended by the team for that individual, as if they had been referred. Subjects were then randomised to a treatment arm, in which the interventions were to be implemented by a research nurse over the next three months. This nurse worked in the community, linking closely with each patient's general practitioner. For those in the control arm, the general practitioner was informed of the patient's depression and its level of severity, but not given specific management guidelines.

Table 10.1 shows the seven most frequent interventions suggested, illustrating the multifaceted approach. An average of 10 visits of approximately 45 minutes was made to each of the depressed patients in their homes over three months by the research nurse. She spent a total of seven hours in face-to-face contact and an additional two hours in liaison with the general practitioner, secondary care personnel or social services for each subject in

Table 10.1 Interventions required of CPN for depression in community residents

	Percentage of cases
Trial of new antidepressant	44
Review medication with GP	28
Increase social network	60
'Counselling' life problems	39
'Counselling' family relationships	30
Behavioural therapy	37
Review of physical health	51

Source: Blanchard *et al.* 1995

the intervention arm. In fact the nurse was only able to implement 50 per cent of the recommended interventions. She was completely successful in the face-to-face counselling or brief psychotherapy that she conducted herself. Noticeable was the difficulty in introducing antidepressant medication (in the main, this was due to the patients' reluctance to take them) and in increasing social networks. Over the same period, the general practitioners made no new interventions for the subjects in the control group, despite being alerted to their patients' depression. There was a beneficial effect upon depression score in the intervention group compared to the control group after three months, both when depression level was measured by a screening scale and by standardised interview. This effect was not associated with the number of contacts the nurse had with the patient, nor explained by those elderly people who lived alone, i.e., it did not seem to reflect a non-specific effect of a friendly person visiting. A *post hoc* analysis indicated the most benefit was derived by the subgroup who had experienced depression for more than two years. Subsequent follow-up, at least six months after the intervention had stopped, has shown that benefits persisted.

There are several lessons from this study of depression and its community treatment. The first is that coordinated active intervention will benefit depression. An important ingredient of this intervention seems to have been the brief psychological therapies carried out by the nurse focusing on particular problems for the older person or in improving family contacts. These approaches are underdeveloped for older people and need promotion. It was also clear that subjects in this study were reluctant to take antidepressant medication, as were some general practitioners to prescribe them.

Therefore, more information for the older patient about these medications and education for primary care staff is necessary. The last conclusion from the study has been supported by a survey of over 400 United Kingdom general practitioners, which indicated that at least 80 per cent would like more information on how to treat their elderly patients with depression (Collins *et al.* 1995).

Anxiety

There have been no specific treatment studies on the management of anxiety states in the older patient in primary care. Evidence does exist for the effectiveness of behaviour therapy for phobic disorders and of cognitive behaviour therapy for patients with depression, generalised anxiety and panic (King and Barrowclough, 1991). Benzodiazepines are still, however, being widely prescribed for older patients with neurotic disorder, despite dangers of long-term dependence; 15 per cent of those over 65 are being prescribed an hypnotic or anxiolytic. Buspirone may be a safer alternative for those with persistent 'psychic' anxiety (Robinson *et al*. 1988), while patients who show disabling behavioural responses leading to avoidance of feared situations may need referral for psychological help. In an ideal situation, such help would be available within primary care.

Cognitive impairment and dementia

The primary care team has often been criticised for inadequate activity and ineffectiveness in the detection and management of patients who are showing cognitive impairment or developing dementia. Early diagnosis means that reversible pathologies can be detected and treated. Then, for those who are developing dementia, families can be helped to understand the nature of the condition and, in particular, the personality and behaviour changes that are likely to occur leading to less blame and anger. The primary care team should refer families to social services for home-based support, if and when required. Adequate information, therefore, should be available within the primary care setting concerning the potential roles of local social services and voluntary agencies, which can be both practical provision of home help and Meals on Wheels, and emotional, providing respite and carer group meetings for support of carers.

Once dementia is diagnosed and established, the primary care team should monitor the progress, both of the patient and the carer. In particular, it is important to respond to sudden deteriorations which may not reflect the dementia, but the onset of a concurrent physical illness. Treatment will restore the patient to the earlier state. Second, the primary care team must be aware of the carer's mental health; depression rates being 30–50 per cent in co-resident carers (Levin *et al*. 1990). Help with certain problematic behaviours, such as restlessness at night, which the carer might find intolerable, can be offered. Finally, the arrival of anti-dementia drugs will provide a new avenue of treatment; general practitioners may have the responsibility for prescribing these medications.

Psychosis

The older patient with paranoid delusions will have been brought to the general practitioner's attention by others. The doctor or nurse in a primary care team is in an ideal position to establish a relationship of trust with the patient. Without colluding with the patient's delusions, it is possible and important to convey an understanding of the importance of the worry it is causing. Thus, provision of time for the patient to explain their difficulties and regular contacts are more important than an accurate, but off-putting, statement that the patient is suffering from a mental illness and needs treatment. In a situation of regular contact and trust, antipsychotic medication can usually be introduced as a means of relieving distress without recourse to a hospital admission.

Relationship to secondary services

The large number of elderly patients with psychiatric disorders in the community will inevitably mean that, as in other age groups, most should be detected and treated at the primary care level. Referral to psychiatric services can only be an option for a minority, even when (as in the United Kingdom) there is a network of specialist psychiatrists, nurses and psychologists dedicated to the elderly mentally ill. Referral for help for depression is necessary if the patient is suicidal or if there has been no response to active pharmacological or psychological approaches within primary care. Expert help may also be required for those whose depression accompanies a physical illness, when medication is difficult to implement. For those with dementia, referral can be made to confirm diagnosis, but may be more essential for help in the management of accompanying symptoms, such as delusions, severe depression or particular behaviour problems. However, a liaison consultation arrangement in primary care, with sessions provided by members of an old-age psychiatry team is becoming common in the United Kingdom, with the hope that this will obviate a number of outpatient referrals and admissions.

The frail, older patient

The very old who have become frail and dependent through intellectual impairment, immobility or hearing and visual loss may be admitted to nursing or residential care. Some of these institutions employ their own medical staff, but for others – particularly in the residential sector – the resident is often expected to maintain contact with his or her own general practitioner. There may be a general practitioner appointed to look after the health of all the residents. In the United Kingdom, the majority of older people admitted to residential care suffer from dementia, but, in addition, around 40 per cent of those residents without advanced dementia who can be assessed, are suffering from depression (Mann *et al.* 1984). This depression not only brings impaired quality of life for the residents, but makes the patient more dependent and show more 'difficult' behaviour for the staff. The use of neuroleptic medication to achieve sedation for patients with behaviour problems still seems to be widespread (Mann *et al.* 1984). However, detection of psychiatric disorders, in addition to the difficulties of diagnosis, can be hampered by lack of direct access by a general practitioner to a resident; the home care staff often decide whom a doctor does or does not see.

Depression in the frail elderly also responds to active intervention. Banerjee *et al.* (1996) conducted a random-control trial of treatment of major depression amongst the housebound elderly, frail enough to require home care services. This is an overlapping group, in terms of levels of disability, with those found in residential care. The prevalence of major depression had been estimated to lie between 26–44 per cent in a sample in South London, but only 16 per cent of those depressed were being prescribed antidepressant medication. Thirty-three of the 66 patients entered into a trial, were randomised and received an individual package of care, consisting of antidepressants (79 per cent), review and improvement of physical health (76 per cent), increased social contact (69 per cent) and personal counselling (59 per cent) – the most common components of the treatment packages. The control group received usual general practitioner care, after notification of depression. During the six-month follow-up, two of the control group were referred to local old age services, but there had been no primary care initiated additional treatments started. After the six months, 58 per cent of those in the intervention group had recovered from depression and 82 per cent had shown an improvement in depression score, compared to 25 per cent and 47 per cent respectively in the control group. Furthermore, in 17 per cent of the control group the depression score had worsened, compared to none in the intervention group.

This study provided powerful evidence of the effectiveness of a pragmatic psychiatric intervention in a group where natural recovery is not expected and in whom the presence of many adverse factors might indicate that depression could not be alleviated. Effective elements of the packages could not be identified from this study, although it is noteworthy that success in introducing antidepressant medication (78 per cent) was considerably greater than in the previously reported community study (37 per cent).

Conclusions

The primary care team deals with a large volume of psychiatric morbidity amongst older patients, which is complicated in presentation by concurrent physical illnesses and many adverse social factors. Detection and management strategies are limited in their effectiveness at the moment and underresearched. The use of screening scales and teaching materials will be likely to help. However, the evidence from two controlled trials of pragmatic co-ordinated interventions for depression shows that effective care is possible, but the components are multifaceted and delivery probably multidisciplinary. The recruitment and training of nurses specifically to work with older patients in primary care might be an important step forward in recreating this research success. Even in the United Kingdom, where old age psychiatry services are well-developed, secondary care can only provide a limited relief to the problems present in primary care. Liaison consultation with members of a specialist psychiatry team working in primary care may enable staff to become more enthusiastic and, therefore, efficient in this field of work.

References

Banerjee, S., Shamash, K., Macdonald, A.J.D. and Mann, A.H. (1996) Randomised controlled trial of effect of interventions by psychogeriatric team on depression in frail elderly people at home. *British Medical Journal*, 313, 1058–1061.

Bird, A.S., Macdonald, A.J.D., Mann, A.H., Philpott, M.P. (1987) Preliminary experience with SELF-CARE-D: A self-rating depression questionnaire for use in elderly, non-institutionalised subjects. *International Journal of Geriatric Psychiatry*, 2, 31–38.

Blanchard, M.R., Waterreus, A. and Mann, A.H. (1994) The nature of depression among older people in inner London and the contact with primary care. *British Journal of Psychiatry*, 164, 396-402.

Bowers, J., Jorm, A.F., Henderson, A.S. and Harris, P. (1990) General practitioners' detection of depression and dementia in elderly patients. *Medical Journal of Australia*, 153, 192–196.

Butler, R.N. (1969) Ageism: another form of bigotry. *Gerontologist*, 9, 243–6.

Christensen, R. and Blazer, D. (1984) Epidemiology of persecutory ideation in an elderly population in the community. *American Journal of Psychiatry*, 157, 228–231.

Collins, E., Katona, C. and Orrell, M. (1995) Management of depression in the elderly by general practitioners: II. Attitudes to ageing and factors affecting practice. *Family Practice*, 12, 12–17.

Cooper, B., Bickel, H. and Schäufele, M. (1992) The ability of general practitioners to detect dementia and cognitive impairment in their elderly patients: a study in Mannheim. *International Journal of Geriatric Psychiatry*, 7, 591–598.

Copeland, J.R.M., Dewey, M.E. and Griffith-Jones, H.M. (1986) A computerised psychiatric diagnostic system and case nomenclature for elderly subjects. GMS and AGECAT. *Psychological Medicine*, 16, 89–99.

Copeland, J.R.M., Beekman, A.T.F., Hooijer, C., Jordan, A., Lawlor, B.A., Lobo, A., Magnusson, H., Mann, A. *et al.* (1999) Depression in Europe: the geographical distribution among older people: the EURODEP collaboration. *British Journal of Psychiatry* 174, 312–321.

Crawford, M.J., Prince, M., Menezes, P. and Mann, A.H. (1998) The recognition and treatment of depression in older people in primary care. *International Journal of Geriatric Psychiatry*, 13, 172–176.

Donoghue, J.M. and Tylee, A. (1996) The treatment of depression: prescribing patterns of antidepressants in primary care in the United Kingdom. *British Journal of Psychiatry*, 168, 164–168.

Donoghue, J., Katona, C. and Tylee, A. (1998) The treatment of depression: anti-depressant prescribing for elderly patients in primary care. *Pharmacology Journal*, 260, 500–502.

Gask, L. (1992) Training general practitioners to detect and manage emotional disorders. *International Review of Psychiatry*, 4, 293–300.

Georgotas, A., Friedman, E., McCarthy, M., Mann, J., Krakowski, M., Sigel, R. *et al.* (1983) Resistant geriatric depressions and therapeutic response to monoamine oxidase inhibitors. *Biological Psychiatry*, 18, 195–205.

Gerson, R.H. (1985) Present status of drug therapy in late life *Journal of Affective Disorders*, Suppl. 1, S23–S31.

Gurland, B., Golden, R., Teresi, J. and Challop, J. (1984) The SHORT-CARE: an efficient instrument for the assessment of depression, dementia and disability. *Journal of Gerontology*, 39, 166–169.

Henderson, A.S., Jorm, A.F., MacKinnon, A., Christensen, H., Scott, L.R., Korten, A.E. and Doyle, C. (1993) The prevalence of depressive disorders and the distri-bution of depressive symptoms in later-life: a survey using Draft ICD-10 and DSM-III-R. *Psychological Medicine*, 23, 719–729.

Hodkinson, H.M. (1972) Evaluation of a mental test score for assessment of mental impairment in the elderly. *Age and Ageing*, 1, 233–238.

Hoffman, A., Rocca, W.A. *et al.* (1991) The prevalence of dementia in Europe: a col-laborative study of 1980–1990 findings. *International Journal of Epidemiology,* 20, 736–748.

Iliffe, S., Booroff, A., Gallivan, S., Goldenberg, E., Morgan, P. and Haines, A. (1990) Screening for cognitive impairment in the elderly using the Mini-Mental State Examination. *British Journal of General Practice*, 40, 277–279.

Katona, C.L.E., Freeling, P., Hinchliffe, K. *et al.* (1995) Recognition and management of depression in late life in general practice. A consensus statement. *Primary Care Psychiatry*, 1, 107–113.

Kennedy, G., Kelman, H., Thomas, C. *et al.* (1989) Hierarchy of characteristics asso-ciated with depressive symptoms in an urban elderly sample. *American Journal of Psychiatry,* 146, 220–225.

King, P. and Barrowclough, C. (1991) A clinical pilot study of cognitive-behavioural therapy for anxiety disorders in the elderly. *Behavioural Psychotherapy*, 19, 337–345.

Krasucki, C., Howard, R. and Mann, A. (1998) The relationship between anxiety dis-orders and age. *International Journal of Geriatric Psychiatry*, 13, 79–99.

Krasucki, C., Ryan, P., Ertan, T., Howard, R., Lindesay, J. and Mann, A. The F.E.A.R.: a rapid screening instrument for generalised anxiety in elderly primary care attenders. *International Journal of Geriatric Psychiatry* 14, 60–68.

Levin, E., Sinclair, I. and Gorbach, P. (1990) *Families, Services and Confusion in Old Age*. Aldershot: Avebury.

Lindesay, J., Briggs, K. and Murphy, E. (1989) The Guy's/Age Concern Survey: prevalence rates of cognitive impairment, depression and anxiety in an urban elderly community. *British Journal of Psychiatry*, 155, 317–329.

Macdonald, A.J.D. (1986) Do general practitioners 'miss' depression in elderly patients? *British Medical Journal*, 292, 1365–1367.

Manela, M., Katona, C. and Livingston, G. (1996) How common are the anxiety dis-orders of old age? *International Journal of Geriatric Psychiatry*, 11, 65–70.

Mann, A.H., Graham, N. and Ashby, D. (1984) Psychiatric illness in residential homes for the elderly: a survey in one London borough. *Age and Ageing*, 13, 257–265.

O'Connor, D.W., Pollitt, P.A., Hyde, J.B., Brook, P., Reiss, B.B. and Roth, M. (1988) Do general practitioners miss dementia in elderly patients? *British Medical Journal*, 297, 1107–1110.

OPCS (Office of Population Censuses and Surveys) (1995) *National Morbidity Statistics from General Practice. Fourth National Study 1991–1992.* HMSO: London.

Post, F. (1982) Functional disorders. I. Description, incidence and recognition, in R. Levy and F. Post (eds) *The Psychiatry of Late Life* pp. 176–196, Oxford: Blackwell.

Prince, M.J., Harwood, R., Thomas, A. and Mann, A.H. (1997a) Gospel Oak V. Impairment, disability and handicap as risk factors for depression in old age. *Psychological Medicine*, 27, 311–321.

Prince, M.J., Harwood, R., Thomas, A. and Mann, A.H. (1997b) Gospel Oak VI. Social support deficits, loneliness and life events as risk factors for depression in old age. *Psychological Medicine*, 27, 323–332.

Robinson, D., Napoliello, M.J. and Shenck, L. (1988) The safety and usefulness of buspirone as an anxiolytic drug in elderly versus young patients. *Clinical Therapeutics*, 10, 740–746.

Robins, L.N. and Regier, D.A. (eds) (1991) *Psychiatric Disorders in America: The Epidemiological Catchment Area Study*, Free Press, New York.

Schonfield, L., Garcia, J. and Streuber, P. (1985) Factors contributing to mental health treatment of the elderly, *Journal of Applied Gerontology*, 4, 30–39.

Weismann, M.M., Myers, J.K., Tischler, G.L. *et al.* (1985) Psychiatric disorders (DSM-III) and cognitive impairment among the elderly in a US urban community. *Acta Psychiatrica Scandinavica*, 71, 366–379.

Williamson, J., Stokoe, I., Gray, S., Fisher, M., Smith, A. and McGhee, A. (1964) Old people at home: their unreported needs. *Lancet*, 1, 1117–1120.

Yesavage, J., Rose, T. and Lum, O. (1983) Development and validation of a geriatric depression screening scale: a preliminary report. *Journal of Psychiatric Research*, 17, 37–49.

11

CLINICAL PRACTICE GUIDELINES FOR THE DIAGNOSIS AND MANAGEMENT OF COMMON MENTAL DISORDERS IN PRIMARY CARE

Deborah J. Sharp

Introduction

Clinical practice guidelines, CPGs, are 'systematically developed statements to assist practitioners' and patients' decisions about appropriate health care for specific clinical circumstances' (Field and Lohr, 1992). Ideally CPGs should identify recommendations for appropriate and cost-effective management of clinical conditions or the appropriate use of clinical procedures with the principal aim of providing good performance (Effective Health Care, 1994). The essential prerequisite for improved quality of care is that the guideline is valid by which it is meant that adherence will increase the likelihood of obtaining the expected health outcome at the expected cost (Field and Lohr, 1992). In 1993, the Department of Health identified clinical guidelines as a means of improving clinical practice (NHS Management Executive, 1993). In 1999, the guideline industry is flourishing in the UK, with several organisations set up for the sole purpose of developing clinical practice guidelines. In general, however, the majority of clinical practice guidelines in the UK are developed by ad-hoc groups who come together for the task of developing a guideline in a particular clinical area.

It seems inevitable that guidelines will become a major part of primary care in the future, but guidelines for this setting must be developed to match the needs of both practitioners and patients (Grol, 1993). There are some tensions here. Research has shown that there is much greater compliance with guidelines if they are developed internally by the people who are going to use them (North of England Study of Standards and Performance in General Practice, 1992). However internal guidelines are less likely to be valid than external guidelines because local groups lack the clinical, managerial and technical skills to produce guidelines (Grimshaw and Russell, 1993a).

Initially guidelines were consensus based, around evidence produced by the consensus panel. More recently, it has become clear that guidelines are more likely to be valid if they are based on the results of systematic reviews of the evidence, if they are developed by national multidisciplinary groups representing the interests of key stakeholders and if the recommendations are explicitly linked to evidence (Grimshaw and Russell, 1993a). Systematic reviews are the business of the Cochrane Collaboration, and in the context of this chapter, the responsibility of the Cochrane Collaboration Depression, Anxiety, and Neurosis Review Group (CCDAN), which is concerned with the evaluation of health care relevant to mood disorders, anxiety disorders, somatoform disorders, chronic fatigue syndrome, dissociative disorders and eating disorders (CCDAN, 1998).

Developing mental health guidelines in the USA

Mental health has not until recently been an area in which many guidelines have been developed. However the Agency for Health Care Policy and Research, AHCPR, in the USA has produced two national guidelines on depression and dementia (Depression Guideline Panel, 1993; Costa *et al.* 1996).

Depression

The Clinical Practice Guideline for Depression in Primary Care was developed with support from AHCPR by an independent multidisciplinary panel made up of private sector clinicians and other experts to assist all primary care practitioners (PCPs) in the diagnosis and treatment of depression. Depression was chosen as a topic by AHCPR because of:

- its prevalence in primary care settings
- most therapy being carried out by primary care physicians
- the range of effective treatments available
- the large body of scientific evidence on which to base the guideline
- the need to improve the recognition and treatment of depression in primary care
- depression resulting in significant morbidity and mortality.

The panel used an explicit science-based methodology and expert clinical judgement to develop specific statements on patient assessment and management of depression. Extensive literature searches were conducted and critical reviews and syntheses used to evaluate empirical evidence and significant outcomes. Where the literature was incomplete or inconsistent in a particular area, the recommendations reflected the professional judgement of panel members and consultants. AHCPR encourages practitioners and patients to use the information in the guideline in the expectation that this will make a positive contribution to the quality of care in the USA. But just how the average PCP would use this in a consultation with a depressed patient is not clear. Volume 1, 'Detection and Diagnosis' is more than 80 pages long, Volume 2, 'Treatment', 120 pages and the executive summary for each 7–8 pages long. In the UK, research has shown that whilst the utilisation of guideline information is complex, key issues for their use include preference for certain formats including the potential for shared decision making as well as the restricted time available for information seeking in the light of clinical uncertainty (Langley *et al*. 1998).

Dementia

Dementia is the other mental health topic covered by the AHCPR series of guidelines (Costa *et al*. 1996), and although it is not aimed solely at the PCP, they are the professional most likely to see these patients and therefore benefit most from the use of a CPG in this area. The format is similar to the one on depression although the executive summary is more accessible ($2\frac{1}{2}$ pages long) but the whole document runs to 73 pages with a further 70 pages of appendices which include the bibliography and mental state tests. The guideline focuses on:

- triggers to alert the clinician to make an assessment for early dementia
- how to undertake an initial assessment
- a flow chart for early recognition and early assessment including the assessment of depression and delirium
- the interpretation of results and appropriate actions
- the role of neuropsychiatric testing.

The guideline recognises that although research on dementia is advancing rapidly, there is no unequivocally effective treatment (unlike depression). However its premise is that correct early diagnosis of dementia can have substantial benefits for patients and their families. It recognises that in some instances clinicians may diagnose dementia or Alzheimer's disease where it does not exist or may misdiagnose or not recognise early signs perhaps dismissing them as part of normal ageing. Two particularly useful clinical tools for the PCP are present in the guideline: a table of symptoms that might indicate dementia, and an algorithm for undertaking an assessment of suspected Alzheimer's disease and related dementias.

Evaluation of depression guidelines

Although the USA has led the field in developing national, multidisciplinary, evidence-based guidelines for common mental disorders in primary care, much less attention has been paid to ensuring effective methods of dissemination and implementation. Very few controlled trials of the impact of CPGs for mental disorders in primary care settings have been reported. In an attempt to evaluate how the AHCPR guidelines for depression in primary care might improve short-term outcomes for patients as well as being acceptable to patients and doctors, a trial of usual care versus a multifaceted educational intervention for patients and physicians was conducted (Katon *et al.* 1995). The intervention required patients to take a much more active role in their health care and provided PCPs with an educational session on depression, monthly case conferences and case by case consultations between psychiatrists and PCPs. The enhanced care group showed improved adherence to treatment with antidepressants and improved satisfaction with care for major and minor depression but a more favourable clinical outcome only for major depression. Nested within this trial, a study to investigate whether the educational intervention would have any effect on physicians' behaviour after its discontinuation found no enduring effect, which has implications for the implementation of CPGs in terms of the resources required for continued physician training (Lin *et al.* 1997). A similar result was achieved in another randomised trial (Schulberg *et al.* 1997) where the treatment principles espoused in the AHCPR guideline were evaluated in four academically affiliated health centres. Nortryptiline and interpersonal psychotherapy were provided under strict conditions to patients with major depression and were found to be more effective than usual care from a PCP, thus providing empirical support for the guideline recommendations.

Although not a rigorous empirical testing of guidelines, a review of the role of psychotherapy in the treatment of major depression as described in the American Psychiatric Association (APA) guideline (American Psychiatric Association, 1993) and the AHCPR guideline (Depression Guideline Panel, 1993) was undertaken (Persons *et al.* 1996). The overall conclusion of the review was that both CPGs understated the value of the different psychotherapies in the treatment of depressed patients and that the APA guideline overstated the use of combined psychotherapy and pharmacotherapy. In general it was more favourably disposed towards the AHCPR guideline, possibly because it had taken a more empirical approach to its task than did the APA. Attention is also drawn to the potential biases that arise from randomised controlled trials whose inclusion criteria do not always reflect general clinical practice.

Development and evaluation of mental health guidelines in the UK

A systematic review of rigorous evaluations of the effect of clinical guidelines on medical practice (Grimshaw and Russell, 1993b) identified 59 published evaluations that met strict criteria for scientific rigour. It found that all but four reported significant improvements in the process of care after introduction of the guideline and all but two of the 11 that assessed the outcome of care, reported significant improvement. However none of the guidelines under scrutiny were concerned with either the process or outcome of mental health care.

Defeat Depression Campaign

Encouraged by the Defeat Depression Campaign, spearheaded by the Royal Colleges of General Practitioners and Psychiatrists and the 1992 consensus statement on depression (Paykel and Priest, 1992), work in the mental health field began to take off. The major aims of the campaign were to improve antidepressant prescribing especially the dose and duration of the prescription, to improve knowledge of psychosocial interventions, especially cognitive behavioural approaches and to offer criteria for referral to secondary care. These messages were disseminated using a booklet and a laminated yellow card to all GPs. In 1993, an Effective Health Care Bulletin on the treatment of depression in primary care was published (Effective Health Care, 1993a) which summarised the results of a systematic review of which therapies were effective in the management of depression in primary care. The main recommendation, in the light of the conclusion that more research was required to provide evidence on the effectiveness of a variety of management strategies, was the development of CPGs for the detection and management of depression in primary care involving a wide range of health service organisations, professionals, voluntary groups and consumers.

Recent mental health guideline developments in the UK

A new publication, 'Guidelines – summarising clinical guidelines for primary care' covering clinical guidelines from the UK and Europe, is regularly being sent to each general practice in the UK. The guidelines are classified according to whether they have been prioritised and approved by the Clinical Outcomes Group of the NHS Executive or have simply been developed by clinicians and sponsored by the relevant professional bodies. In addition there are summaries of ad-hoc working party guidelines.

The guideline for mental health promotion in high-risk groups (Effective Health Care, 1997) stresses the need for early identification of people vulnerable to mental health problems such as new parents, children, those who become unemployed, and carers. It highlights the role of the primary care team in this task. The guideline for alcohol misuse (Effective Health Care, 1993b) summarises the evidence from clinical trials for the effectiveness of brief interventions and suggests more energy is expended by primary care in using simple screening instruments to detect heavy drinkers and offer brief therapies. Another guideline on alcohol (Plinius Maior Society, 1996) offers a more explicit model for detecting, discussing and assessing alcohol problems in primary care. The Alzheimer's Disease Society has developed a guideline for GPs to improve the management of dementia (Alzheimer's Disease Society, 1993). As well as sections on treatment and referral, it includes the Abbreviated Mental Test Score as well as a table of the clinical features distinguishing dementia, acute confusional state and depression. A guideline for the treatment of depressive illness with antidepressants (British Association of Psychopharmacology, 1993), takes as its starting point the problem of missed depression and covers recognition/diagnosis before considering in detail choosing the right antidepressant in terms of likely efficacy, suicide risk, dose, side-effects and cost considerations.

Also included are three summary guidelines from ad-hoc working parties. The first on old age depression (Banerjee et al. 1996), considers the problem of people living in residential homes who are at particular risk of depression. They offer a step by step plan for agreeing the need to improve the detection and management of residents with depression with managers and briefly rehearse the arguments for and against pharmacological and psychosocial interventions. The second is another guideline for the recognition and management of depression in primary care (Neurolink, 1996) and is no different in its coverage – recognition, diagnosis, drug treatment, counselling and cognitive treatments, and referral, but does include a table outlining the use of antidepressants in different patient groups. The final guideline in this section is again concerned with alcohol misuse (UK Alcohol Forum, 1997) and used a multidisciplinary group which included a solicitor, a health economist and a community alcohol services director amongst its members.

Guidelines for dementia

With the increasing number of elderly in the population, the prevalence of dementia is set to rise, making it an ideal area for guideline development particularly as new drugs are becoming available and there is the need to further integrate health and social care. A clinical guideline has been developed making recommendations for the management of behavioural and psychological aspects of dementia in Scotland (SIGN, 1998). The guideline was developed along the lines advocated by AHCPR and includes a special section on the issue of consent to treatment for patients with dementia. It is expected that the guideline will be adjusted locally after discussions involving groups of appropriate staff and managers. A similar document has been prepared by the North of England Evidence Based Guideline Development Project on the primary care management of dementia (Eccles et al. 1998). This guideline, unlike the one from SIGN, includes recommendations for the cognitive aspects of dementia and is aimed specifically for use in general practice. Neither has been rigorously evaluated in terms of establishing validity.

148

Evaluation of CPGs for common mental disorders in the UK

There have been few evaluations of mental health guidelines in the UK. A survey using the NHS research register as a database for research being conducted in 1966 (Dowie, 1998), found 13 studies in general practice undertaking robust evaluations of guidelines, of which two were for the diagnosis and management of common mental disorders – depression (the Hampshire Depression Project, Stevens *et al.* 1997) and dementia (the Bristol Dementia Guidelines Project, Trickey *et al.* 1998). In the Hampshire Depression Project, the guideline was developed as part of a comprehensive educational programme about the recognition and management of depressive illness in primary care. The model employed in this project was informed by the experience gained in east London, where guidelines for the care of asthmatic and diabetic patients introduced into 27 practices using a practice-based programme of education, produced some improvements in the management of patients in the following year (Feder *et al.* 1995). The full Hampshire Depression Project guidelines are 24 pages long with a four-page summary. They were developed by a steering committee including academic representatives from public health, primary care and psychiatry following a comprehensive review of previous consensus statements and guidelines. The educational programme consisted of the guidelines, introduced through practice-based seminars and further consolidated by team negotiated follow-up sessions. A full evaluation of the effectiveness of the programme is underway in a randomised controlled trial involving 56 general practices.

The Bristol Dementia Guideline Project has been carried out along similar lines. The guidelines were developed using a formal consensus method, the Nominal Group Technique, with a national panel of experts and local stakeholders. They covered the areas of diagnosis, needs assessment and management and were developed for use by the primary care team both in the primary care setting (e.g when undertaking an over-75 check) and at the primary/secondary care interface. They were formatted to gain wide acceptability in primary care, as either a laminated A4 sheet or as an A5 booklet with a flow chart. They are currently being evaluated in a randomised controlled trial in 36 practices in the South and West with implementation at practice level by the researchers. It is hoped that their use will increase the recognition of early dementia by primary care professionals and improve the care that patients and their carers receive.

Guidelines for psychological therapies

It is not only individual disorders that are the focus of CPGs – they can equally well be directed at specific therapeutic interventions. CORE, the centre for Clinical Outcomes Research and Effectiveness, funded by the Department of Health, with a multiprofessional national steering group, is developing a guideline to provide guidance to GPs and others who wish to decide whether referral for counselling or psychotherapy is appropriate to the needs of a particular patient. It takes further the work done in North London under the auspices of the local medical audit advisory group (Cape *et al.* 1998). The guideline is using systematic reviews of available evidence and consensus methods where evidence is insufficient or unavailable.

Appraising the quality of guidelines

In terms of formal evaluations of the multiplicity of guidelines for depression in primary care, there is still very little published despite the fact that the Clinical Outcomes Group has commissioned the use of a specific 'Appraisal Instrument for Clinical Guidelines' (Cluzeau *et al.* 1997). Its purpose is to provide a transparent and standardised method for assessing the quality of clinical guidelines. It contains 37 questions divided into three dimensions: rigour of development, context and content, and application.

The appraisal instrument has been used to assess a sample of the guidelines developed in the UK for the management of depression in primary care (Littlejohns *et al.* 1999). The guidelines were identified by a national postal survey and an electronic search. All national guidelines and a random sample (6/36) of local guidelines were appraised. For rigour of development the range of scores was 18.3–56.7 (mean 33.1); for context and content 16.7–78.3 (mean 46.2) and for applicability 4.17–72.0 (mean 25.5). The maximum possible score was 100 if all referees thought the guideline had fulfilled all criteria in each domain. Most guidelines covered similar areas reflecting the consensus statement (Paykel and Priest, 1992), suggesting that its message had been widely disseminated. It also supports the view that the most cost-effective method of developing CPGs is to provide a national template that can then be adapted for local use.

An international perspective: ICD10-PHC

WHO has developed ICD10-PHC – 'Diagnosis and management of mental disorders in primary care' (WHO, 1996) – as the first of its clinical tools to assist PCPs and community health workers to deal appropriately with mentally ill persons. It was designed by an international group of PCPs, mental health workers, public health experts, social workers, psychiatrists and psychologists with a special interest in mental health in primary care. As well as classifying 24 of the most common mental health problems encountered in primary care, in a fashion that corresponds to Chapter 5 of the Tenth Revision of the International Classification of Disease (ICD10), it provides guidance on diagnosis, advises on counselling, recommends treatment and indicates when referral might be necessary. The guideline was designed to be easy to understand, brief and reliable and was initially presented as a set of flip cards for evaluation in national field trials with diagnosis guidelines on one side and management on the other (Üstün *et al.* 1995). David Goldberg and Greg Simon were the chief consultants to the project and collaborated with colleagues from 14 countries in designing the package which was subjected to field trials all over the world.

The UK field trial for ICD10-PHC took place in four centres and involved 50 GPs who attended a series of three workshops over a five-week period (Goldberg *et al.* 1995). The workshops informed GPs about the content of ICD10-PHC, invited them to use the flip cards in role-play scenarios and provided them with diaries in which to record their mental health consultations. Baseline and final data collection provided information on changes in GP behaviour over the five-week period. The guideline was generally well received and resulted in an increase in GPs' interest in mental disorders, and their confidence in making diagnoses. Use of the depression card, increased the range of symptoms considered when making a diagnosis of depression, increased the threshold for prescribing antidepressants and added to the management strategies suggested for depressive illnesses.

Further developments of ICD10-PHC

A project in Bristol has undertaken a more in depth evaluation of ICD10-PHC in a 'before and after' study of the detection and management of depression in primary care (Upton *et al.* in press). In this study, GPs' diary diagnoses of depression were validated on a 10 per cent sample using the computerised Clinical Interview Schedule (CIS). Although use of the guidelines made no improvement to the overall detection of mental health problems nor the accuracy of diagnoses nor prescribing of antidepressants, there was a significant increase in the number of patients diagnosed with depression. The GPs also made increased use of psychological interventions for certain groups of patients.

In line with the original intentions of WHO, local adaptations and evaluations of ICD10-PHC are currently taking place. The Evaluation of Guideline Outcomes study (EGO), funded by the Department of Health (EGO, 1997), has taken the original guidelines and utilised a robust consensus method, the Nominal Group Technique, to adapt them for use by GPs and two community mental health teams in south Bristol. The study is evaluating their impact in a randomised controlled trial on three main outcomes: unmet need in patients with severe mental illness, referrals from primary to secondary care and detection of psychiatric morbidity by GPs. Another study is taking a slightly different direction, utilising findings from previous work that showed that simply providing GPs with GHQ scores or CIS symptom profiles had no effect on patient outcomes (Lewis *et al.* 1996). This study is linking patients' psychiatric symptoms as recorded by the computerised CIS with personalised treatment guidelines based on ICD10-PHC and also generated by the computer (ITAS, 1997). It takes as its starting point the need for GPs to be given guidance not only with diagnosis but specifically the management of each individual patient. The computer generated guideline is placed in the patient's record for the GP to use at the next consultation. It remains to be seen whether this mode of implementation is effective.

Conclusions

This chapter has attempted to summarise some of the work on guideline development, implementation and evaluation for common mental disorders in primary care. In so doing, it has described some national and international initiatives utilising state of the art evidence-based methodology as well as some more local guideline developments by ad-hoc groups using less explicit methodological underpinning. It is only possible to attach a value to these two different approaches by undertaking rigorous, empirical evaluations to ascertain if they can deliver the health gain they promise.

Mental health is an enormously wide clinical area and in this respect quite different to asthma or hypertension, two other disorders which constitute a high workload in primary care and for which guidelines are commonly used. As such, it will take some time before guidelines are developed for each distinct disorder, simply because the research base is still sparse in terms of high quality randomised controlled trials on which to base systematic reviews. Compliance with clinically valid and scientifically based guidelines can lead to improved patient outcomes but there is still a problem in changing physicians' behaviour. Implementation strategies are crucial and need to take account not only of doctors' views but also patients' perceptions of likely costs or benefits.

Despite the fact that guideline development in the UK is still at a relatively early stage, general practitioners (GPs) are being inundated by a tidal wave of guidelines (Hibble *et al.* 1998), and now there are guidelines for guidelines (Eccles *et al.* 1996). In order to help clinicians make better decisions, they need to be simple, patient-specific and user-friendly (Jackson and Feder, 1998).

Depression is the most common mental disorder encountered in primary care. We have known for some time that recognition alone does not alter outcome. We now know that strict adherence to a CPG can, at some cost, improve outcome. The key to long-term success in this field will be better patient education, more systematic monitoring of the process of care and easier access to the range of psychological therapies that are increasingly being shown to be effective. The guideline is no better than the doctor who uses it and the setting in which it is employed.

References

Alzheimer's Disease Society (1993) *Guidelines for GPs: Management of Dementia.*

American Psychiatric Association (1993) Practice guidelines for major depressive disorder. *American Journal of Psychiatry* 150 (Suppl 4), 1–26.

Banerjee, S., Blanchard, M., Drinkwater, C. *et al.* (1996) Old age depression, in *Guidelines – Summarising Clinical Guidelines for Primary Care*, Medendium Publishing, Berkhamsted.

British Association of Psychopharmacology (1997) Guidelines for the treatment of depressive illness with antidepressants. *Journal of Psychopharmacology* 7, 19–23.

Cape, J., Hartley, J., Durrant, K. *et al.* (1998) Development of local clinical practice guidelines to assist GPs, counsellors and psychological therapists in matching patients to the most appropriate psychological treatment. *Journal of Clinical Effectiveness* 3, 116–124.

CCDAN (Cochrane Collaboration, Depression, Anxiety and Neurosis Review Group) (1998) Coordinator: N. Khin. Auckand, New Zealand.

Cluzeau, F., Littlejohns, P., Grimshaw, J. and Feder, G. (1997) *Appraisal Instrument for Clinical Guidelines.* St George's Hospital Medical School, London.

Costa, P.T. Jr, Williams, T.F., Somerfield, M. *et al.* (1996) *Recognition and Initial Assessment of Alzheimer's Disease and Related Dementias. Clinical Practice Guideline no 19.* AHCPR, US Department of Health and Human Resource, Rockville, MD.

Depression Guideline Panel, AHCPR (1993) *Depression in Primary Care Clinical Practice Guideline, Number 5.* US Department of Health and Human Resource, Rockville, MD.

Dowie, R. (1998) A review of research in the United Kingdom to evaluate the implementation of clinical guidelines in general practice. *Family Practice* 15, 462–470.

Eccles, M., Clapp, Z., Grimshaw, J., Adams, P., Higgins, B., Purves, I. and Russell, I. (1996) Developing valid guidelines: methodological and procedural issues from the North of England Evidence Based Development Project. *Quality in Health Care* 5, 45–50.

Eccles, M., Clarke, J., Livingstone, M. *et al.* (1998) North of England evidence based guideline development project for the primary care managment of dementia. *British Medical Journal* 317, 802–808.

Effective Health Care (1993a) *Treatment of Depression in Primary Care*, vol. 1 (5).

—— (1993b) *Brief Interventions and Alcohol Use*, vol. 1 (5).

—— (1994) *Implementing Clinical Practice Guidelines: Can guidelines be used to improve clinical practice?*, vol. 1 (8).

—— (1997) *Mental Health Promotion in High Risk Groups*, vol. 3 (3).

EGO (Evaluating Guideline Outcomes) (1997) 'An intervention to improve targeting of secondary mental health services and the management of psychiatric disorders in primary care by defining referral thresholds in "shared ownership" general practitioner guidelines', Department of Health, Mental Health Initiative, Grant No. JR126/06/34.

Feder, G., Griffiths, C., Highton, C., Eldridge, S., Spence, M. and Southgate, L. (1995) Do clinical guidelines introduced with practice based education improve care of asthmatic and diabetic patients? A randomised controlled trial in general practice in east London. *British Medical Journal* 311, 1473–1478.

Field, M. and Lohr, K. (eds) (1992) *Guidelines for Clinical Practice – From Development to Use.* Washington DC: National Academy Press.

Goldberg, D., Sharp, D. and Nanayakkara, K. (1995) The field trial of the mental disorders section of ICD-10 designed for primary care (ICD10-PHC) in England. *Family Practice* 12, 466–473.

Grimshaw, J. and Russell, I. (1993a) Achieving health gain through clinical guidelines 1: Developing scientifically valid guidelines. *Quality in Health Care* 2, 243–248.

—— (1993b) Effect of clinical guidelines on medical practice: a systematic review. *Lancet* 342, 1317–1322.

Grol, R. (1993) Development of guidelines for general practice. *British Journal of General Practice* 43, 146–151.

Guidelines – Summarising Clinical Guidelines for Primary Care (1998) Berkhamsted: Medendium Publishing.

Hibble, A., Kanka, D., Pencheon, D. *et al.* (1998) Guidelines in general practice: the new Tower of Babel. *British Medical Journal* 317, 862–863.

ITAS (Information Technology Assessment Study) (1997) 'A randomised controlled trial of a computerised clinical decision support system for the management of psychiatric disorder in primary care', NHS R&D Primary/Secondary Care Interface Programme. Grant No. 2/58.

Jackson, R. and Feder, G. (1998) Guidelines for clinical guidelines. *British Medical Journal* 317, 427–428.

Katon, W., Von Korff, M., Lin, E. *et al.* (1995) Collaborative management to achieve treatment guidelines *JAMA* 273, 1026–1031.

Langley, C., Faulkner, A., Watkins, C., Gray, S. and Harvey, I. (1998) Use of guidelines in primary care – practitioners' perspectives. *Family Practice* 15, 105–111.

Lewis, G., Sharp, D., Bartholomew, J. and Pelosi, A. (1996) Computerised assessment of neurotic disorder in primary care: effect on clinical outcome. *Family Practice* 13, 120–126.

Lin, E., Katon, W., Simon, G. *et al.* (1997) Achieving guidelines for the treatment of depression in primary care: Is physician education enough? *Medical Care* 35, 831–842.

Littlejohns, P., Cluzeau, F., Bale, R., Grimshaw, J., Feder, G. and Moran, S. (1999) The quantity and quality of clinical practice guidelines for the management of depression in primary care in the UK. *British Journal of General Practice* 49, 205–210.

NHS Management Executive (1993) *Improving clinical effectiveness*, EL (93)115.

Neurolink (1996) *Depression: a guide to its recognition and management in general practice.* Medendium Publishing, Berkhamsted.

North of England Study of Standards and Performance in General Practice (1992) Medical audit in general practice: effect on doctors, clinical behaviour and health of patients with common childhood conditions. *British Medical Journal*, 304, 480–488.

Paykel, E.S. and Priest, R.G. (1992) Recognition and management of depression in general practice: consensus statement. *British Medical Journal* 305, 1198–2002.

Persons, J., Thase, M. and Crits-Christoph, P. (1996) The role of psychotherapy in the treatment of depression. *Archives of General Psychiatry* 53, 283–290.

Plinius Maior Society (1996) *Alcohol Risk Assessment and Intervention in Primary Care*, Plinius Maior Society, Brussels.

Schulberg, H., Block, M., Madonna, M. *et al.* (1997) The usual care of major depression in primary care practice. *Archives of Family Medicine* 6, 334–339.

SIGN (Scottish Intercollegiate Guidelines Network) (1998) *Interventions in the Management of Behavioural and Psychological Aspects of Dementia*, Royal College of Physicians, Edinburgh.

Stevens, L., Kinmonth, A.-L., Peveler, R. and Thompson, C. (1997) The Hampshire Depression Project: development and piloting of clinical practice guidelines and education about depression in primary health care. *Medical Education* 31, 375–379.

Trickey, H., Harvey, I., Wilcock, G. and Sharp, D. (1998) Formal consensus and consultation: a qualitative method for development of a guideline for dementia. *Quality in Health Care* 7, 192–199.

UK Alcohol Forum (1997) *Guidelines for the Management of Alcohol Problems in Primary Care and General Psychiatry*, Tangent Medical Education, High Wycombe.

Upton, M., Evans, M., Sharp, D., Goldberg, D. An evaluation of ICD10-PHC mental health guidelines in detecting and managing depression within primary care. *British Journal of Psychiatry*, in press.

Üstün, B., Goldberg, D., Cooper, J. *et al.* (1995) New classification for mental disorders with management guidelines for use in primary care: ICD10-PHC chapter five. *British Journal of General Practice* 45, 211–215.

WHO (1996) *Diagnostic and Management Guidelines for Mental Disorders in Primary Care ICD10 Chapter V Primary Care version*, Hogrefe and Huber, Gottingen.

12

COMPUTERISED ASSESSMENTS FOR PSYCHIATRIC DISORDER

Glyn Lewis and Ita Lyons

Information and Communication Technologies (ICTs) is a new name for a newish set of technological advances. ICTs have revolutionised many areas of our lives but have had relatively little impact on the practice of clinical medicine. There are potentially many applications of this technology in clinical work but we shall discuss its application to the assessment of patients and its possible use in clinical settings, particularly in relation to the 'common mental disorders' (Goldberg and Huxley, 1992) of anxiety and depression seen in primary care.

Measuring psychiatric disorder

Psychiatrists have acknowledged the difficulty of accurately measuring psychiatric disorder for many years and there are now a multitude of different standardised methods for assessing psychiatric disorder. These range from the lengthy semi-standardised interviews administered by mental health professionals such as the Schedule for Clinical Assessment in Neuropsychiatry (SCAN) (Wing *et al.* 1990) to brief self-administered questionnaires like the General Health Questionnaire (GHQ) (Goldberg, 1972). The GHQ has now become one of the most widely used self-administered questionnaires to assess common mental disorders (Goldberg and Williams, 1988).

One of the important strengths of the GHQ was that its development and subsequent use was based upon an acute recognition that the reliability and validity of psychiatric assessments needed to be studied with great care. This has usually been done by comparing the GHQ with longer and more detailed assessments, usually administered by a psychiatrist. Overall, the GHQ appears to perform well with sensitivities and specificities of about 70 per cent to 80 per cent in most studies (Goldberg and Williams, 1988). Psychiatry, like many other medical disciplines, does not have a 'gold standard' measure of disorder. This raises problems for assessing common mental disorder compounded by the observation that symptoms appear to be continuously distributed in the community. Nevertheless, there has been

156

a widespread assumption (at least amongst psychiatrists) that standardised assessments carried out by psychiatrists are more valid than the GHQ or similar self-administered questionnaires.

The development and widespread use of the GHQ and similar self-administered questionnaires was an important prerequisite to developing self-administered computerised assessments. These are essentially branching multiple-choice self-administered questionnaires. They can provide a more detailed assessment of psychopathology and allow some questions to be asked only when relevant. In the UK the most widely used self-administered computerised assessment is based upon the Clinical Interview Schedule (CIS) (Goldberg et al. 1970). The CIS was designed for administration by psychiatrists but has been revised and altered so as to be suitable for lay interviewers (CIS-R) (Lewis et al. 1992). If a standardised interview can be administered by a lay interviewer it is therefore suitable for administration by a computer. Therefore the Diagnostic Interview Schedule (DIS) (Robins et al. 1981), Composite International Diagnostic Interview (CIDI) (Robins et al. 1988) and CIS-R have all been adapted for computerised use. The current evidence suggests the level of agreement between computerised assessments and clinician-administered interviews is of the same order of magnitude as the agreement one would expect between two clinician-administered interviews. There is also little evidence of any systematic bias between the two methods (Lewis, 1994; Greist et al. 1987; Lewis et al. 1988; Levitan et al. 1991; Erdman et al. 1992).

The arguments for and against the use of these self-reported structured questionnaires has been debated at length (Robins, 1985; Lewis et al. 1992). These arguments will not and never should be settled as the reliability of measuring psychiatric symptoms remains quite poor and there are suggestions that different assessments lead to somewhat different estimates of prevalence. Nevertheless, for measuring the common mental disorders seen in the community, these structured interviews appear to perform quite well. In contrast, there are still severe doubts about the ability of self-reported information to assess disorders where insight is substantially impaired such as in psychotic illness.

Using computers has a number of potential advantages in research studies. They eliminate the possibility of observer bias and reduce fieldwork costs. Data entry and coding are performed automatically. The use of computerised assessments in research seems assured. In contrast, their use in clinical practice seems more problematic.

Questionnaires versus interviews

Questionnaires are often seen as quick, cheap and rather 'dirty' alternatives to the 'gold standard' of psychiatrist administered interviews. Self-administered questionnaires rely upon a literate populace (though they can be administered by interviewer) (Sen and Mari, 1986) and concerns about validity rest upon the difficulty in knowing how the subject interprets the questions. In contrast, observer-rated information could be subject to observer bias, particularly if the rater is encouraged to use his or her judgement in coming to decisions about the presence or absence of psychopathology. Self-administered computerised assessments, like the lay interviewer self-report interviews upon which they are based, lie somewhere in between these two extremes. Current questionnaires such as the shorter versions of the GHQ can be very short and do not ask directly about psychiatric symptoms. In contrast, the computerised questionnaires can be lengthier and because they 'branch' allow a more interrogative style of questioning, more reminiscent of clinical interviewing.

There has been relatively little investigation of the possibility that self-administered questionnaires have a systematic bias in identifying common mental disorder compared to standardised interviews. Such studies require large numbers of subjects and all the existing studies are underpowered. Mari and Williams (1986) examined the association between various socio-demographic factors and being a false positive among 'true' non-cases and being a false negative among true cases. They found that women and those with less education were more likely to report symptoms on the GHQ and SRQ (Symptom Reporting Questionnaire) (Harding et al. 1980) than on the Clinical Interview Schedule. Ludermir (1998) found similar results in a different part of Brazil using the SRQ compared to a standardised psychiatric interview. A similar methodology was used in another South American study but in this case the CIS-R, a fully standardised interview administered by lay interviewers, was used (Araya et al. 1992). A computerised assessment was used in a UK study though, and, in contrast to the South American studies, there appeared to be a bias that led to *under*-reporting in lower socio-economic groups (Stansfeld and Marmot, 1992).

These preliminary findings suggest that all the South American studies found a similar ascertainment bias in the GHQ or SRQ irrespective of whether the lengthier assessment was self-reported or clinician administered. This supports the idea that the important distinguishing factor between self-administered questionnaires and self-administered computerised assessments concerns the nature of the questions rather than the manner in which the questions are asked. On balance, self-administered computerised assessments probably behave in a similar way to standardised interviews when assessing common mental disorders. However, we need to better understand the reasons why different methods of assessment appear to lead to somewhat different prevalence estimates.

Researcher versus clinician

The ultimate aim of medical research is to inform the prevention or treatment of illness. However, the needs of research are sometimes at odds or perceived to be in conflict with the needs of clinical practice. The reliability of psychiatric diagnoses (Cooper *et al.* 1972) before the advent of standardised interviews was poor. The impetus to improve standardisation and reliability of psychiatric diagnosis was driven primarily by the needs of research so that investigators in different countries could communicate with each other and ensure comparability of clinical samples. Nevertheless, reliability of diagnosis is of great clinical importance. Patients and their relatives require a consistent diagnostic approach and confidence in the medical profession can be undermined if different professionals give different diagnoses.

The term Evidence Based Medicine (EBM) (Evidence-Based Medicine Working Group, 1992) is relatively recent, though the idea that medical practice should be based upon empirical evidence has a longer history. If empirical research is to inform clinical practice then the diagnoses used in research studies have also to be used in clinical practice. The diagnostic manuals such as ICD-10 and DSM-IV are now bulky tomes that do not fit easily into the work of busy specialist clinicians let alone primary care physicians. There is a challenge to ensure that diagnostic habits in research studies remain of relevance to clinical practice. Studies of aetiology benefit from relatively specific and narrow criteria as this ensures that all the cases really have the disease. In contrast, clinicians tend to prefer diagnoses with higher sensitivity, particularly if there are relatively harmless treatments available. If clinical trials are to be relevant to clinical practice, it is important that they include categories of patients that are relevant for clinicians.

One possible way to surmount this dilemma is by encouraging the use of research methods within clinical practice. For example, the GHQ was originally developed for use in research studies as a rapid and economical case-identification questionnaire. It also has potential for similar use within primary care to identify probable cases of psychiatric disorder (Goldberg, 1986; Wright, 1994). Similarly, there is potential for using self-administered computerised assessments in order to provide more clinical information about psychiatric disorder to primary care physicians without necessarily elongating the clinical consultation (Pelosi and Lewis, 1989). Self-administered computerised assessments were often developed primarily for their use in research. However, they might also have clinical applications especially in primary care.

Case finding in primary care

Much of the psychiatric morbidity seen in primary care is not detected, diagnosed or treated by the primary care physician. This observation has been made in many countries with quite different health care systems. One of the main approaches towards improving detection rates has been to improve the knowledge and training of primary care physicians, especially in their interviewing methods (Goldberg *et al.* 1980; Gask, 1992). However, this

159

valuable approach will only lead to a modest improvement in the rates of detection. Even trained psychiatrists working in primary care have relatively low rates of detection so it is clear that the difficulty of detection of psychiatric disorder cannot be remedied by a simple improvement in knowledge or experience.

One of the main contributions towards poor detection is the reluctance of patients to disclose emotional symptoms to the doctor. About 80 per cent of new presentations who have psychiatric disorder complain to their doctor of physical symptoms. The presentation of physical symptoms is closely associated with lower rates of detection (Goldberg and Bridges, 1988; Weich et al. 1995). There is therefore an increasing interest in the characteristics of patients and the potential influence of their attitudes and values on the likelihood that they will volunteer emotional symptoms to the doctor (Kessler et al. 1998).

Administration of the GHQ in primary care is a quick and simple way of improving detection rates in primary care but it has not been adopted as a routine method of case-finding except by a handful of practitioners. There are probably a number of reasons why this is so. First, the GHQ does not produce information that is clinically very usable. As discussed above, the GHQ and similar questionnaires do not focus on symptoms and diagnoses and it is not very clear how the results feed through into clinical decision making. Second, there is a widespread, and possibly unjustified view that the important and more severe cases of psychiatric disorder *are* detected in primary care. There is evidence that the more severe conditions are *more* likely to be detected, but some of the more severe cases are still missed. Third, and possibly most important, there is still equivocal evidence that detection using the GHQ improves outcome.

Johnstone and Goldberg's (1976) study provided the first evidence that screening with the GHQ could produce clinical benefit. However, the findings have not been consistently replicated. One likely reason is that primary care physicians need education and guidance in how to use the GHQ (Rand et al. 1988) and when the physicians are not active members of the research team, effects of GHQ feedback alone are more difficult to find (Lewis et al. 1996; Dowrick and Buchan, 1995). Another possible reason, is that many of those who are 'cases' on the GHQ might not have severe enough illness to benefit from pharmacological treatment (Kendrick, 1996).

Self-administered computerised assessments might be a way to circumvent this difficulty. As discussed above, the assessments correspond much more closely to the clinician-based standardised interview and it is possible to obtain standardised diagnostic information via this route. This would both be more clinically meaningful for the clinicians and also enable management guidelines for psychiatric disorder to be based upon the same kind of assessments that are used in randomised controlled trials. Using computerised assessments would appear to be a way of crossing both the secondary–primary care interface and the research–clinical practice divide. Empirical evidence about effectiveness in particular diagnostic groups or at certain severity of symptoms can be easily transferred to clinical guidelines in primary care if the implementation of those guidelines in primary care is based upon a standardised assessment. It should also be possible to computerise the management guidelines themselves.

Computerised assessments as a clinical tool

Over the last few years we have developed self-administered computerised assessments as a clinical tool and investigated the effectiveness of them on patient outcome. The system we have been using has been christened PROQSY (PROgrammable Questionnaire SYstem). It consists of a program which administers a separate questionnaire file prepared on a word processor. The patient is presented with a series of multiple-choice questionnaires and has to press one of the number keys on a conventional keyboard to answer. It has proved acceptable to almost all literate and sighted patients who find it acceptable and easy to use.

Our main approach towards evaluating this tool has been to link the computerised assessment with case-finding with the GHQ. As noted above, one possible reason for the inconsistent clinical effectiveness of GHQ feedback is that the GHQ does not produce information that is readily interpretable by the primary care physician. In contrast, computerised assessments such as PROQSY can summarise clinical symptoms, suggest probable diagnoses and enquire of other clinically relevant information such as suicide risk, sleep disturbance, etc. We therefore designed a randomised controlled trial with three groups: (1) 12-item GHQ feedback alone; (2) 12-item GHQ case-finding followed by PROQSY feedback; (3) no feedback. In Johnstone and Goldberg's (1976) original study they were able to randomise only those subjects that had not been detected by the primary care physician. Unfortunately, this was not feasible in our study. Therefore all those who presented and scored 2 or above on the 12-item GHQ were randomised to the three groups. About 70 per cent of the subjects who were randomised to PROQSY completed the assessment and they were then asked to return to the general practitioner in order to discuss the findings. There was no further education and training of the physician.

There was some evidence in this study for a beneficial effect of the PROQSY feedback at six weeks. The statistical results were only of borderline statistical significance and the effect size was small. By six months there appeared to be no real difference between any of the groups. It is worth noting that there was no evidence that GHQ feedback was of any clinical benefit in this study in which the physicians had no additional training in use of the GHQ. Of equal importance was the finding that there was no difference in the number of consultations with the primary care physician over the following six months despite the protocol that asked the patients to return to the doctor to discuss the PROQSY results (Lewis *et al*. 1996). A similar finding was reported in Johnstone and Goldberg (1976). This suggests that case-finding did not increase the overall number of consultations by any significant amount and therefore possibly does not greatly increase the workload on primary care physicians.

These results were not convincing enough on their own to encourage the use of case finding followed by computerised assessments in routine clinical practice. However, there are a number of reasons why one might expect a smallish effect-size in this study. First, all the cases amongst the attenders were entered, so many of those in the trial would have been known to the primary care physicians and actively treated. Second, some of those who scored 2 or over on the GHQ would have had short-lived illness or otherwise be 'false positives'. This group would have 'recovered' spontaneously or their GHQ scores would not have altered. Third, only 70 per cent of those randomised to PROQSY actually completed the assessment. Given the suggestion of a positive effect together with a number of factors that would have reduced the size of effect, the results of the study were encouraging enough for us to plan a follow-up study.

Guidelines and computers

There has been a proliferation of clinical guidelines in many western countries, across a range of specialities (Kosecoff *et al*. 1987; Haines and Feder, 1992; Grimshaw and Russell, 1993). These are designed to provide guidance on optimal management. Primary care physicians have been particularly interested in these given their need to manage a wide variety of conditions across the whole spectrum of human disease. Collaboration between GPs and specialists in the UK has led to the introduction of clinical guidelines for conditions ranging from asthma and diabetes to alcohol dependence (Haines and Hurwitz, 1992). Guidelines for the management of anxiety and depression in primary care are already widely available (Paykel and Priest, 1992; Effective Health Care, 1993; AHCPR 1993; World Health Organization, 1996).

One of the main difficulties with the enormous proliferation of guidelines is that individual primary care physicians are now faced with a vast array of guidelines from a large variety of organisations. Hibble and colleagues (Hibble *et al*. 1998) identified all the available guidelines retained by primary care physicians in the Cambridge and Huntingdon Health Authority. They found 855 different guidelines 'a pile 68 cm high and weighing 28 kg'. Of these guidelines, 160 were more than 10 pages long. This example illustrates that guidelines on their own are difficult to incorporate into the busy work of a primary care physician dealing with the whole range of medical conditions. There appears to be some potential for using technology to help doctors manage this information and make the relevant pieces of information available when needed.

It therefore appears unsurprising that consensus statements based on expert opinion have little impact on clinician behaviour, particularly when disseminated solely through publication in journals (Kosecoff et al. 1987; Grilli and Lomas, 1994; Lomas et al. 1989; Grol, 1990). Guidelines appear most likely to be acted upon if those who are to use them participate in their development ((North of England Study of Standards and Performance in General Practice, 1992a, 1992b), and if doctors are given patient-specific reminders about treatment at the time of consultation (Grimshaw and Russell, 1993; Haines and Feder, 1992). Guidelines which were introduced in the context of rigorous evaluations are also more likely to improve the outcome of medical care (Grimshaw and Russell, 1993). On the basis of these results the most effective advice to offer GPs would be locally agreed guidelines which are tailored for the individual patient.

Computer-based clinical decision support systems (CDSSs) are capable of combining patient information with treatment guidelines to produce patient-specific prompts (Johnston et al. 1994). The application of this technology in psychiatry has been limited by the difficulty of obtaining standardised clinical data on which to base these guidelines, given the extreme variability in doctors' clinical assessments. It is therefore possible to base computerised decision support systems on a standardised assessment of psychiatric disorder, itself administered by computer. We therefore chose to further develop the computerised assessment PROQSY, to incorporate these features. We are currently carrying out a randomised controlled trial to investigate the cost-effectiveness of the new system.

Development and evaluation of computerised decision support

The previous version of PROQSY was further developed in order to generate the common ICD-10 diagnoses that are seen in primary care including major depression, generalised anxiety, phobias and panic. However, primary care physicians are also concerned with the psycho-social environment. We therefore included questions to cover recent life events (Brugha and Cragg, 1990) in addition to questions concerning finances, employment, marital relationship (when appropriate) and housing.

The next step in development was to link the results of this comprehensive psychosocial assessment with clinical guidelines in order to generate some specific advice related to that patient. Clinical guidelines have been developed for some of these disorders, particularly depression, but in general these have arisen through consensus rather than upon systematic review of the literature. In the main we based our clinical guidelines on ICD-10 PHC (World Health Organization, 1996). In addition, we attempted to provide guidance on the severity of disorder above which pharmacological treatment would be prescribed. Almost all the Randomized Controlled Trials (RCTs) of depression have included subjects who scored more than 18 on the Hamilton Rating Scale for Depression (HRSD) (Hamilton, 1960). One of the advantages of using a standardised assessment administered by computer is that severity can be assessed fairly reliably, in contrast to the difficulties within a primary care consultation. We therefore incorporated a recommendation that a patient with a score on the CIS-R of 20 or over would probably benefit from antidepressant medication (Hotopf et al. 1997).

In our current study that is being carried out in collaboration with Deborah Sharp, Scott Weich and Keith Lloyd, attenders in primary care are recruited if they score 3 or more on the 12-item GHQ. The individuals who agree to take part then complete PROQSY under the supervision of the research assistant. Those who score over the usual threshold of 12 or more on the CIS-R are randomised either to no further action or to the intervention. In the intervention group, the primary care physician is given the results of the assessment summarised on one sheet of A4 paper. They are provided with a list of the clinical symptoms together with their severity, including suicidal thoughts. There is a summary of recent life events together with possible sources of help. For example, if someone has recently been bereaved the assessment lists the telephone number of the relevant local voluntary group. There is further guidance about the use of medication and behavioural programmes based upon the probable diagnosis.

The subjects will be followed up for six months and asked to complete the 12-item GHQ together with questions assessing quality of life, and service use. When the study is completed, we will be able to examine the cost-effectiveness of the intervention, best described as case-finding together with feedback from a self-completed computerised assessment.

We have received many encouraging comments from the primary care physicians who are involved in this study. The feedback from the computerised assessment can often be useful and can give consultations a new focus and direction, even when the physician is aware of a psychiatric disorder. Another potential use of PROQSY might be as a source of additional information for patients who have already been identified as probable cases of common mental disorder.

Conclusions

Self-administered computerised assessments are useful research tools and may have important clinical applications. At best, this brave new world could provide an important bridge between research results and the clinical 'coalface'. Future randomised studies on the treatment and management of common mental disorders in primary care could define eligibility for randomisation using computerised assessments. The same computerised assessments could easily be made available within primary care providing standardised information about patients and linking the implementation of clinical guidelines directly to the results of the research. Who knows what the future holds? Perhaps ICTs will change the practice of medicine.

References

AHCPR (1993) *Depression in Primary Care: Volume 2. Treatment of Major Depression. Clinical Practice Guideline Number 5*, US Dept of Health and Human Services, Rockville, MD.

Araya, R.I., Wynn, R. and Lewis, G. (1992) A comparison of two self–administered questionnaires in primary care in Chile. *Social Psychiatry and Psychiatric Epidemiology* 27, 168–173.

Brugha, T.S. and Cragg, D. (1990) The list of threatening experiences: the reliability and validity of a brief life events questionnaire. *Acta Psychiatrica Scandinavica* 82, 77–81.

Cooper, J.E., Kendell, R.E., Gurland, B.J., Sharpe, L., Copeland, J.R.M. and Simon, R. (1972) *Psychiatric Diagnosis in New York and London: a Comparative Study of Mental Hospital Admissions*, London: Oxford University Press.

Dowrick, C. and Buchan, I. (1995) Twelve month outcome of depression in general practice: does detection or disclosure make a difference? *British Medical Journal* 311, 1274–1276.

Effective Health Care (1993) The treatment of depression in primary care. *Effective Health Care Bulletin* 5.

Erdman, H.P., Klein, M.H., Greist, J.H., Skare, S.S., Husted, J.J., Robins, L.N., Helzer, J.E., Goldring, E., Hamburger, M. and Miller, J.P. (1992) A comparison of two computer-administered versions of the NIMH Diagnostic Interview Schedule. *Journal of Psychiatric Research* 26, 85–95.

Evidence-Based Medicine Working Group (1992) Evidence-based medicine. A new approach to teaching the practice of medicine. *Journal of the American Medical Association* 268, 2420–2425.

Gask, L. (1992) Training general practitioners to detect and manage emotional disorders. *International Review Journal of Psychiatry* 4, 293–300.

Goldberg, D.P. (1972) *The Detection of Psychiatric Illness by Questionnaire. Maudsley Monograph 21*, 1st edn. Oxford University Press: Oxford.

—— (1986) Use of the General Health Questionnaire in clinical work. *British Medical Journal* 293, 1188–1189.

Goldberg, D.P. and Bridges, K. (1988) Somatic presentation of psychiatric illness in primary care setting. *Journal of Psychosomatic Research* 32, 137–144.

Goldberg, D. and Huxley, P. (1992) *Common Mental Disorders: a Bio-Social Approach*, London, Routledge.

Goldberg, D.P. and Williams, P. (1988) *The User's Guide to the General Health Questionnaire*, Windsor, NFER–NELSON.

Goldberg, D.P., Cooper, B., Eastwood, M.R., Kedward, H.B. and Shepherd, M. (1970) A standardised psychiatric interview for use in community surveys. *British Journal of Preventive and Social Medicine* 24, 18–23.

Goldberg, D., Smith, C., Steele, J.J. and Spivey, L. (1980) Training family doctors to recognise psychiatric illness with increased accuracy. *Lancet* ii, 521–523.

Greist, J.H., Klein, M.H., Erdman, H.P., Bires, J.K., Machtinger, P.E. and Kresge, D.G. (1987) Comparison of computer- and interviewer-administered versions of the Diagnostic Interview Schedule. *Hospital and Community Psychiatry* 38, 1304–1311.

Grilli, R. and Lomas, J. (1994) Evaluating the message: the relationship between compliance rate and the subject of a practice guideline. *Medical Care* 32, 202–213.

Grimshaw, J.M. and Russell, I.T. (1993) Effect of guidelines on medical practice: a systematic review of rigorous evaluations. *Lancet* 342, 1317–1322.

Grol, R. (1990) National standard setting for quality of care in general practice: attitudes of general practitioners and response to a set of standards. *British Journal of General Practice* 40, 361–364.

Haines, A. and Feder, G. (1992) Guidance on guidelines. *British Medical Journal* 305, 785–786.

Haines, A. and Hurwitz, B. (1992) *Clinical Guidelines. Occasional Paper No 58*, London: Royal College of General Practitioners.

Hamilton, M. (1960) A rating scale for depression. *Journal of Neurology, Neurosurgery and Psychiatry* 23, 56–62.

Harding, T.W., De Arango, M.V., Baltazar, J., Climent, C.E., Ibrahim, H.H.A., Ladrigo-Ignacio, L., Srinivasa Murthy, R. and Wig, N.N. (1980) Mental disorders in primary health care: a study of their frequency and diagnosis in developing countries. *Psychological Medicine* 10, 231–241.

Hibble, A., Kanka, D.P.D. and Pooles, F. (1998) Guidelines in general practice: the new Tower of Babel? *British Medical Journal* 317, 862–863.

Hotopf, M., Sharp, D. and Lewis, G. (1997) What's in a name? A comparison of four psychiatric assessments. *Social Psychiatry and Psychiatric Epidemiology* 33, 27–31.

Johnston, M.E., Langton, K.B., Haynes, R.B. *et al.* (1994) Effects of computer-based clinical decision support systems on clinician performance and patient outcome. *Annals of Internal Medicine* 120, 135–142.

Johnstone, A. and Goldberg, D. (1976) Psychiatric screening in general practice: a controlled trial. *Lancet* i, 605–608.

Kendrick, T. (1996) Prescribing antidepressants in general practice. *British Medical Journal* 313, 829–830.

Kessler, D., Lloyd, K., Lewis, G. and Pereira Gray, D. (1998) Symptom attribution and the recognition of depression and anxiety in general practice. *British Medical Journal*, 318, 436–440.

Kosecoff, J., Kanouse, D.E. and Rogers, W.H. (1987) Effect of the National Institute of Health consensus development program on physician practice. *JAMA* 258, 2708–2713.

Levitan, R.D., Blouin, A.G., Navarro, J.R. and Hill, J. (1991) Validity of the computerized DIS for diagnosing psychiatric inpatients. *Canadian Journal of Psychiatry* 36, 728–731.

Lewis, G. (1994) Assessing psychiatric disorder with a human interviewer or a computer. *Journal of Epidemiology and Community Health* 48, 207–210.

Lewis, G., Pelosi, A.J., Glover, E., Wilkinson, G., Stansfeld, S.A., Williams, P. and Shepherd, M. (1988) The development of a computerised assessment for minor psychiatric disorder. *Psychological Medicine* 18, 737–745.

Lewis, G., Pelosi, A.J., Araya, R. and Dunn, G. (1992) Measuring psychiatric disorder in the community: a standardised assessment for use by lay interviewers. *Psychological Medicine* 22, 465–486.

Lewis, G., Sharp, D., Bartholomew, J. and Pelosi, A.J. (1996) Computerised assessment of common mental disorders in primary care: effect on clinical outcome. *Family Practice* 13, 120–126.

Lomas, J., Anderson, G.M. and Domnick-Pierre, K. (1989) Do practice guidelines guide practice? The effect of a consensus statement on the practice of physicians. *New England Journal of Medicine* 321, 1306–1311.

Ludermir, A.B. (1998) Socioeconomic status, employment, migration and common mental health disorders in Olinda, Northeast Brazil. Doctoral thesis, University of London.

Mari, J.J. and Williams, P. (1986) Misclassification by psychiatric screening questionnaires. *British Journal of Psychiatry* 158, 368–374.

North of England Study of Standards and Performance in General Practice (1992a) Medical Audit in General Practice: 1. Effect on doctors' clinical behaviour for common childhood conditions. *British Medical Journal* 304, 1480–1484.

North of England Study of Standards and Performance in General Practice (1992b) Medical Audit in General Practice: 2. Effects on health of patients with common childhood conditions. *British Medical Journal* 304, 1484–1488.

Paykel, E.S. and Priest, R.G. (1992) Recognition and management of depression in general practice: consensus statement. *British Medical Journal* 305, 1198–1202.

Pelosi, A.J. and Lewis, G. (1989) The computer will see you now. *British Medical Journal* 299, 138–139.

Rand, E., Badger, L. and Coggings, D. (1988) Towards a resolution of contradictions: utility of feedback from the GHQ. *General Hospital Psychiatry* 10, 189–196.

Robins, L.N. (1985) Epidemiology: reflections on testing the validity of psychiatric interviews. *Archives of General Psychiatry* 42, 918–924.

Robins, L.N., Helzer, J.E., Croughan, J. and Ratcliff, K.S. (1981) National Institute of Mental Health Diagnostic Interview Schedule; its history, characteristics and validity. *Archives of General Psychiatry* 38, 381–389.

Robins, L.N., Wing, J.K., Wittchen, H.-U., Helzer, J.E., Babor, T., Burke, J., Farmer, A.E., Jablensky, A., Pickens, R. and Regier, D.A. (1988) The Composite International Diagnostic Interview. An epidemiologic instrument for use in conjunction with different diagnostic systems and in different cultures. *Archives of General Psychiatry* 45, 1069–1077.

Sen, B. and Mari, J.J. (1986) Psychiatric research instruments in the transcultural setting: experiences in India and Brazil. *Social Science and Medicine* 23, 277–281.

Stansfeld, S.A. and Marmot, M.G. (1992) Social class and minor psychiatric disorder in civil servants: a validated screening survey using the General Health Questionnaire. *Psychological Medicine* 22, 739–749.

Weich, S., Lewis, G., Mann, A.H. and Donmall, R. (1995) The somatic presentation of psychiatric morbidity in general practice. *British Journal of General Practice* 45, 143–147.

Wing, J.K., Babor, T., Brugha, T., Burke, J., Cooper, J.E., Giel, R., Jablensky, A., Regier, R. and Sartorius, N. (1990) SCAN: Schedules for Clinical Assessment in Neuropsychiatry. *Archives of General Psychiatry* 47, 589–593.

World Health Organization (1996) *Diagnosis and Management Guidelines for Mental Disorder in Primary Care*, Hogrefe and Huber, Seattle.

Wright, A. (1994) Should general practitioners be testing for depression? *British Journal of General Practice* 44, 132–135.

Part IV

TRAINING IN MENTAL HEALTH SKILLS IN PRIMARY CARE

13

A COURSE IN MENTAL HEALTH SKILLS FOR GENERAL PRACTITIONERS IN MANCHESTER

Linda Gask

Background and development

The need for family doctors in the UK to receive training in mental health skills has been well documented (Horder 1983; Pullen *et al.* 1994). About 40 per cent of British general practitioners (GPs) train formally in a psychiatric post as part of the two years of specialist attachment in their training (Pereira Gray 1994) but the training needs of future GPs are quite different from those of psychiatrists. Failure to recognise and meet these needs has resulted in low satisfaction with psychiatric attachments in some GP training schemes (Kelly and Murray 1991; Turton *et al.* 1995). Some training in psychiatry occurs during the year-long training attachment to general practice. The extent of this varies from post to post, and depends on the nature of the practice, the interest of the GP trainer and the skills and knowledge of the local GP vocational training course leader.

The increasing emphasis on the role of GPs in the management of non-psychotic and so called 'minor' mental illness in UK primary care (Gask *et al.* 1997; Goldberg and Gournay 1997), reserving specialist services for the severely mentally ill, means that there is a greater need than ever before, for the development of appropriate knowledge and skills within primary care by both GPs and the extended primary care team. Surveys of the perceived training needs of experienced general practitioners support the need for GP education that focuses on skill acquisition (Turton *et al.* 1995; Kerwick *et al.* 1997).

The Manchester context

The University Department of Psychiatry in Manchester has been associated with the development of mental health skills training for general practitioners for more than 20 years. Seminal work carried out by Marks, with Goldberg and Hillier (1979) that involved asking consecutive patients to complete the General Health Questionnaire and direct observation of GPs consulting, concluded that both personality factors and GP interviewing skills were important determinants of ability to recognise emotional disorders. They identified ten key interviewing skills which determined whether a patient's emotional distress would be recognised (see Table 13.1). As interview techniques were potentially easier to change than the personality of the doctor, work began to focus on ways of improving the interviewing skills of GPs in order to achieve both an increase in detection and improved management of mental health problems in primary care.

But how could interview skills be improved? During a visit to the USA in the late 1970s, David Goldberg conducted a controlled trial of one-to-one video feedback of primary care residents interacting with patients. This study demonstrated significant improvement in the residents' recognition of psychiatric disorder. This appeared to be due to significant changes in doctors' interviewing skills (Goldberg *et al.* 1980a, b).

At about the same time, the effectiveness of video techniques for teaching specific psychiatric interviewing skills to medical students was demonstrated by Maguire, again with Goldberg and other colleagues (Maguire *et al.* 1978). They showed that methods which involved students listening to or watching either audiotapes or videotapes of their interviews were more effective than didactic teaching and that provision of a model or written structure for the interview was also important. Members of this group took advantage of the video expertise developed in Manchester during the early 1980s and further

Table 13.1 Ten aspects of a GP's interview style which are related to ability to assess a patient's emotional problems accurately

Early in the interview:
- Makes good eye contact
- Clarifies presenting complaint
- Uses directive questions for physical complaints
- Begins with open-ended questions moving to closed questions later

Interview style:
- Makes empathic comments
- Picks up verbal cues
- Picks up non-verbal cues
- Does not read notes during the taking of the history
- Can deal with overtalkativeness
- Asks fewer questions about past history

Source: Goldberg and Huxley (1980)

developed the video-based teaching model, incorporating opportunities for videotape demonstration and role-play and successfully applying it to the acquisition of both psychotherapeutic and psychiatric interviewing skills by psychiatrists in training (Maguire *et al.* 1984; Harrison and Goldberg 1993) and to the training of general practitioners. When Art Lesser, a psychiatrist from McMaster University in Canada, who had developed the model of Problem-Based Interviewing (Lesser 1985) spent a year as Visiting Professor in the department in 1985, the techniques of group video-feedback with general practitioners were introduced.

The GP context: training in primary care.

However, neither communication skills training nor the concepts of video-feedback were unknown within general practice. One of the key research projects in the field of doctor–patient communication, which led to development of the concepts of 'doctor-centred' and 'patient-centred' consultations had itself been carried out in Manchester within the Department of General Practice in the 1970s (Byrne 1976). In certain centres in the UK, particularly around the Tavistock Clinic in North London, psychiatrists and psycho-therapists had been working with groups of GPs in order to help them to understand and work with their patients with mental health problems along the lines developed by Balint (1964). But such groups only attracted a minority of highly motivated GPs. By the late 1970s psychiatrists were beginning to develop outreach clinics in general practice (Mitchell 1985).

Video and audio feedback techniques for the development of communication skills were first introduced into primary care education in the United Kingdom in the 1970s. The model developed by David Pendleton, a psychologist working with the Royal College of General Practitioners and based in the Oxford Region, was particularly influential (Pendelton *et al.* 1984) but it would be some years before video feedback was widely accepted within GP training and most GP teachers (in common with teachers based in departments of psychiatry and general practice in medical schools) did not possess the necessary skills to provide video-feedback teaching effectively.

Group video-feedback methods

The group training approach adopted in Manchester during 1985 was developed by Art Lesser over a long period of working with GPs (Lesser 1981). In his earlier work, Lesser had only worked with audiotapes, but in the groups that he conducted in Manchester with GP trainees, he was introduced to working with videotapes. He also introduced his model of Problem-Based Interviewing (PBI) (Lesser 1985) which formed the framework for the skills which the GP needed to acquire in the group and began from the principle that patients consulted doctors with problems not diagnoses. PBI eschewed traditional history-taking approaches to the interview and emphasised the importance of following up key cues that the patient offered during the consultation.

The PBI group feedback method devised by Lesser shares the group approach to discussion of patients with the Balint group approach (Balint 1964) but differs in its use of recordings of the consultation and practical emphasis on what to say to the patient in the 'here and now' of the consultation being viewed. Lesser was keenly aware of the limited appeal of the Balint group to the majority of GPs who find the psychoanalytic theory difficult to relate to and do not wish to commit to attendance for a prolonged period of time.

The advantages of recordings

Recording of consultations are particularly powerful because they allow us access to three key sources of information:

1   What the patient tells the doctor; the events, symptoms and feelings that the patient talks about; formal medical history taking really only emphasises this as a source of information, and then only in a limited way as the importance of attending to verbal cues given by the patient is not focused upon.
2   What the doctor 'sees'; in other words not only the appearance and behaviour of the patient, but also how the vocal tone of the patient may change when he or she is talking about different topics or feelings.
3   How the doctor feels; doctors' own feelings in consultations are a useful source of information and may say something about how other key people in the patient's life might react to him or her.

Ground rules

The approach to feedback is structured but not concerned with rating the behaviour of doctors against a 'gold standard'. Instead the group aims to utilise the feedback process for the rehearsal of new skills. They watch a recording of a real or role-played consultation featuring a group member, together with the group facilitator. Anyone in the group may stop the tape, but if they do so they must offer constructive criticism, that is, what they would have said or done themselves at that point in the interview. Other basic rules of feedback include letting the person who features in the recording comment first and always attempting to provide positive feedback first before offering suggestions for improvement. The videotape feedback session is seen as a medium for improving the skills of all members of the group because they are all asked to imagine themselves in the position of the person who has been recorded. When the technique is combined with role-play of brief scenarios to learn new skills (see below), all members of the group have indeed been in exactly the same situation only minutes earlier.

Over the last decade the basic approach we use has not radically changed but we have sought to clarify what skills can be taught using this model (Gask et al. 1991). We have also delineated the skills required to teach it (Gask et al. 1992; Gask 1998) in order to simplify dissemination of the model and train more group facilitators. The recent groups however have a shorter life span than our earlier ones and we have also compressed the experience into two-day residential workshops. It seems likely, though, that having the opportunity to practise new skills between sessions may be important. The skills for the recognition and management of emotional problems that can be taught using this model are summarised in Tables 13.2 and 13.3.

Table 13.2 Detection skills

- Beginning the interview
- Picking up and responding to verbal cues by:
  - *Asking open-ended questions*
  - *Asking for clarification*
  - *Asking for an example*
- Picking up and responding to non-verbal cues by:
  - *Commenting on cue*
  - *Demonstrating empathy*
- Making supportive or empathic comments
- Asking about health beliefs
- Maintaining appropriate control of the interview

Table 13.3 Management skills

- Ventilation of feelings
- Provision of information/education
- Making links, e.g. between:
  - *Somatic symptoms and psychological problems*
  - *Problems and behaviours*
- Negotiation
- Motivating change in behaviour
- Problem-solving
- Conjoint interviewing

Training packages for developing specific skills

The range of problems captured on videotape of routine consultations is often limited. Distressed patients may be reluctant or unable to give informed consent to be recorded and some types of problem are uncommon. Production of training packages to teach specific skills for management of patients who have somatic presentation of emotional distress (Goldberg *et al.* 1989), alcohol problems (Lewis and Gask 1994), depression (Gask *et al.* 1998), management of anxiety (Morriss *et al.* 1998a) and suicidal patients (Morriss *et al.* 1999c) has provided us with material to demonstrate new approaches to the consultation. These packages have proved more acceptable to many experienced GPs than training designed primarily to improve their interviewing skills.

Our specific skill training workshops employ multiple techniques including:

- brief didactic presentation using slides with clearly presented models for the consultation;
- group discussion of own case material;
- modelling of the *key strategies and component microskills* of a simple assessment and/or management model with specially prepared videotapes;
- paired-role-play in which every member of the group role-plays a scenario to rehearse a specific skill with a partner (this can either be triggered from a scenario on the tape or from specially prepared, brief written role plays); and
- *video-feedback in small groups* using group members own tapes of real patients with problems that are relevant to the workshop, or tapes recorded during the workshops, either of their paired-role-play with another professional or with an actor playing the patient. The combination of modelling, role-play and video feedback seems to be particularly powerful.

Evaluation

We have approached evaluation primarily from two perspectives:

- Is it possible to use the method of training to change clinician behaviour?
- Does this change, if it occurs, result in improved outcome?

Objective assessment of behaviour change has required 'blind' rating of real or role-played videotaped consultations recorded both before and after the training course. This has been supplemented by subjective feedback from the widest possible range of informants including course participants, patients (real or role-played) and course tutors.

A variety of outcome measures have been employed including not only clinical outcome tools but also measures of patient satisfaction and economic outcome.

The basic group video-feedback method was effective in improving the psychiatric interviewing skills of both GP trainees (Gask et al. 1988) and experienced GPs (Gask et al. 1987). We were also able to demonstrate that change in GP behaviour was associated with significantly improved accuracy in assessment of emotional problems. The change in skills of experienced GPs was maintained over a two-year follow-up period (Bowman et al. 1992).

Specific training packages are effective in improving the way that GPs manage patients who present with somatised forms of emotional distress (Gask et al. 1989; Kaaya et al. 1992) and depression (Gask et al. 1998). We now also have evidence of the effectiveness of packages for the training of primary care attached nurses in anxiety management (Morriss et al. 1999a) and front-line community workers in the assessment and management of suicidal risk (Morriss et al. 1999c).

Thus far, we have conducted two major studies of clinical outcome, one of basic PBI teaching with a retrospectively selected contemporary control group of doctors undergoing similar training minus PBI (Gask and Goldberg 1993), and a second study of the impact of the somatisation training package which utilised a before/after design in which doctors acted as their own controls (Morriss et al. 1999b, 1998).

In the first of these studies (Gask and Goldberg 1993) doctors who had received video-feedback training appeared to be most effective with patients who were both significantly anxious and depressed although there was a trend for all patients in the index group to have a better outcome. In some way it appeared that training helped these doctors to 'contain' the anxiety of their patients and this finding was confirmed by patient satisfaction ratings.

Evaluation of the somatisation training package (Morriss et al. 1998, 1999b) revealed that social outcome was significantly better for patients who were at least partially able to accept that their problems had a psychosocial origin. There was no improvement in outcome for patients who were convinced their symptoms had a solely physical origin, and no significant impact on either group in terms of changes in patient satisfaction. However the most striking outcome was a 15 per cent reduction in total health costs (including the cost of the training itself) in the three-month period in the after-training cohort compared to the before-training cohort.

Our findings have not been uniformly positive. In our first evaluation of the depression training materials (Gask et al. 1995) with GP trainees, ability to assimilate the skills was limited and there was evidence of decrease in 'patient satisfaction' from role-players' ratings. This suggested that the doctors needed more opportunity to practise new skills. The package for management of somatisation known as 'reattribution' is also currently being rewritten following its extensive evaluation.

Table 13.4 The Manchester studies: summary of outcomes

Participants	n	Skill	Design	Outcomes
Problem-based interviewing				
GP trainees (1988)	14	Problem-Based Interviewing (PBI)	before/after	*behaviour:* learned skills; increased accuracy in assessment of emotional problems.
Newly qualified GPs (1993)	16	PBI	8 trained + 8 matched controls. Follow-up of patients ($n = 101$)	*clinical outcome:* improved for anxious and depressed. *patient satisfaction:* increased.
Experienced GPs (1987 and 1992)	10	PBI	before/after/ 2 years	*behaviour:* learned skills. Retained on follow-up.
GP trainers (1991)	21	PBI and How to teach PBI	before/after. Randomised into 3 groups for second stage	*behaviour:* learned skills. Greatest improvement in teaching ability occurred after basic PBI group experience alone.
'Reattribution'				
GP trainees (1989 and 1992)	20 20	Managing Somatisation	before/after	*behaviour:* learned skills. *patient satisfaction (role-play):* increased.
Experienced GPs (1997)	8	Managing Somatisation	before/after and follow-up of patients at each stage ($n = 215$)	*behaviour:* learned skills. *clinical and social outcome* improved for 'part' somatisers. *economic outcome:* reduction in total health costs. *patient satisfaction:* no change.
Depression				
GP trainees (1995)	15	Assessing and managing depression	before/after	*behaviour:*limited impact on skills *patient satisfaction (role play):* reduced for some dimensions.
Experienced GPs (1997)	10	Assessing and managing depression*	before/after	*behaviour:* learned skills. *patient satisfaction (role-play):* increased.

Note: * Randomised controlled trial of depression training (clinical and economic outcome) in progress.

Earlier before–after comparisons are now being followed by randomised-controlled trials of training, which are considerably more expensive and difficult to mount in primary care settings. Nevertheless a randomised-controlled trial of the impact of a course in the assessment and management of depression on patient outcome is currently underway and will report during 1999. Results of evaluations of training carried out to date are summarised in Table 13.4.

A comprehensive course in psychiatry for family doctors in Manchester: 12 years on

The Manchester Course in Psychiatry for Family Doctors was established in 1985 (Creed 1987) to meet the needs of GP trainees (now called GP registrars) during their attachment in psychiatry. Important early elements of the course emphasised the development of interviewing skills appropriate to the general practice setting, and a development of awareness and understanding of how primary care and members of the psychiatric team interact from the perspective of primary care.

The course is now based in Preston in Central Lancashire, in the University of Manchester Department of Community Psychiatry (35 miles north of Manchester) to increase its accessibility to the whole North-West Region. Although primarily focusing on those in hospital posts, the course has always included a number of GP registrars in their practice year who will not have the opportunity to do a six-month attachment in psychiatry as part of their training.

Content of the course

The content of the course at its inception was greatly influenced by Lesser (1985) and has continued to focus on the recognition and management of common problems presenting in primary care. The main aim is to provide the family doctor with a conceptual structure and practical advice for what he or she can do in primary care, not what a specialist could do if the patient were referred.

The 1998 course consisted of eight separate days made up of workshops of full or half-day duration (see Table 13.5) each concerned with a different topic. The workshops are, as far as possible, jointly facilitated by a psychiatrist with an interest in the psychiatry of primary care and a general practitioner with an interest in mental health problems.

A variety of teaching methods are employed including brief lecture/demonstrations, videotape demonstration, small group work, discussion, video-feedback and role play. The impact the workshop elements have on development of skills on the topics of depression and somatisation have been evaluated independently during past courses (Goldberg et al. 1989;

Table 13.5 Course in mental health skills for general practitioners

Week	Morning session	Afternoon session
1	Course aims/goals Introduction to mental health problems in the community	Problems of the elderly
2	Assessing and managing depression	
3	Problems in children and young people	
4	Physical presentation of psychological problems	
5	Alcohol problems	
6	Behavioural treatments in primary care	
7	Managing major mental illness	Personality disorders
8	Sexual problems	Drug problems

Gask *et al*. 1989, 1995; Kaaya *et al*. 1992). Recent research has examined how far the course currently meets the perceived training needs of GP registrars (Ratcliffe *et al*. 1999). Several of the sessions incorporate opportunities for the group to discuss case presentations from general practitioners of patients with psychiatric problems in the primary care setting and also to discuss their own problem cases.

Conclusion

Over 20 years, the Department of Psychiatry in Manchester has been involved in development and evaluation of new approaches to the training of GPs in mental health skills. The work continues in the present. The twice-yearly course for registrars in general practice (GP trainees) draws on the expertise and materials developed during this period. This remains one of only two such courses designed to meet the particular needs of trainee GPs during their psychiatry attachments in the UK. Dissemination of the training materials produced in Manchester for the UK Defeat Depression Campaign between 1991 and 1996 has ensured that many GPs, both experienced and in training, around the UK are familiar with the Manchester approach. Current and future challenges include development of more effective ways of integrating training with the provision of support and supervision across the interface between primary and secondary care in order to ensure maximal and continuing effectiveness, and further development of the skills of the nurses and other mental health workers who also work in primary care alongside the general practitioner.

References

Balint, M. (1964) *The Doctor, his Patient and the Illness,* Pitman, London.

Bowman, F., Millar, T., Goldberg, D. and Gask, L. (1992) 'Improving the psychiatric skills of general practitioners: is the effect of training maintained?', *Medical Education* 26, 63–68.

Byrne, P. (1976) *Doctors Talking to Patients: Study of Verbal Behaviour of General Practitioners Consulting in their Surgeries,* HMSO, London.

Creed, F. (1987) 'Course in psychiatry for family doctors', *Bulletin of the Royal College of Psychiatrists* 11, 193–194.

Gask, L. (1998) 'Small group videofeedback teaching methods', *International Journal of Psychiatry and Medicine* 28, 97–113.

Gask, L. and Goldberg, D. (1993) 'Impact on patient care, satisfaction and clinical outcome of improving the psychiatric skills of general practitioners', *European Journal of Psychiatry* 7, 203–218.

Gask, L., McGrath, G., Goldberg, D. and Millar, T (1987) 'Improving the psychiatric skills of established general practitioners: evaluation of group teaching', *Medical Education* 21, 362–368.

Gask, L., Goldberg, D., Lesser, A.L. and Millar, T. (1988) 'Improving the psychiatric skills of the general practice trainee: an evaluation of a group training course', *Medical Education* 22, 132–138.

Gask, L., Goldberg, D., Porter, R. and Creed, F. (1989) 'The treatment of somatisa- tion: evaluation of a training package with general practice trainees', *Journal of Psychosomatic Research* 33, 698–703.

Gask, L., Boardman, A.P. and Standart, S. (1990) 'Teaching Communication Skills: A problem-based approach', *Postgraduate Education for General Practice* 2, 7–15.

Gask, L., Goldberg, D., Boardman, A.P., Craig, T., Goddard, C., Jones, O., Kiseley, S., McGrath, G. and Millar, T. (1991) 'Training general practitioners to teach psychiatric interviewing skills: an evaluation of group training', *Medical Education* 25, 444–445.

Gask, L., Usherwood, T. and Standart, S. (1992) 'Training teachers to teach com- munication skills: a problem-based approach', *Postgraduate Education for General Practice* 3, 92–99.

Gask, L., Williams, B. and Harrison, J. (1995) 'Teaching cognitive-behavioural skills to general practice trainees: a pilot study of training', *Primary Care Psychiatry* 1, 201–205.

Gask, L., Sibbald, B. and Creed, F. (1997) 'Evaluating models of working at the inter- face between mental health services and primary care', *British Journal of Psychiatry* 170, 6–11.

Gask, L., Usherwood, T., Thompson, H. and Williams, W. (1998) 'Evaluation of a teaching package for the assessment and management of depression in general practice', *Medical Education,* 32, 190–198.

Goldberg, D. and Gournay, K. (1997) *The General Practitioner, the Psychiatrist and the Burden of Mental Health Care.* Maudsley Discussion Paper number 1. Institute of Psychiatry, London.

Goldberg, D. and Huxley, P. (1980) *Mental Illness in the Community,* Tavistock, London.

Goldberg, D.P., Smith, C., Steele, J.J. and Spivey, L. (1980a) 'Training family doctors to recognise psychiatric illness with increased accuracy', *Lancet* ii, 521–523.

Goldberg, D.P., Steele, J.J. and Smith, C. (1980b) 'Teaching psychiatric interviewing skills to family doctors', *Acta Psychiatrica Scandinavica* 62, 41–47.

Goldberg, D., Gask, L. and O'Dowd, T. (1989) 'The treatment of somatisation: teach- ing the skills of reattribution', *Journal of Psychosomatic Research* 33, 689–695.

Harrison, J. and Goldberg, D. (1993) 'Improving the interview skills of psychiatry trainees', *European Journal of Psychiatry* 7, 31–40.

Horder, J. (1983) 'Psychiatric training for future general practitioners', *Practitioner* 227, 86–87.

Kaaya, S., Goldberg, D. and Gask, L. (1992) 'Teaching the skills of 'reattribution': a replicated study', *Medical Education* 26, 138–144.

Kelly, D.R. and Murray, T.S. (1991) 'Twenty years of vocational training in the West of Scotland', *British Medical Journal* 302, 28–30.

Kerwick, S., Jones, R., Mann, A. and Goldberg, D. (1997) 'Mental health training priorities in general practice', *British Journal of General Practice* 47, 225–227.

Lesser, A.L. (1981) 'The psychiatrist and family medicine: a different training approach', *Medical Education* 15, 398–406.

—— (1985) 'Problem-based interviewing in general practice: a model'. *Medical Education* 19, 299–304.

Lewis, B. and Gask, L. (1994) *Focus on Alcohol*, videotape training package, Department of Postgraduate Medical Studies: University of Manchester.

Maguire, G.P., Roe, P., Goldberg, D., Jones, S., Hyde, C. and O'Dowd, T. (1978) 'The value of feedback in teaching interviewing skills to medical students', *Psychological Medicine* 8, 697–704.

Maguire, P., Goldberg, D., Hobson, R., Margison, F., Moss, S. and O'Dowd, T. (1984) 'Evaluating the teaching of a method of psychotherapy', *British Journal of Psychiatry* 144, 515–580.

Marks, J.N., Goldberg, D.P. and Hillier, V.F. (1979). 'Determinants of the ability of general practitioners to detect psychiatric illness', *Psychological Medicine* 9, 337–353.

Mitchell, A.R.K. (1985) 'Psychiatrists in primary health care settings', *British Journal of Psychiatry* 147, 371–379.

Morriss, R., Gask, L., Smith, C. and Battersby, L. (1999a) 'Training practice nurses to assess and manage anxiety disorders: a pilot study', *Nursing Times Research* 4, 131–142.

Morriss, R., Gask, L., Ronalds, C., Downes-Grainger, E., Thompson, H. and Goldberg, D. (1999b) 'Clinical and patient satisfaction outcomes of a new treatment for somatised mental disorder taught to general practitioners', *British Journal of General Practice* 49, 263–267.

Morriss, R., Gask, L., Battersby, L., Franceschini, A. and Robson, M. (1999c) 'Teaching frontline health and voluntary workers to assess and manage suicidal patients: a controlled before and after evaluation of a new training package', *Journal of Affective Disorders* (in press).

Morriss, R., Gask, L., Ronalds, C., Downes-Grainger, E., Thompson, H., Leese, B. and Goldberg, D. (1998) 'Economic outcome of a new treatment for somatised mental disorder taught to general practitioners', *Family Practice* 15, 19–25.

Pendleton, D., Schofield, T., Tate, P. and Havelock, J. (1984) *The Consultation: an Approach to Learning and Teaching.* Oxford University Press, Oxford.

Pereira Gray, D. (1994) 'General practice and psychiatry – a general practice perspective', in: I. Pullen, G. Wilkinson, A. Wright and D. Pereira Gray (eds) *Psychiatry and General Practice Today*, Gaskell, London.

Pullen, I., Wilkinson, G., Wright, A. and Pereira Gray, D. (eds) (1994) *Psychiatry and General Practice Today*, Gaskell, London.

Ratcliffe, J., Gask, L., Creed, F. and Lewis, B. (1999) 'Psychiatric training for family doctors: What do GP registrars want and can a brief course provide this?', *Medical Education* (in press).

Turton, P., Tylee, A. and Kerry, S. (1995) 'Mental health training needs in general practice', *Primary Care Psychiatry* 1, 197–199.

14

THE EDUCATION OF GENERAL PRACTITIONERS IN THE MANAGEMENT OF MENTAL DISORDERS

Gavin Andrews and Caroline Hunt

The problem

Encouraged by the work of Goldberg and empowered by having such a simple and useful measure as the General Health Questionnaire (Goldberg and Blackwell 1970) we embarked on a series of studies in general practice. We surveyed patients and doctors in a stratified sample of Sydney general practitioners to answer the first question 'How many patients have which disorders?' The general practitioners noted that 13 per cent of their patients came for emotional or social reasons that day (Chancellor *et al*. 1977). This figure surprised us, for it was lower than the prevalence of mental disorders in the community which we had established to be about 20 per cent (Andrews *et al*. 1977) and certainly much lower than the 47 per cent of the general practitioners' patients who scored as positive cases on the GHQ completed in the waiting room prior to seeing their doctor. This led us to do a further survey to ask why psychiatric disorders are missed and of those that are recognised how are they managed (Brodaty *et al*. 1982a; Brodaty *et al*. 1982b). We decided that something needed to be done. Keen to improve the ability of general practitioners to identify and manage people with emotional disorders we conducted a controlled trial of brief psychotherapy in general practice (Brodaty and Andrews 1983) and began to provide some training for general practitioners in interviewing and counselling (Brodaty *et al*. 1981). The conclusions from this body of work were that we should establish a formal postgraduate training programme for general practitioners and that this should be informed by reliable data from a national survey that focused on prevalence, disability and health service utilisation of people with mental disorders. Both these goals have now been achieved.

The national survey of the mental health of Australians was completed in 1998 (Australian Bureau of Statistics 1998; Andrews *et al.* 1999). Approximately 10,600 people participated in the adult household survey. The interview used the Composite International Diagnostic Interview v2.1 to enumerate people with common mental disorders (six anxiety, two affective and four substance-use disorders) and contained screening questions for psychosis, personality disorder, neurasthenia and cognitive impairment. It also collected information about common physical disorders, and the disability and health service use reported by the respondents. Collateral surveys have examined the situation in children and explored the psychotic disorders in more detail.

Most Australians enjoyed good mental health but 18.6 per cent reported symptoms that satisfied the criteria for an ICD-10 diagnosis of one of the common mental disorders in the previous 12 months; 9.6 per cent met criteria for an anxiety disorder, 7.2 per cent for an affective disorder and 7.7 per cent for a substance-use disorder. Comorbidity was common, one in three of those satisfying criteria for one disorder meeting criteria for more than one. Screening instruments for neurasthenia (1.5 per cent), cognitive impairment (1.3 per cent), psychosis (0.5 per cent) and personality disorder (6.1 per cent) were also included. Comorbidity with anxiety and depression was common, and the final figure for adults meeting criteria for any mental disorder in the past twelve months was 22.6 per cent. There were significant variations in risk of reporting a mental disorder by age and by sex and type of disorder. Confining attention to the anxiety, affective and substance-use disorders, disorders of greatest concern to general practitioners, the highest rates were found in persons aged 18-24 (27 per cent) and the lowest in persons aged 65 and over (7 per cent). Overall the rates of mental disorder were similar in males and females but males were twice as likely to report substance-abuse disorders (11 per cent vs 4.5 per cent) while females were significantly more likely to report symptoms consistent with anxiety (12 per cent vs 7 per cent) and depressive disorders (9.1 per cent vs 5.2 per cent). The prevalence of substance-use disorders declined rapidly with age, being rare, even in men, after 45, but the anxiety and affective disorders were most frequent throughout the reproductive span 18 to 54. In summary, the mental health of young people was worse than is commonly reported and the mental health of the elderly much better. Clearly general practitioners need to be alert to the needs of the young. The socio-demographic correlates were as expected – the lowest rates of mental disorder were found in those who were married and in employment, a causal chain that is undoubtedly bi-directional.

The survey also asked about common chronic physical disorders. Nearly 40 per cent of adults reported a chronic physical disorder but, unlike mental disorders, physical disorders increased with age – from 23 per cent in the 18–24 year old group to 77 per cent in the 65 and older group.

Thus the elderly, who are mentally healthy, attend general practitioners often for their physical disorders whereas young adults, who have real mental health problems, are physically healthy and find no reason to attend general practitioners. The comorbidity between mental and physical disorders, while statistically significant, is insufficient to redress this bias. There is a significant need for GPs to refocus their attention on the young.

When many people think of one in five adults meeting criteria for a mental disorder they are sceptical. But anxiety and depressive disorders, like high blood pressure and arthritis, are common and, like those two conditions, are seldom talked about. Nevertheless anxiety and depression do disable. The survey included a number of measures of disability of which the most transparent is the number of days in the last 28 that the respondent reported that they could not carry out their usual daily activities fully. On average people with physical disorders and no mental disorders and those with mental disorders and no physical disorders reported equivalent (2.6) days out of role. People with comorbid mental and physical disorder reported rates double this, with depression and a physical disorder increasing the disability to an average of 6.2 days out of role every 28 days. The effect of the common mental disorders on the productivity of the nation is considerable.

Just how many people consulted GPs? Only 30 per cent of people with a mental disorder consulted their general practitioner about their mental disorder, and a further 7 per cent did not see their GP but consulted a mental health practitioner directly. General practitioners are thus the major points of contact for people with mental disorders and so must be skilled in the management of these conditions. Eighty-five per cent of people with a mental disorder saw a GP during the year but most did not tell their GP about their mental disorder. Thus the big task for general practitioners is the recognition of mental disorders among affected patients who do not mention symptoms of their anxiety, depression or substance-use disorders.

Summary
20 per cent of the adult population have symptoms in any year that meet criteria for a mental disorder. The vast majority attended a general practitioner but only a third actually mention their mental symptoms even though their mental disorders are equally as disabling as the physical diseases for which they do consult.

Educational programmes for general practitioners

Undergraduate programmes

Undergraduate medical education programmes lay the groundwork for knowledge about mental disorders. For example, at the University of New South Wales (UNSW) undergraduate students have a 60-hour course in human behaviour in their second year that provides a grounding in psychological medicine. In the fifth year of their six-year programme they spend eight weeks in psychiatry, time that is equally split between formal didactic teaching and clinical experience in the teaching hospitals. The problem with the UNSW programme, like that of the majority of medical schools in Australia, is that the lecture programme covers the whole gamut of psychiatry and spends only a fifth of the time on anxiety, depressive and substance-use disorders. Of more concern is that the clinical material in the teaching hospitals is heavily weighted towards people with psychotic disorders who need hospitalisation. The typical patient who would appear in general practice, is nowhere to be seen.

The teaching of psychological medicine at University of Sydney is different. Psychiatry there, like most medical schools, used to be taught in the largely theoretical framework of the 'mini psychiatrist model' described above. With the introduction of the Graduate Medical Programme in 1997, psychiatric issues and cases have been incorporated into the problem-based learning format and occur across the four years of the training programme. Emphasis is now on the acquisition of generalist skills in mental health and the focus is on the common disorders. Depression, anxiety, substance-use and eating disorders now have the prominence they deserve. The development of skills early in the course underpins the dedicated term in psychological medicine that takes place in years 3 and 4. This term incorporates the usual psychological medicine topics but, being linked with adolescent health and drug and alcohol studies, is able to provide a rounded and appropriate experience in keeping with the needs identified by the National Survey.

Undergraduate medical programmes in psychiatry are mostly limited by the need to teach about all mental disorders and by the severity and limited range of disorders that bring people to specialised teaching hospitals. There are better alternatives.

Continuing medical education

Most general practitioners in Australia own and operate their own practices and are paid on a fee for service basis by the national health insurance funder. Since 1992 they have been encouraged by the Department of Health to belong to one of the 123 area-wide Divisions of General Practice and most now do. They are also encouraged by the Royal Australian College of General Practitioners to pursue a programme of continuing education, usually organised by the Divisions or by the pharmaceutical industry, and for attendance at which they receive credit points required for continuing registration of their College Fellowship. Few divisions conduct their educational programme in accord with a predetermined curriculum and so, for most, the content of continuing education is influenced by which teacher is available and by about which product the industry is keen to educate them. This is not a good educational model.

Aware of the shortcomings in continuing education, and keen to be able to influence quality among the country's 19,000 GPs the Federal Government has, since 1992, encouraged a partnership between specialists and general practitioners in the care of patients with particular disorders. At the beginning, shared care programmes for patients with mental disorders were identified as a priority area and money was allocated for specific short-term projects in the expectation that funding would not continue. The range of these initial projects is interesting – case conferences with community mental health staff, a mental health workbook for general practitioners, development of a collaborative model for co-operation between general practitioners and mental health professionals, treating anxiety disorders in general practice using cognitive behavioural therapy manuals, a 'flying doctor' for child psychiatry in the outback, and teleconferencing of mental health consultations in remote areas.

A more general need was articulated as the programme developed. General practitioners wanted to develop skills to manage patients with anxiety, depression and somatoform disorders presenting in their practices, and hoped that the collaboration with specialists would lead to this knowledge. Psychiatrists saw that case managers in community mental health centres needed to liaise with GPs and hoped that collaboration would lead to some of the load of caring for people with chronic mental illness being transferred to general practitioners. The disparate expectations of the two groups should have been a recipe for disaster. Progress has been variable, but, to some extent the needs of each group have been satisfied. The overall shared care programme has been quite successful and funding, now at $58 million per annum looks likely to continue. This is about $3,000 per annum for each GP in a Division, of which an unknown amount, but hopefully about 10 per cent, will go to mental health projects. In the 80 or so mental health initiatives that have begun, the money has been largely used to pay project officers and to partly reimburse GPs for the loss of income that occurs when they attend the programme.

Currently each Division is asked to develop a programme of shared care that is sensitive to local needs and to the national health priorities. Mental health is often identified as an area of need and so, across the country, some $6 million per annum is spent on the 80 shared care mental health programmes. What do such programmes entail?

Given such open-ended encouragement, it is not surprising that a wide variety of programmes have developed. Many centres have adopted the shifted outpatient model in which mental health consultants or registrars conduct an out-patient clinic in the general practitioner's rooms, seeing people with psychosis who would normally have been seen at the community mental health clinic, and seeing patients identified by the general practitioners as

187

having a mental disorder who may or may not have otherwise been referred to the hospital outpatients department. In some centres community mental health nurses have functioned in the same role. There are two issues with this model. First, as general practitioners notionally conduct small for-profit businesses and mental health staff are salaried, there have been political and ideological tensions over who would pay for what. Mostly this has been resolved on a quid pro quo basis, for both services are more efficient when they co-operate. Second, many feel that this model does not educate the general practitioners to work independently of the mental health staff and hence is not meeting the aims of the shared care programme, which was to upskill general practitioners.

The shared care liaison service at St Vincent's Hospital (Professor K. Wilhelm) has, to some extent, solved both these difficulties. In addition to providing liaison community psychiatric nurses to assist general practitioners she, and three other psychiatrists (two of whom are from the private sector), conduct Balint type groups in which general practitioners meet regularly to discuss difficult cases and to learn new techniques. Thus the GPs involved in her programme meet to learn and also have patients whose care they share with the staff of the mental health service. Professor Wilhelm is evaluating both the increase in skill levels and the transfer of care and has some preliminary evidence that skill levels are improving and that the cost of patient care is decreasing. Educating general practitioners in the setting of the shared care model is not always that simple. In one centre, general practitioners attended the psychiatric unit for some 20 half-days and while their knowledge of psychiatric disorders improved, their patient skills did not. In another centre, general practitioner skills were not enhanced after a long period of having a registrar do a half-day clinic in their rooms. It does seem that separating the education and patient care components of the shared care programme is worthwhile.

Postgraduate education

Andrews and Brodaty (1980) argued for a model for training general practitioners in counselling and interviewing skills, and in the more complex psychological therapies. It was acknowledged that training in these skills would take time; time to learn the theory, practise the techniques, and then to conduct the therapy under supervision. In 1984, the University of New South Wales allowed, for the first time, fee-paying postgraduate degree programmes to be established. The School of Psychiatry promptly established a Master of Psychotherapy programme, open to psychiatrists, clinical psychologists, general practitioners and other medical specialists who wished to undertake further study in the psychological management of patients with mental disorders. It soon became apparent that the needs of general practitioners and the mental health specialists were different and hence the Master of Psychological Medicine programme was established, catering specifically to the needs of general practitioners.

The aims of the current Master of Psychological Medicine programme are to increase the ability of experienced general practitioners to recognise mental disorders in their patients, to improve their ability to manage many such patients within their own practices, and to facilitate their ability to refer appropriately for more specialised treatment. The course makes use of the principles of problem-based learning and uses real-patient problems as the core of the curriculum. The course took its first enrolments in 1991, and following demand from GPs in rural and remote practice who were otherwise unable to attend, a distance education version commenced in 1998.

Currently the MPM runs over two years in four 14-week semesters. The first semester provides an overview of diagnosis and systems of classification. Clinical case reviews focus on the development of core skills which include interviewing and counselling skills, structured problem solving, motivational interviewing, and reattribution techniques. The second semester covers the recognition and management of mood, anxiety, stress-related and somatoform disorders. The third semester focuses on chronic psychiatric disorders and problems (somatisation, chronic pain, schizophrenia, personality disorders, dementia), recognition of psychiatric presentations of organic disorders, good clinical care of life-threatening illness, managing acute presentations and the requirements of the mental health legislation. Clinical case reviews focus on longer-term management plans and good clinical care of patients with these more intractable problems and disorders. The fourth semester, which is by far the most popular, covers problems relating to children and the family, marital relationships, and behavioural disorders (sleep, eating, sexual, substance). Clinical case reviews in this semester focus primarily on childhood, family and marital problems. There is a fifth component to the course, a project report. Planning for this begins in the third semester, with lectures on research methods and then detailed supervision is given as each student identifies a topic, plans the methodology, does the research and completes the writing up. Few general practitioners have ever done any original work of this type and it is this segment of the course that seems to be the most difficult for them, although after completion it is the segment of which they are most proud.

All students enrolled in the Sydney-based Master's programme attend for 5 hours, 7.30am to 12.30pm, each week during semester. The format for each week is consistent across the semesters and involves a didactic lecture and discussion, a skills training session, and case reviews, where each student brings audiotaped consultations from their own practice for supervision and peer review, the content of the consultations and the sessions varying in accord with the focus of the semester. Frequent attendance at the University is not feasible for doctors in rural and remote practice and therefore a distance education programme was instituted in 1998. That course structure brings all students to the city for 40 hours of intensive teaching at the beginning of each semester, 40 hours in which the content of the semester is overviewed and the skills essential to the semester taught. The didactic lectures are provided to the students on videotape supported by associated reading material. Web-based tutorials run throughout the semester and feature discussion of clinical issues raised by the lecture topics, based on case vignettes. The case review sessions are run by closed telephone conference calls that are sufficiently secure to allow doctors to play the tape-recordings of their consultations during the 60-minute call.

The Master of Psychological Medicine relies on fees from student enrol-ments to cover an annual expenditure of $100,000. The costs of the course include a full-time academic, a half-time administrative assistant, guest lecturers, telephone conferencing, and course materials for students. The course fees are now $9,000, or $2,250 per semester, a deterrent for many general practitioners who are, in the profession of medicine, relatively low income earners. Furthermore, under the current fee-for-service system of pay-ment, enrolment in the course results in a loss of income for GPs as they attend classes, complete the course work and do the work for the project report. We calculate that the course involves more than 1,000 post-graduate assessable hours, which, even when spread over two years, is a considerable slice out of the doctors' working week. The direct financial penalties of fees and earnings forgone from doing the course are thus considerable. Most post-graduate programmes enable successful graduates to advance profession-ally and increase their earnings. The consequences of doing the MPM are different, there is no increase in income for, as doctors incorporate the skills they learn for improved management of patients with mental disorders, their practice changes. They tend to spend more time with patients with psychological problems, which is a further threat to the income of a doctor who is paid on a fee-for-service basis.

Given the aforementioned financial pressures on students, and external pressures from competing models of education, the task of enrolling 20 new local students each year to meet the real costs of the course is not to be taken lightly. Nevertheless, the Universities in Australia are committed to improving the recognition and management of people with mental disorders by general practitioners. All are involved in the shared care programmes and two others, the University of Melbourne and the University of Western Australia, currently offer fee-paying certificate courses to general practitioners.

Providing resource material

Educating general practitioners in the recognition and management of patients with mental disorders is dependent on there being adequate resource materials available.

Management of mental disorders

This is a 700-page two-volume book that was initially written for community mental health nurses. It is now in a second edition (Treatment Protocol Project 1997) and this edition has already sold 10,000 copies in Australia. A United Kingdom edition is in preparation. The book is now used as the text in two medical undergraduate programmes and in the UNSW Master of Psychological Medicine programme. It is widely used as a handbook by general practitioners who are not undertaking any educational programme. Even psychiatrists and clinical psychologists are purchasing the book. Why is this book so successful? For twelve months before the first edition was published the books were trialled in community mental health clinics and revised in the light of comments received to ensure that the book was of practical use. The books became the vade mecum for practising clinicians, in part because the text, deliberately freed of references, was so accessible and in part because each chapter is backed by resource material – like outcome measures to evaluate progress in treatment and information pamphlets for patients and their families – resource materials that could be photocopied and used within each clinic.

'Counselling and management skills in clinical practice'

The shared care programmes have made it clear that general practitioners require both knowledge and skills – but how do you transmit skills without hands-on training? 'Counselling and Management Skills in Clinical Practice' (Treatment Protocol Project 1998) is an interactive CD-Rom that uses case histories of four typical patients to teach five clinical skills. The cases are acute depression, chronic depression, panic disorder and somatoform disorder. The skills are interviewing skills based on the micro counselling model; informing patients about their illness; how to prescribe; and two psychological management skills: hyperventilation control and structured problem-solving. The disk is accompanied by a moderator's guide which allows any psychologically-aware clinician to use the CD-Rom to teach these five skills to groups of clinicians. It has proven surprisingly popular with groups of general practitioners being prepared to give up a Saturday afternoon to learn skills that they have identified as being likely to improve their practice efficacy.

Conclusions

Some 20 per cent of the population suffer from a mental disorder and while most of these people consult a GP each year only 30 per cent do so for a mental health reason. Thus general practitioners need to develop skills to recognise the presence of mental disorder, even when it is not the focus for the consultation. This is especially important in the young for their rates of mental disorder are unacceptably high. What is the best way to alert the general practitioners about the knowledge and skills required? One can ensure that all general practitioners have basic resource material. The *Medical Journal of Australia*, in conjunction with the Commonwealth Department of Health, has recently distributed a booklet on mental disorders to all general practitioners. The two-volume book, the *Management of Mental Disorders*, has been purchased by half the country's GPs and, because of the resource materials it contains, is likely to be in active use. The CD-Rom on clinical skills will be bundled with the next edition of the *Management of Mental Disorders*. Shared-care programmes in mental health probably involve 10 per cent of general practitioners. Their level of expertise will rise and while there is as yet no firm evidence of such improvement, the appropriate research is underway. The graduates of the University Masters' programmes are few in number and will not affect the overall quality of care, unless, as some already do, they become educators of their colleagues. General practitioners do prefer to learn practice skills from other general practitioners. Maybe this is the proper role for the graduates of the university courses.

References

Andrews, G. and Brodaty, H. (1980) The general practitioner as psychotherapist. *Medical Journal of Australia*, 2, 655–659.

Andrews, G., Schonell, M. and Tennant, C. (1977) The relation between physical, psychological, and social morbidity in a suburban community. *American Journal of Epidemiology*, 105, 324–329.

Andrews, G., Hall, W., Teesson, M. and Henderson, S. (1999) *The Mental Health of Australians*, Australian Government Printing Office, Canberra.

Andrews, G., Slade, T. and Issakidis, C. (in press) Technical update on the National Survey of Mental Health and Wellbeing: Revised prevalence rates. *Australian and New Zealand Journal of Psychiatry*.

Australian Bureau of Statistics (1998) *Mental Health and Wellbeing Profile of Adults, Publication Number 4326.0*. Australian Bureau of Statistics: Canberra.

Brodaty, H. and Andrews, G. (1983) Brief psychotherapy in family practice: a controlled prospective intervention trial, *British Journal of Psychiatry* 143, 11–19.

Brodaty, H., Andrews, G. and Austin, A. (1981) Training in interviewing and counselling, *Medical Journal of Australia* 1, 593–594.

Brodaty, H., Andrews, G. and Austin, A. (1982a) Psychiatric illness in general practice II: How is it managed? *Australian Family Physician*, 11, 682–686.

Brodaty, H., Andrews, G. and Kehoe, L. (1982b) Psychiatric illness in general practice I: Why is it missed? *Australian Family Physician*, 11, 625–631.

Chancellor, A., Mant, A. and Andrews, G. (1977) The general practitioner's identification and management of emotional disorders. *Australian Family Physician*, 6, 1137–1143.

Goldberg, D.P. and Blackwell, B. (1970) Psychiatric illness in general practice. *British Medical Journal*, 2, 439–441.

Treatment Protocol Project (1997) *Management of Mental Disorders*, 2nd edition. ISBN 0 9587052 0 8. World Health Organization Collaborating Centre for Mental Health and Substance Abuse: Darlinghurst. NSW.

—— (1998) *Counselling and management skills in clinical practice.* CD ROM, World Health Organization Collaborating Centre for Mental Health and Substance Abuse: Darlinghurst. NSW.

15

TRAINING THE WHOLE PRIMARY CARE TEAM

Andre Tylee

Introduction

It is a great privilege to have worked with David Goldberg over the last 13 years or so. When I was developing my Mental Health Foundation research fellowship protocol in 1984 I went to see him in Manchester and immediately felt welcomed and encouraged to study the recognition of depression by GPs. Incidentally, he also introduced me to his research fellow working on the training of GPs, Linda Gask with whom I have also worked closely ever since. David Goldberg has inspired countless other researchers and teachers similarly over the years and continues to support me in my efforts to develop whole-team, primary-care skills-based training at the Institute of Psychiatry. He also inspires many of the participants on my courses with the microskills needed to work with patients who somatise their distress.

Several other authors in this book have outlined how common mental health problems are in primary care and the need for good quality skills training for the general practitioner (GP) and the whole primary health care team (PHCT). There is also a need to improve the mental health components of undergraduate training and post basic training for the GP registrar before entering a lifetime of general practice. In this chapter I will describe the perceived mental health training needs of GPs in England and Wales and training programmes that have occurred over the last decade or two (many of which David Goldberg has initiated). I will also describe some of the current barriers to training of English GPs and some strategies for overcoming them. The importance of assessing the learning needs of the whole primary health care team will be discussed using a 'bottom-up' rather than a 'top-down' approach.

Real need

A quarter of everyday GP consultations are with people who have a mental health problem (Shepherd *et al.* 1966), and these patients consult more frequently. Goldberg and Huxley (1980) described pathways to care for patients with mental health problems describing two filters that operate in primary care (i.e. recognition and referral). Around 90 per cent of patients with mental health problems are managed solely in primary care. Primary care is usually the first port of call in a crisis and arrangements can be made for follow up over many years. Practice nurses (PNs) are increasingly involved in the care of mental illness. This mirrors the chronic disease management of conditions like asthma and diabetes although unlike these conditions there is as yet no financial reward in the UK. Practice nurses often administer depot medication and have related training needs which are being increasingly recognised. The Royal College of General Practitioners (RCGP) in 1996 established its Unit for Mental Health Education in Primary Care in the Section of Epidemiology and General Practice at the Institute of Psychiatry and its activities in promoting practice-based multi-professional training will be described later in this chapter.

Recent legislation in the White Paper 'Choice and Opportunity' (Department of Health 1996) allows primary care in England to pilot new forms of organisation of primary care services. Primary Care Groups (PCGs) in England now commission services. GPs are also likely to be providing care for patients with mental illness at primary care sites. GPs are increasingly identifying training needs around provision of services and commissioning good mental health care.

In the UK, there is an increasing role for other professionals in the PHCT whether medical (e.g. GPs, practice nurses, health visitors, community nurses, practice counsellors, psychologists, community psychiatric nurses) or non-medical (e.g. practice receptionists, practice managers, computer operators, etc.).

The PHCT needs to relate well to its community mental health team (CMHT) often through a link-worker. The two teams need to develop joint protocols for referrals and good quality communication about patients' needs. One aim of education must surely be to improve teamwork and improve the communication at the interface between the teams. In 1991, 48 per cent of practices in six health authorities had a link with community psychiatric nurse, 21 per cent with a social worker, 17 per cent with a counsellor, 15 per cent with a psychologist, and 16 per cent with psychiatrist (Thomas and Corney 1992).

Strathdee and Jenkins (1996) estimated that a GP with an average list size of 2,000 patients will have 4–12 patents with schizophrenia, 6–7 patients with affective psychosis, 4–5 patients with organic dementia, 60–100 patients with depression, 70–80 patients with anxiety and other neuroses, 50–60 patients with situational problems and 5–6 patients with drug or alcohol disorders.

The World Health Organization (WHO) survey of psychiatric disorder in primary care settings (Üstün and Sartorius 1995) demonstrated that

195

psychological problems are common with an average prevalence of 24 per cent in consecutive attenders. Most common were depressive disorders, anxiety disorders, alcohol use disorders and somatoform disorders. Psychological reasons for consulting were only given as the main reason for the visit in 5.3 per cent.

Goldberg and Gournay (1998) examined the spectrum of primary care mental health disorders by prevalence, likelihood of spontaneous remission and response to drug treatments and talking treatments. They described four categories of mental disorder. Group 1 includes severe mental illness such as schizophrenia, bipolar disorder and dementia. These conditions have a low prevalence, a low spontaneous remission rate and respond to drugs and psychosocial treatments. Group 2 contains the higher prevalence mixed anxiety and depression, pure depression, and generalised anxiety disorder. These conditions respond to drug treatment and 'talking' treatments such as cognitive therapy. Spontaneous remission is moderate to low. Group 3 comprises conditions of variable prevalence grouped together by response to talking treatments such as phobic disorders, obsessional compulsive disorders, post traumatic stress disorder and mild eating disorders and are unlikely to spontaneously remit. Some conditions in this group go unrecognised (e.g, phobias, mild eating disorders). Group 4 comprises adjustment disorders and bereavement disorders, both of which remit if left and for which there is little evidence to date of beneficial outcome for talking treatments or drug treatments. There will clearly be a variety of learning needs around these conditions depending on their prior training and experience.

Current training

Current professional training for mental health staff tends to be uni-professional (Sainsbury Centre for Mental Health 1997). Many GPs have had no training in mental health since undergraduate days as there is no requirement to undertake further training. Around 50 per cent of GP registrars undertake a psychiatry attachment, although it is debatable how relevant some of these jobs are to primary care. GPs choose their own educational activity which is likely to be based on perceived need and preference rather than real need.

Perceived training need

A survey of randomly selected GPs in England and Wales (Turton et al. 1995) found that 35 per cent of respondents had attended any course on mental health in the previous three years. 63 per cent of respondents had completed vocational training with half of these involving a psychiatric post. Of those who had received vocational training, 39 per cent had found it to be of uncertain or little value in helping them meet the mental health needs of their patients. Respondents rated their own competence in mental health skills and rated themselves average. Skills in which GPs felt confident included depression recognition. Every respondent rated themselves average or above average at recognising depression. When asked which topics they 'personally and definitely' would like further training in they listed in decreasing order; psychodynamic counselling (25 per cent), stress management techniques (20.8 per cent), cognitive techniques (15 per cent), management of addictions (13.3 per cent), how to help the long-term mentally ill (10 per cent), when to prescribe psychotropic drugs (9.2 per cent) and assessment of suicide risk (7.5 per cent). This list is mainly skills based; 42 per cent wanted no training at all. In another survey undertaken to delineate the extent of professionals who undertook counselling in their surgeries (Sibbald *et al*. 1993), 19 per cent of the GP respondents indicated an interest in mental health (personal communication from B. Sibbald). The challenge is how to attract the other 80 per cent.

Kerwick with Goldberg and colleagues (Kerwick *et al*. 1997) elicited perceived training need in inner London GPs. The most frequently requested topics were psychiatric emergencies, somatization, counselling skills, 'heart-sink' patients (i.e. how to deal with those patents who make their doctors' hearts sink), psychosexual problems and stress management each of which was chosen by at least 40 per cent of the respondents. Preferred formats for teaching were small group work alone or allied to a lecture.

Training changes behaviour

Allery and colleagues (Allery *et al*. 1997) interviewed general practitioners and consultants to ascertain factors which doctors attribute to changing their practice. The three most frequently mentioned reasons were organisational factors, education and contact with professionals.

Gotland

Evidence that a mental health educational intervention can change GP behaviour and possibly improve patient outcome comes from Gotland (Rutz *et al*. 1989a). The training programme was associated with decreases in psychiatric inpatient care (by 65 per cent), and sick leave frequency (by 50 per cent) of depressed patients (Rutz *et al*. 1989b). There was a 60 per cent reduction in the number of suicides (mainly in females with major depression who had been in contact with the GPs) although numbers were small because of the small population base (Rutz *et al*. 1989b). Whilst the use of anti-depressants increased in Sweden they increased significantly more on Gotland (Rutz *et al*. 1990). Prescriptions for sedatives decreased by 8.2 per cent (Rutz *et al*. 1990). A fading out of the educational effect other than for the prescribing of anti-depressants was seen largely because nine of the original

18 GPs who had taken part in the educational programme left (Rutz *et al*. 1992). The Gotland model inspired similar interventions or campaigns such as the Defeat Depression campaign organised jointly by the Royal Colleges of Psychiatrists and General Practitioners between 1992–1996 described in more detail later in this chapter. One educational intervention for GPs about anxiety disorders in Germany (Wittchen 1995), over two seminars, showed increased recognition, improved attitudes, changes in referrals and more patients treated in primary care. In the longer term outcome was still maintained at one year.

Consultation review

One teaching method shown to change behaviour is that of reviewing consultations using audio-tape or video-tape with medical students (Maguire *et al*. 1978), psychiatrists (Goldberg *et al*. 1994) and GPs (Pendleton *et al*. 1983). Primary care residents in Charleston, Carolina who were given video-feedback changed their interviewing behaviour and improved at detecting psychiatric illness (Goldberg *et al*. 1980). Gask working with Goldberg and colleagues subsequently integrated the Carolina work with the problem-based interviewing approach of Lesser from MacMaster University (Lesser 1985; Gask 1992). She and her colleagues demonstrated that video-feedback training could improve the accuracy of GP trainees (Gask *et al*. 1980) and experienced general practitioners (Gask *et al*. 1987) and such changes persisted over time (Bowman *et al*. 1992). GP trainers can teach these skills to trainees (Gask *et al*. 1991). These findings have been replicated in the USA (Gask 1992). Whewell and colleagues (Whewell *et al*. 1988) also found that video-feedback improved detection. The Gask approach uses recent real-life material (or relevant role-play), a supportive peer group atmosphere, facilitation, skill rehearsal, a learner centred approach and learners are encouraged to use their own feelings (Gask 1992).

Skill demonstration and rehearsal

Interviewing, assessment or therapeutic skills can be taught using skill demonstration and skill rehearsal. The effect of deficient interviewing skills are demonstrated in the first of two training packs 'Depression. From Recognition to Management' developed for the Defeat Depression Campaign (see Appendix). This package also demonstrates how a GP can elicit the symptoms of depression in everyday practice. The second videopackage (see Appendix) focuses on talking skills and demonstrates problem solving if the problems are soluble, coping strategies when the problems seem insoluble and basic cognitive skills where there is automatic negative thinking. Actors and GPs demonstrate microskills for skill rehearsal. Other teaching packages (see Appendix) that employ this method have been produced on reattribution skills in somatisation disorders and alcohol problems.

The package on somatisation has been shown to improve: picking up non-verbal cues, using empathic comments, asking about social and family factors, acknowledgement of the reality of symptoms and making the link between somatic symptoms and psychological problems (Gask *et al.* 1989).

A package on child and adolescent psychiatry developed for GP registrars, consists of three video-based sessions on the assessment and management of psychiatric problems in early childhood, schoolchildren and adolescents. The objectives encouraged participants to develop more positive attitudes towards the subject, to improve identification skills and to improve knowledge.

The training for nurses in the recognition and management of depression in old age comprises a video, training manual and nurse interview schedule to help nurses and other members of the PHCT learn how to detect depression in the elderly (Mann *et al.*, see Appendix).

Other RCGP Unit for Mental Health Education training packages

Other training packages that the RCGP Unit for Mental Health Education has developed in conjunction with other agencies include 'Schizophrenia in General Practice' (RCGP Unit/SANE-Schizophrenia a national emergency), and a 'Training for GPs on Suicide Awareness' (RCGP Unit/the Samaritans). The schizophrenia package contains acetates with accompanying notes for the lecturer and is based on the deliberations of a working party convened by SANE and a UK-wide consultation exercise with nearly 200 health professionals. The suicide training package is a template for GP trainers and Samaritans to jointly run a one-day experiential workshop to explore the skills and attitudes needed to elicit and assess suicide ideation and intent. The Samaritans are essential because of the possibility of participants being moved by personal experience of this sensitive issue and requiring time to express this on a one-to-one basis.

Other training approaches

Case report

Balint groups are a well known method of learning by small groups of GPs using case reports (Balint 1979). Although the intention of these groups is to achieve change in the participants' personality and psychotherapeutic skills, this has only been described by anecdote.

Training courses/research projects

Researchers have assessed the ability of GPs to use behavioural anxiety management techniques (Catalan *et al.* 1984), problem-based approaches for major depression (Mynors Wallis *et al.* 1995); psychotherapy skills (behavioural and psychodynamic) (Andrews and Brodaty 1980); re-attribution skills in somatisation (Mental Health Foundation 1997); structured assessments in the long-term mentally ill (Kendrick *et al.* 1995); psychosexual skills (Mathers *et al.* 1994); and counselling skills for GP trainees (Havelock *et al.* 1992). These training courses have relied on the enthusiasm of a particular researcher/trainer. Participants are often motivated to undergo training, may already have an interest in the subject and are willing to be evaluated. This, of course, has profound implications for further dissemination by less motivated trainers to less motivated learners and these projects have not been replicated in other centres. One study (Thompson *et al.* 1996) is attempting to replicate the Gotland findings in a randomised controlled trial design with a larger more representative GP population and the results are awaited.

'Top down' training programmes for general practitioners

In the USA, the Depression Awareness Recognition and Treatment (D/ART) campaign was established in 1985 to provide training for health and mental health professionals and to enhance public awareness about depression (Davidoff 1996). The Professional Education program included a $2\frac{1}{2}$ day course on the epidemiology, biological aspects, diagnosis, treatment and management of depression which was subsequently modified for primary care groups. Participant evaluations indicated 'high levels of satisfaction with the courses and positive opinions about the potential application of the knowledge gained to clinical situations' (Davidoff 1996).

In the UK the Royal College of Psychiatrists (RCPsych) and the Royal College of General Practitioners (RCGP) ran the Defeat Depression Campaign from 1992-1996 (Paykel *et al.* 1997). The aims were to educate general practitioners about recognition and management of depression, to educate the general public about depression and to reduce stigma. A media campaign was aimed at the general public using leaflets, books and tapes. Conferences were organised on the recognition of depression, the management of depression, depression in the elderly, depression in the young, postnatal depression, depression in ethnic groups and depression in the workplace and in health professionals. The meetings on depression recognition and management led to a consensus statement (Paykel and Priest 1992) as did the meeting on depression in the elderly (Katona *et al.* 1995). The first consensus statement was sent to all GPs and psychiatrists and a book was published by the RCGP and sent to the members of the RCGP and the RCPsych (Wright 1993). Evaluation of the impact of educational materials on a random one-in-fourteen sample of GPs in England and Wales on awareness of the campaign, awareness and use of campaign materials and ratings of usefulness of the campaign in relation to other educational activities is being written up.

A parallel initiative was jointly organised by the RCGP, the Department of Health and the Mental Health Foundation. A Senior Mental Health Educational Fellowship was established in 1992 and I was appointed to the role (Secretary of State, *Health of the Nation* 1992). The objective was to improve training in mental health received by GPs in England by targeting the 239 district GP tutors. After initial piloting, 11 out of the 14 regions in England created regional mental health educational fellowship posts. A new national cascade was constructed (Turton and Tylee 1995; Kerwick and Jones 1996). Regional fellows provided support on average to 15 district GP tutors (regions had between 5 and 22 tutors) and met for peer support. Training packages were produced and strategies were developed to increase the quality of training available. During the lifetime of the Fellowship it metamorphosed from a predominantly pedagogic model to a predominantly andragogic model (Singleton and Tylee 1996a). This was chiefly because of difficulties gaining widespread acceptance within the GP tutor network. Most GP tutors have limited time in which to plan and execute all learning activity and this requires as much administrative time. As a result of this experience the focus has now changed with establishment of the RCGP Unit for Mental Health Education in Primary Care at the Institute of Psychiatry. The aim remains to improve recognition and management of mental illness by general practitioners and PHCTs. The Unit supports pairs of teachers who are chiefly GPs and nurses or psychologists or counsellors who wish to work as pairs to provide whole team training to practices led by learning needs. A new mental health management course which is modular over one year has been set up. Pairs are taught to elicit true learning need and then are supported in their efforts to help the practices to meet those needs. Ninety-four teachers have so far been through the courses and more are planned so that a network of well over 100 teachers in England will soon exist. District Health Authorities and the new primary care groups are increasingly seeing the benefit from having a pair of trainers who can look after their training needs.

Continuing medical education

Kerwick and Jones (1996) reviewing the literature on continuing medical education (CME), find evidence that it can improve clinical performance and even patient outcome although the effects are modest so that more rigour in evaluation is required, as is attention to reproducing effects. Laxdal (1982) has emphasised the importance of assessing educational needs to improve effectiveness of CME programmes. She emphasises that needs assessment must include the characteristics of the learner and their perceived needs, well-defined criteria and standards of performance to be achieved with clear educational objectives and prioritisation. A survey (Singleton *et al.* 1999) of GP tutors in England indicated that three-quarters of the speakers delivering courses are not themselves based in primary care and that the most popular courses are one-hour lectures at local postgraduate centres. Only 34 per cent of respondents teach more than four times a year with only 8 per cent teaching more than once a month. Most of their workload was administrative (Singleton *et al.* 1999). GP tutors were established around 15 years ago mainly by faculties of the RCGP to develop the CME infrastructure and when a new postgraduate education allowance was introduced as part of overall contractual changes within the profession in 1990 (Health Departments of Great Britain 1989) these posts became more widely established. To qualify for the allowance, GPs are required to attend 25 days training over five years at registered courses whereby the registration or accreditation of the courses is the responsibility of the regional directors of postgraduate general practice education. The content of these courses simply needs to be reflect three categories, health promotion, clinical and practice management.

Learner-centred education

Traditional didactic methods of training have been increasingly challenged as a means of changing GPs' behaviour (Horder *et al.* 1986). The practical difficulties of a heavy workload, family commitments, and inflexible partnership arrangements can frustrate ambitions to continue purposeful learning or pursue a higher degree (Wright 1994) and a more flexible learner-centred approach to helping doctors keep up to date or develop their careers has been advocated (Kerwick and Jones 1996; Branthwaite *et al.* 1988; Coles 1994; Pietroni 1992; Stanley *et al.* 1993; Royal College of General Practitioners 1993), although many GPs remain unconvinced (Kelly and Murray 1994). Stanley and colleagues (Stanley *et al.* 1993) proposed a model for systematic reading, reflection and audit with formal education being complementary and motivating. As reading plays such an important role in self-directed learning it is essential to have critical reading skills and there are early indications that introducing these skills into the membership examination has already changed the reading behaviour of trainees (Wright 1994). An RCGP working party into higher professional training recommended a modular approach to CME whereby learners build up portfolios over time that include many types of self-directed learning with the help of an educational mentor, approaches such as diaries, commentaries on read material and performance review (Royal College of General Practitioners 1993). One major implication however is that there is no formal tradition of available mentorship and it would be costly to implement a system of mentors, who would themselves need training in facilitation skills (Wright 1994).

Multi-disciplinary practice-based training

With the ever-increasing shift for PHCTs to provide mental health care in the community the public have a right to expect the PHCT workers to be trained adequately for this role. Tomorrow's GPs will need greater clinical and inter-personal skills, epidemiological skills for assessing the health of populations, practice management skills and skill in operating quality assurance systems. Therefore they will need to promote multi-disciplinary learning (Irvine 1993). The practice is the best venue for CME (Reiss *et al.* 1981; Owen *et al.* 1989; Stanley 1992; Al-Shehri *et al.* 1993) because it focuses training on everyday practice problems, teamwork, communication and practice management issues. Multidisciplinary audit, peer review, development of guidelines and protocols, use of screening instruments, use of paper-based or computer-aided prompts are several practice based approaches that can be used (Kerwick and Jones 1996): One paper-based prompt that may, in the future be developed into computer prompts and additional educational material is the ICD10 chapter Primary Care Version (World Health Organization 1996). Practice teams often require facilitation, which is why the RCGP Unit for Mental Health Education has focused on training practice-friendly pairs of mentors to be sensitive to the whole team's training needs and to provide support when required, using a multi-layered approach to facilitate change. Pairs of mentors are more likely to 'model' inter-professional teamwork. The pair can function as key local opinion leaders. The RCGP Unit for Mental Health Education in Primary Care is evaluating this new approach and developing new methods of evaluation. In this way it is hoped that the pioneering work of David Goldberg may be built upon and disseminated throughout British general practice.

References

Allery, L.A., Owen, P. and Robling, M.R. (1997) Why general practitioners and consultants change their clinical practice: a critical incident study. *British Medical Journal* 314, 870–874.

Al-Shehri, A., Stanley, I. and Thomas, P. (1993) Continuing education for general practice. 2. Systematise learning from experience. *British Journal of General Practice* 43, 249–253.

Andrews, G. and Brodaty, H. (1980) General practitioner as psychotherapist. *Medical Journal of Australia* 2, 655–659.

Balint, E. (1979) The Balint group approach. *Journal of the Royal Society of Medicine* 72, 467–469.

Bowman, F., Goldberg, D., Millar, T. *et al.* (1992) Improving the psychological skills of experienced general practitioners: Do effects of training persist? *Medical Education* 26, 63–68.

Branthwaite, A., Ross, A., Henshaw, A. *et al.* (1988) *Continuing Education for General Practitioners*. Occasional paper 38. London: RCGP.

Catalan, J., Gath, D. and Edmonds, G. (1984) The effects of non-prescribing of anxio-lyytics in general practice: 1. Controlled evaluation of psychiatric and social outcome. *British Journal of Psychiatry* 144, 593–602.

Coles, C. (1994) Learner-centred education in primary care. *Postgraduate Education for General Practice* 5, 19–25.

Davidoff, I. (1996) The Depression Awareness, Recognition and Treatment (DART) Program. The first 10 years: a record of achievement, report: available from National Institute of Mental Health, 5600 Fishers Lane, Room 10-85, Rockville, MD 20857.

Department of Health (1996) *Choice and Opportunity*. HMSO, London.

Gask, L. (1992) Training general practitioners to detect and manage emotional disorders. *International Review of Psychiatry* 4, 293–300.

Gask, L., Goldberg, D., Lesser, A. *et al.* (1980) Improving the psychiatric skills of the general practice trainee, an evaluation of a group training. *Medical Education* 22, 132–138.

Gask, L., McGrath, G., Goldberg, D. *et al.* (1987) Improving the skills of established general practitioners. *Medical Education* 21, 362–368.

Gask, L., Goldberg, D., Porter, R. *et al.* (1989) The treatment of somatisation: evaluation of a teaching package with general practice trainees. *Journal of Psychosomatic Research* 33, 697–703.

Gask, L., Goldberg, D., Boardman, J. *et al.* (1991) Training general practitioners to teach psychiatric interviewing skills: an evaluation of group training. *Medical Education* 25, 444–451.

Goldberg, D. and Gournay, K. (1998) *The general practitioner, the psychiatrist and the burden of mental health care*. Maudsley Discussion Document. Maudsley, London.

Goldberg, D. and Huxley, P. (1980) *Mental illness in the community*. Tavistock, London.

Goldberg, D., Smith, C., Steele, J.J. *et al.* (1980) Training family doctors to recognise psychiatric illness with increased accuracy. *Lancet* ii, 521–523.

Goldberg, D., Hobson, R., Maguire, P. *et al.* (1994) The clarification and assessment of a method of psychotherapy. *British Journal of Psychiatry* 144, 567–580.

Havelock, P., Nathan, R. and Cooper, Y. (1992) A course in counselling for GP trainees. *Postgraduate Education in General Practice* 3, 34–40.

Health Departments of Great Britain (1989) *General Practice in the NHS. The 1990 Contract*. London, HMSO.

Horder, J., Bosanquet, N. and Stocking, B. (1986) Ways of influencing the behaviour of general practitioners. *Journal of the Royal College of General Practice* 36, 517–521.

Irvine, D. (1993) Educating general practitioners. The new demands of general practice require substantial educational change. *British Medical Journal* 307, 696–697.

Katona, C., Freeling, P., Hinchcliffe, K. *et al.* (1995) Recognition and management of depression in late life in general practice: consensus statement. *Primary Care Psychiatry* 1, 107–113.

Kelly, M.H. and Murray, T.S. (1994) General practitioners' views on continuing medical education. *British Journal of General Practice* 44, 469–471.

Kendrick, A., Burns, T. and Freeling, P. (1995) Randomised controlled trial of teaching general practitioners to carry out structured assessments of their long term mentally ill patients. *British Medical Journal* 311, 93–98.

Kerwick, S. and Jones, R. (1996) Educational interventions in primary care psychiatry. *Primary Care Psychiatry* 2, 107–117.

Kerwick, S., Jones, R., Mann, A. *et al.* (1997) Mental health care training priorities in general practice. *British Journal of General Practice* 47: 225–227.

Laxdal, O.E . (1982) Needs assessment in continuing medical education: a practical guide. *Journal of Medical Education* 57, 827–834.

Lesser, A.L. (1985) Problem based interviewing in general practice: a model. *Medical Education* 19, 299–304.

Maguire, P., Roe, P., Goldberg, D. *et al.* (1978) The value of teaching interview skills to medical students. *Psychological Medicine* 8, 695–704.

Mathers, N., Bramley, M., Draper, K. *et al.* (1994) Assessment of training in psychosexual medicine. *British Medical Journal* 308, 969–972.

Mental Health Foundation (1997) *Briefing* 7, Mental Health Foundation: London.

Mynors Wallis, L.M., Gath, O.H., Lloyd-Thomas, A.R. *et al.* (1995) Randomised controlled trial comparing problem solving treatment with amitriptyline and placebo for major depression in primary care. *British Medical Journal* 310, 441–445.

Owen, P.A., Allery, L.A., Harding, K. *et al.* (1989) General practitioners continuing medical education within and outside their practice. *British Medical Journal* 299, 238–240.

Paykel, E.S. and Priest, R.G. (1992) Recognition and management of depression in general practice; consensus statement. *British Medical Journal* 305, 1198–1202.

Paykel, E.S., Tylee, A., Wright, A. *et al.* (1997) The Defeat Depression Campaign: Psychiatry in the public arena. *American Journal of Psychiatry* 154, 59–65.

Pendleton, D., Schofield, T., Tate, P. *et al.* (1983) *The consultation: an approach to learning and teaching.* Oxford University Press, Oxford.

Pietroni, R. (1992) New strategies for higher professional education. *British Journal of General Practice* 42, 294–296.

Reiss, B.B., Berrington, R.M., Stuart, D.R.M. *et al.* (1981) Practice educational meetings: a new influence in general practice. *British Medical Journal* 283, 1025–1027.

Royal College of General Practitioners (1993) *Portfolio-based learning in general practice.* Occasional paper 63. RCGP, London.

Rutz, W., Walinder, J., Eberhard, G. *et al.* (1989a) An educational programme on depressive disorders for general practitioners on Gotland: background and evaluation. *Acta Psychiatrica Scandinavica* 79, 19–26.

Rutz, W., von Knorring, L. and Walinder, J. (1989b) Frequency of suicide on Gotland after systematic postgraduate education of general practitioners. *Acta Psychiatrica Scandinavica* 80, 151–154.

Rutz, W., von Knorring, L., Walinder, J. *et al.* (1990) Effect of an educational program for general practitioners on Gotland on the pattern of prescription of psychotropic drugs. *Acta Psychiatrica Scandinavica* 82, 399–403.

Rutz, W., von Knorring, L. and Walinder, J. (1992) Long-term effects of an educational program for general practitioners given by the Swedish Committee for the Prevention and Treatment of Depression. *Acta Psychiatrica Scandinavica* 85, 83–88.

Sainsbury Centre for Mental Health (1997) *Pulling Together. The future roles and training of mental health staff.* Sainsbury, London.

Secretary of State (1992) *Health of the Nation.* London: HMSO.

Shepherd, M., Cooper, B., Brown, A. *et al.* (1966) *Psychiatric Illness in General Practice.* Oxford University Press, Oxford.

Sibbald, B., Addington-Hall, J., Brenneman, D. *et al.* (1993) Counsellors in English and Welsh general practices: their nature and distribution. *British Medical Journal* 306, 29–33.

Singleton, A. and Tylee, A. (1996a) Continuing medical education in mental illness: a paradox for general practitioners. *British Journal of General Practice* 46, 339–341.

Singleton, A., Smith, F. and Tylee, A. (1999) Teachers or administrators? A survey of GP tutors. *Education for General Practice* 10, 140–146.

Stanley, I. (1992) Practice-based small group learning postgraduate education in general practice. *Postgraduate Education in General Practice* 3, 89–91.

Stanley, I., Al-Shehri, A. and Thomas, P. (1993) Continuing education for general practice. 1. Experience, competence and the media of self-directed learning for established general practitioners. *British Journal of General Practice* 43, 210–214.

Strathdee, G. and Jenkins, R. (1996) Purchasing mental health care for primary care. In G. Thornicroft and G. Strathdee (eds) *Commissioning Mental Health Services.* HMSO, London.

Thomas, R. and Corney, R. (1992) A survey of links between mental health professionals and general practice in six district health authorities. *British Journal of General Practice* 42, 358–361.

Thompson, C., Stevens, L., Ostler, K. *et al.* (1996) The Hampshire Depression Project: A methodology for assessing the value of general practice education in depression. *International Journal of Methods in Psychiatric Research* 6, S27–S31.

Turton, P. and Tylee, A. (1995) Evaluation in setting up a large scale educational programme: principles and problems. *Education for General Practice* 6, 226–229.

Turton, P., Tylee, A. and Kerry, S. (1995) Mental health training needs in general practice. *Primary Care Psychiatry* 1, 197–199.

Üstün, T.B. and Sartorius, N. (1995) *Mental illness in general health care. An international study.* Chichester: Wiley.

Whewell, P., Gore, V. and Leach, C. (1988) Training general practitioners to improve their recognition of emotional disturbance in the consultation. *Journal of the Royal College of General Practitioners* 38, 259–262.

Wittchen, H.U. (1995) Short and long term effectiveness of a training programme for recognition. *Primary Care Psychiatry* 1, 45–52.

World Health Organization (1996) *Diagnostic and Management Guidelines for Mental Disorders in Primary Care.* ICD-10 Chapter V Primary Care Version. Hogrefe and Huber, Seattle.

Wright, A. (1993) *Depression: Recognition and management in general practice.* RCGP, London.

Wright, A. (1994) Modular continuing medical education: our flexible friend? *British Journal of General Practice* 44, 146–147.

Appendix: Teaching packages

Alcohol

The teaching packages referred to in the text and some others are here listed. These packages are the main ones that have been used within the National Teach the Teachers training programme. Because the course is learner-centred, the overriding principle employed is to use relevant sections of each package in response to training need.

Health Education Board for Scotland. *DRAMS Skills for Helping Problem Drinkers.* Edinburgh, SHEG.

Lewis, B. and Gask, L. *Focus on Alcohol.* North West Region Postgraduate General Practice, NHS Executive.

Available from Dr Lewis 01706 58905.

Child and adolescent psychiatry

Garralda, M.E., Bernard, P., Hughes, T. and Tylee, A. *A teaching package in child and adolescent psychiatry for general practitioner registrars.*
Available from Professor Garralda, St Mary's Hospital, Norfolk Place, London (0171 725 1145).

Old age depression

Mann, A., Blanchard, M. and Tylee, A. *Training for Nurses in the Recognition and Management of Depression in Old Age.*
Available from Professor Mann, Institute of Psychiatry (0171 919 3150).

Depression

Gask, L., Goldberg, D., Tylee, A. and Freeling, P. (1992) *From Recognition to Management.* Defeat Depression Campaign.
Gask, L., Scott, J. and Standart, X. (1992) *Counselling skills in depression.* Defeat Depression Campaign.

For availability contact the RCGP Unit (0171 919 3150)

Suicide

Tylee, A. and Guenault, J. *Training for GPs on Suicide Awareness.*
RCGP Unit (0171 919 3150).

Schizophrenia

Tylee, A., Armstrong, E., *et al. Schizophrenia in General Practice.*
RCGP Unit (0171 919 3150).

Part V

THE INTERFACE BETWEEN PRIMARY CARE AND SPECIALIST MENTAL HEALTH SERVICES

16

THE LIMITS OF MENTAL HEALTH CARE IN GENERAL MEDICAL SERVICES

Norman Sartorius

Introduction

Texts concerning health care organisation over the past several decades are unanimous in at least one recommendation: that primary and general health care services should take on the responsibility for the treatment (and prevention) of a number of illnesses that have been handled by specialist services (or by nobody) until now. Mental health planners have been particularly vocal in this respect. This is easy to understand. The prevalence of mental disorders in the general population and in general health care services is high and there are effective relatively easy-to-use methods of treatment. Skills and knowledge necessary for the application of these methods can be conveyed in a reasonably short time and the cost of treatment can be kept low. Preventive interventions are also possible – and most of them have to be implemented by general health care services or social sectors other than health. Examples of primary prevention measures range from the iodination of salt to prevent cretinism and appropriate perinatal care to avoid early brain damage, to the avoidance of hospitalisation of the elderly to prevent cognitive and sensory overload: most of them can be suggested by psychiatrists but have to be implemented by others, outside of the mental health system.

The recommendations of the Alma-Ata Conference on Primary Health Care (World Health Organization, 1978) included mental health care as one of the essential elements of primary health care and a number of countries have taken specific steps to provide care to those with a mental illness at the level of primary care. An important factor in accepting this recommendation was the results of studies done in Northern and Western Europe showing that a significant proportion of people with mental illness seek and receive help from general health care services and in particular from general practitioners. Meanwhile, such studies have been carried out in other countries producing similar results (Sartorius *et al*. 1990). An international study of the frequency of mental disorders in primary health care services in developing countries combined the investigation of prevalence with an operational study demonstrating that it is possible to train general and primary health care staff in methods of treatment of several mental disorders and that staff so trained can provide useful and effective service to people contacting the services (Sartorius and Harding, 1983). Other studies since then demonstrated that the mental disorders are frequently seen in general health care services and that many of those seeking help do not receive it because their illness does not get recognised and even when it is recognised appropriate treatment is only provided to a proportion of those ill (Üstün and Sartorius, 1995).

In some developing countries it has been possible to do all that is necessary to introduce mental health care into primary care. National mental health programmes have been drafted and accepted by the government, resources for the training of general health care have been made available and the medicaments for the treatment of some of the most severe mental disorders have been provided on a regular basis. In other countries some of the steps have been taken, but a broad scale application of mental health measures at primary health care level still remains only an objective although all concerned believe that its achievement is of the highest priority. In other countries still, governments and the professionals have not yet fully accepted the notion that mental health care should be provided in the primary health care services and mainly by primary or general health care staff. In many of these situations it is easy to obtain declarative support from the authorities and the professional associations but programmes do not go further than that.

In situations in which there was an extension of mental health care to the periphery there was invariably an individual or group of individuals who were determined to introduce the change and who often succeeded – although on occasion the new strategy is applied only on a limited territory and also often loses sharpness and power in parallel to the departure, ageing or promotion of the individuals who were the leaders of the original programme. This is not to say that progress is not being made: gradually, attitudes change, services are organised differently, training in medical schools is adjusted to the situation in the field and budgetary provisions are beginning to support peripheral mental health care in general health care services.

The above considerations do not only apply to developing countries: many highly industrialized countries are still committed to a model of provision of care in which most of the serious or longer lasting mental disorders are treated by the psychiatric service system and the remaining mental health problems are dealt with by psychiatrists in private practice, by psychologists and by a proportion of general practitioners who seem to have a special interest in mental health matters. Traditional health practitioners[1] see a significant number of people with mental health problems and play an important role in their treatment in both developing and developed countries: their activity however is often not taken into account in official documents reporting on mental health care nor in planning for services.

It is therefore legitimate to ask why it is so difficult to fully implement a strategy of extension of mental health care to the periphery using primary and general health care services. At first glance everybody stands to gain from the acceptance of this way of proceeding. The patients would receive help from clinics which are located close to their domicile. The health services would save money because it would be possible to treat patients under supervision of primary health care workers at their home and the effects of institutional treatment would not come into play. The cultural background and the home situation of the patient and their family would be well known to the service providers which would help to avoid some of the difficulties that usually arise when patients are treated far away from home by individuals who are often not familiar with the culture and the situation in which the patients live. Doctors would feel better because they would know that their field of action has been expanded. The psychiatrists and other mental health specialists could give their attention to therapy-resistant cases, spend some time teaching and doing research. And yet, progress towards the introduction of mental health components into general health care remains slow or has been arrested.

Factors that limit the introduction of mental health components into general health care

An analysis of the reasons for the slow introduction of mental health care into general health services shows that limiting factors belong to the personal, technical, social, administrative and professional domains.

Limiting factors: the personal domain

Factors belonging to this group are undoubtedly the most important and most difficult to manage. They refer to the attitudes and other personal characteristics of the main actors in the process of providing care – the patient, his or her family the service provider and the decision makers in the field of health.

People suffering from mental illness (as well as their families) are aware of the nefarious consequences of being recognised as a 'mental case'. They will therefore – if they suspect that mental illness might be the reason for their suffering – seek help from people who are not part of their immediate social surroundings. Sometimes they will go for treatment to another town or village; sometimes they will see a privately practising psychiatrist although

213

they may have to pay for this treatment themselves. In many countries patients and their families do not believe that the information about a person's illness will stay in the records of the general practitioner: they feel that it is very likely that in one way or another an indiscretion by the nurse, home visitor or even the doctor, will give away the diagnosis or indicate the nature of ailment from which the patient suffers.

Sometimes patients and their families will go to traditional healers who by and large never make the distinction between mental and physical illness but operate using a different system of grouping illnesses. The classification of problems used by traditional healers is usually more comprehensible for the patient and the treatment that is being prescribed is harmonious with cultural beliefs and previous experience of the patient and of the family. Primary health care is closer to most patients than the large and often dehumanised hospitals, but it is still in many cultures a foreign import, far less their own than traditional health practices and practitioners.

The fear of stigma and possible discrimination because of mental illness and the wish to be treated by an acceptable practice are not the only reasons for the selection of someone other than the primary health care provider: to these reasons is added the uncertainty about the knowledge and treatment skills that the general practitioner has and might use to deal with mental illness. This lack of confidence is not without justification: for a very long time general medical practitioners had little training in psychiatry (particularly concerning the treatment of 'banal' mental illnesses such as anxiety states) and were reluctant to treat people suffering from mental illness. The population often sees the general practitioner as a person who can help with emergencies and can treat minor physical illness: when it comes to more complex problems it is felt the general practitioner will act in accordance with a specialist's advice.

The personal reasons that make physicians at primary care level reluctant to handle mental health problems are more complex. In some instances the lack of knowledge and absence of treatment skills drives the general practitioner to refer the patient away. The medical school training in most countries of the world and in most medical schools still lacks emphasis on psychiatric treatment skills for the general practitioner; even such an elementary skill as the mental state examination is not taught in practical exercises. The total number of hours that medical undergraduates spend in direct contact with people who are suffering from mental illness is still abominably low in most medical schools of the world: the total number of hours of instruction about psychiatry is often restricted to 50 hours, most of which are given in lectures.

Stigma and the image of a mental patient also play a role in the reluctance of the general physician to take on the care of the mentally ill: among the elements of the stigmatised image of the mentally ill, the myth of incurability of those who suffer from diseases of the mind may also make the treatment of mental illness less attractive. When a mental disorder and a physical disorder are both present, both the doctor and the patient may prefer to pay attention to the physical illness, thus avoiding talking about mental illness or seeking treatment for it ('tacit collusion').

The working conditions of the majority of general health care personnel are also of importance. In many countries long hours of work, relatively low income, absence of career prospects, excessive administrative demands and other factors, reduce the motivation of the primary health care personnel to do their work. The 'burn-out' syndrome appears to have become common in peripheral health care workers (and some other professionals, e.g. teachers in peripheral schools) and health decision makers in various countries complain that it is becoming exceedingly difficult to introduce any measure requiring additional work or learning into primary health care services. The proposal that general practitioners and other primary health care personnel should participate in service training or refresher courses is usually found acceptable by the administrative heads of the service: the attendance at training courses and the enthusiasm to learn new things however, remains low and incentives other than increase of knowledge have to be provided in most instances.

Similar factors might also be at work in creating the reluctance of health decision makers to promote the introduction of mental health care into general health services. The health decision makers of today have often received inadequate training in psychiatry and may have left their medical school believing that all mental disorders are like those that they have seen during their brief visit to the mental hospital. They know that such patients are rare in general health care services and are therefore not convinced that much would be gained if an intensive effort were to be made to train general practitioners or to reorganise the services. Even when they have a broader comprehension of mental health problems and have accepted data about the prevalence of mental disorders in general health care facilities they do not believe that today's psychiatry has the means to help those patients given the constraints of primary health care activity. They therefore do not do much to help the introduction of psychiatry into primary care. This can be changed: in the All India Institute of Neurosciences and Mental Health in Bangalore (India) for example, health decision makers have been invited for information sessions about mental health and illness which greatly facilitated the introduction of changes into the health service system.

Limiting factors: the technological domain

Technological constraints (using the word technology in its original sense of the application of scientific knowledge) are also of considerable importance in the provision of mental health care in primary care settings. Once research produces methods that can reduce particularly disturbing symptoms of mental illness (e.g. extreme agitation) even more rapidly than is possible using today's techniques, it will be reasonable to expect that general health care services retain patients who show such symptoms. For the time being, the settings in which primary health care is usually practised do not permit the management of acutely disturbed, severely psychotic or aggressive patients *in loco*: referral to a facility which is equipped to deal with this type of behavioural disturbance will be necessary while these symptoms last. The discovery of modern pharmacological means to deal with various types of symptoms of mental disorder has already significantly changed the organisation of services for the mentally ill. Further advances of science and of treatment tools will make the treatment of mental illness in the framework of primary health care much easier and more similar to other interventions in emergency situations often used in primary care settings.

Other technological problems also limit the possibility of transferring responsibility for mental health problems into primary health care. The irregularity of supply of medicaments to the peripheral health services and pharmacies, for example, is a persistent problem in many developing countries and more recently also in countries of Eastern Europe. Transport to a referral centre takes a long time and has to be prepared well in advance: under such conditions it will often be considered safer to send the patient to an inpatient facility even if that is far away, to avoid complications and unsolvable emergencies.

Limiting factors: the social domain

Stigma of mental illness is not limited to the disease or the person who suffers from it. It extends itself to the family of the patient, the medicaments used to treat the disease, to the institutions where people receive treatment for mental illness and to mental health workers. It is pervasive and frightening in its consequences. The idea that a nice primary health care facility could be used to treat mentally ill people is not acceptable for many who receive treatment in the primary care centre (for other types of ailments), to the authorities that run the facility, the population living in the area and, last but not least also to many of the health staff working in the centre. It is certainly possible to overcome these resistances but not in all situations and not without a major effort often involving legal measures, long-lasting disputations and difficulties with colleagues, friends and politicians. The line of lesser resistance is therefore often chosen and even when the architectural and other plans have foreseen that mental health care would be provided in a department of psychiatry located in a general health care facility, things somehow soon change and the treatment of the mentally ill is done elsewhere. The reasons given for this move are remarkably inventive and usually sound very rational, referring to more pleasant surroundings, better access, more space for parking and various other apparent advantages. It is encouraging to watch how the departments of psychiatry in general hospitals previously often located in the basement floor or in a separate building at the far end of the hospital grounds gradually move closer to 'real' medicine departments; unfortunately however, in order to be acceptable to other colleagues in the hospital or the medical school the psychiatrists select the best-behaved patients for admission in the general hospital, sending other patients – who often need particularly careful attention – to other facilities in which the patient/staff ratio and other conditions are considerably worse than in the general hospital wards. This two-tier psychiatry, which has made its appearance in recent years, is a real danger to the discipline as a whole: in often elegant settings there are numerous psychiatrists and other mental health personnel – psychologists, social workers, case managers all dealing with 'attractive' patients – while somewhere else, understaffed and otherwise poorly resourced facilities break down under the load of patients who have diseases that are difficult to manage and are poor, often homeless and with many social problems. The previous battle to enter into the general hospital and general health care facilities will probably now have to be replaced by a battle to open the upper quality mental health facilities to all or most of the patients and to ensure that mental health resources are equitably distributed within psychiatric services, not only between psychiatric and other health services.

Limiting factors: the administrative domain

Resources that are spent on mental health services are in many settings, considerable. Mental hospitals – although often catering only for a small proportion of those with mental illness in the population (among whom many are resident in the hospital for years) – cost a lot of money. Staff in mental hospitals may be low-paid, the food and other facilities for patients may be miserable and the buildings and parks surrounding them may be in need of repair: the annual budget for the institution as a whole (and for its 'sisters' or 'brothers' carrying the name of 'mental health institute' or some other, e.g. 'rehabilitation centre') is nevertheless high and represents a significant proportion, sometimes almost the whole, of the allocation for mental health care in the country. Reformers have for a long time pointed to the resources reserved for the maintenance of mental hospitals stating that the mental health budgets do not necessarily have to be increased to provide better service to a much larger number of patients. All that would have to be done would be to reallocate resources to outpatient services, to the training of general health staff in psychiatry, to the development of half-way institutions, to the strengthening of social services. All in vain: over the years and through many a bitter experience it became clear that (1) it is relatively easy to discharge some of the patients with chronic illnesses and impairments but that it is difficult to discharge all of them; (2) that staff in mental hospitals although not well paid and often lacking prospects of scientific or other careers prefer stability and when given a choice of working outside the hospital or in it, select the latter; (3) that the economy of the villages surrounding the hospital depends on its existence and that their inhabitants can create a lot of opposition to its closure; (4) that there are often considerable difficulties in converting an empty mental hospital with its grounds, into readily available cash to be used exclusively for the development of mental health care; (5) that there are patients who need in-patient care, for a variety of reasons and that, unless or until another mental hospital or in-patient facility has been built, such patients will come back to the mental hospital and that (6) when there are no mental hospital beds, acute wards have to use part of their resources to house chronically-disabled patients, which in turn changes the nature of the acute community service in a major way. Operational research has shown that it is necessary to nearly double the investments in mental health services during the period of emptying the mental hospital so as to build alternative facilities and establish appropriate mental health care in the community (Trieman *et al.* 1998). As a consequence of such experience and findings administrative authorities have become reluctant to begin the process of deinstitutionalisation and the introduction of mental health care in general health services has become dependent on an enlargement of the budget for mental health (naturally at the cost of diminution of some other budget line whose proponents always seem to fight back with vigour). In current times of financial stringency and administrative conservatism it is therefore becoming even more strenuous to introduce such changes and detailed and well reasoned programmes to do so linger idly in many places, waiting for better times.

Limiting factors: professional domain

Most of the knowledge about mental health problems and of the techniques for their treatment are produced by the psychiatric profession. Psychiatrists are engaged in research on mental illness and serve as a bridge to other disciplines carrying out related research. Psychiatrists teach medical students, study the epidemiology of mental disorders and its changes under the impact of new service arrangements, provide forensic psychiatric service and represent – well or not so well – the interests of psychiatric patients and of the discipline of psychiatry before the administrative and academic authorities.

When it is proposed that mental health care should be carried out by general health care services, that biological research into the causes and pathogenesis of mental disorders should be left to fundamental scientists and that rehabilitation of the impaired should be taken on by the rehabilitation services, psychiatrists begin to feel uneasy: those in private practice feel that the patients whom they normally treat will be taken away by the general practitioner and that their income will therefore diminish; those in teaching positions foresee that teachers of other subjects, for example internal medicine, will begin teaching about the recognition and treatment of, say, depression; and those engaged in research see their field of enquiry drastically diminished. Psychiatrists are therefore, in most instances not very ardent supporters of the delegation of mental health tasks to the general health care workers.

The fears that there will not be enough patients to treat and that teaching will be taken over by others are not supported by evidence (Sartorius, 1997). The introduction of treatment of the mentally ill in general health services usually increases the number of those requesting help and there is little movement from the specialist to the generalist and the teachers of other disciplines are rarely keen to begin teaching psychiatry. There is, however, a danger that one of the consequences of a broad-scale reform will be a significant reduction of the resources that are put at the disposal of psychiatry, which might reduce its productivity in terms of new knowledge and in terms of its capacity to provide adequate teaching to medical students and others in the health care system. The reformers should keep this in mind and argue for a strengthening of mental health components of general health care, while maintaining the function of psychiatry which has to support the providers of care at the point of primary contact and has to continue to lead in the development of new knowledge and skills that can be used by others in the health sector.

Overcoming obstacles to the introduction of mental health care into general health care

While it is obvious that some of the factors limiting the introduction of mental health components into general health care are expressions of true dilemmas, others are not. The latter should be removed: at the present state of our knowledge there is no other way but the introduction of mental health care into general health care to increase the probability that those suffering from a mental illness will receive adequate help. In many countries of the world there are very few psychiatrists; their numbers in developing countries range from one psychiatrist per 20,000 inhabitants to one psychiatrist per 10 million population (Alem, 1997). The prevalence of mental disorders in developing and developed countries is high and the total burden of mental disease worldwide is second highest in terms of years lost due to disability produced by disease. No less than one person out of every five who contact general health care services has a psychological disorder as a primary reason for consultation and most of those disorders are amenable to treatment.

Table 16.1 summarises the factors limiting the introduction of mental health care into general health care and proposes interventions that could remove or lessen some of the limitations. In examining this table it is

Table 16.1 Introducing mental health care: limitations and interventions

Domain	Limiting factor	Intervention
Personal	• Reluctance of patient to present problems to general health care worker	• Health education
	• Reluctance of health worker to deal with mental health problems	• Training of health workers to increase their technical competence and change attitudes
Technological	• Imperfection of treatment tools	• Research to produce better treatment interventions, with particular emphasis on the possibility of their use in primary health care
	• Irregularity of supply of medicaments	• Reorganisation of supporting services
Social	• Stigma on mental illness and on mental health services	• Anti-stigma actions within the health care system and in the general population (e.g. in school health programme)
		• Examination of legal provisions concerning discrimination
Administrative	• Transfer of allocations of funds to general health care, earmarked for psychiatry often difficult	• Lobbying for an increase of funding for the mental health programmes
		• Development of long-term gradual programme of diminution of in-patient services and their replacement by outpatient service
Professional	• Reluctance of psychiatrists to participate in programmes of introduction of mental health care into general care	• Involvement of psychiatric society as well as general practitioners in planning for change and provision of incentives for training of general health care staff

important to remember that there is usually more than one limiting factor at work and that the measures listed are examples of a variety that have been used in different settings to reduce some of them.

Conclusion

As in many other instances, programmes and strategies are important for any change. At the same time however, it is useful to recall that people change faster in response to emotional and social pressures than they do in response to logic and public health imperatives. Change to new ways of doing things should therefore, wherever possible be proposed by leaders who have the confidence of the profession and of the population because of their knowledge, previous achievements, personality and political skills. Transfer of responsibility for care is also a transfer of power – an operation that will involve readjustments and often sacrifice. A vast majority of those involved in changes are reasonable people, of reasonably good will. Proceeding with respect for concerns and wishes of all involved and carefully choosing the pace and manner of achieving change is therefore an indication of good sense and a guarantee that changes will survive and last after the reformers have left the field.

Note

1 'Traditional health practitioner' refers to an individual who has not completed formal training in a recognised medical school and/or is not officially permitted to treat people with mental illness.

References

Alem, A. (1997) *Mental Health in Rural Ethiopia*, Umeå University Press, Umeå.

Sartorius, N. (1997) Psychiatry in the framework of primary health care: a threat or boost to psychiatry? *American Journal of Psychiatry*, June supplement, 154, 67.

Sartorius, N. and Harding, T.W. (1983) The WHO collaborative study on strategies for extending mental health care I. Genesis of the study. *American Journal of Psychiatry*, 140, 1470.

Sartorius, N., Goldberg, D., de Girolamo, G., Costa e Silva, J.A., Lecrubier, Y., and Witchen, H.U. (eds) (1990) *Psychological Disorders in General Health Care*, Hogrefe and Huber, Bern, Toronto, Lewiston (NY).

Trieman, N., Hughes, J. and Leff, J. (1998) The TAPs Project 42: the last to leave hospital – a profile of residual long-stay populations and plans for their resettlement. *Acta Psychiatrica Scandinavica*, 98, 354–359.

Üstün, T.B. and Sartorius, N. (eds) (1995) *Mental Illness in General Health Care*, John Wiley and Sons, Chichester.

World Health Organization (1978) *Primary Health Care: Report of the International Conference on Primary Health Care*, Alma Ata, 6–12 September 1978, WHO, Geneva.

17

CO-ORDINATING PRIMARY CARE WITH COMMUNITY MENTAL HEALTH SERVICES

Graham Thornicroft and Michele Tansella

Introduction

An historical perspective helps us to establish the changing relationships between primary medical care and community psychiatry. A WHO Working Group report in 1973 stated that 'the primary medical care team is the cornerstone of community psychiatry'. The influence of Michael Shepherd's seminal work on this conclusion is clear. Some sixteen years later another WHO Working Group reported that 'the further development of a comprehensive community-based network of mental health and psychiatric services in Member States was considered to be an indispensable precondition for the overall improvement of mental health care in primary health care settings' (WHO, 1990). The change in the perspective can be summarised as follows: from the view that primary care is a necessary and essential ingredient for community psychiatry, to the view that an improved community psychiatric service is necessary to provide better mental health care in general practice. The influence of David Goldberg upon this latter conclusion is equally clear. In addition, he was instrumental in building upon the insights of Michael Shepherd by broadening the field of research from conspicuous morbidity (which was the subject of the noted monograph by Michael Shepherd *et al.* 1966), to a consideration of total morbidity. As a consequence, a new conceptualisation became possible, which included both patients not correctly identified by family doctors as mentally ill (false negatives), and those who are wrongly identified by their GPs (false positives).

In this final chapter we shall refer to the wider arena of agencies and organisations who deliver services to people who are mentally ill, and we shall indicate that the particular boundary between primary and secondary health care services is only one example of the multiple interfaces that exist between all the elements of this wider array. In other words, we shall describe a whole system of care, made up of separate service components, and we shall locate the primary–secondary care elements as parts (vital parts) of the larger system. Moreover, we shall offer the reader a scheme including three stages in this area of applied research: (1) descriptive studies, (2) effectiveness or intervention studies, and (3) dissemination research (to modify the terminology of Von Korff in this volume). This dynamic, moving from a description of serious public health problems, through specifying effective interventions, to ensuring their widespread dissemination, is in fact a description of the range and historical importance of David Goldberg's contributions over the last 30 years.

This research pathway, in which David Goldberg was in effect one of the earliest proponents of evidence-based medicine, includes an increasing recognition that what really matters is how far individual patients benefit from treatments and from services, and therefore one of the key research endeavours is to accurately measure the outcomes of treatments and care, rather than being content with process description alone.

In this chapter we shall stress two central points. First, a key task is to shift the balance from research upon the recognition of mental disorders by staff in primary care settings, to studies on the treatment of recognised cases. This will entail a move in focus from the *processes* of assessment and referral by the GP, to a strict measure of patient *outcomes*, compared between different treatments. Second, we shall underscore the importance of translating successful models of treatment into widespread implementation programmes, which are themselves subject to evaluation. This takes the field from the multi-site trial mode (efficacy) into the local/regional implementation mode, in those areas of practice where sufficiently robust evidence exists to underpin such large scale policy and practice changes (effectiveness). We shall then conclude by discussing briefly the implications for improved co-ordination between primary care and specialist mental health care in a public health perspective. In this chapter, we shall refer mainly to services provided in economically more developed countries.

Defining co-ordination

In relation to health services, we can distinguish between cross-sectional and longitudinal co-ordination. The first refers to the co-ordination of information and services within an episode of care (both within and between services). The latter refers to the interrelationships between staff and between agencies over a longer period of treatment, often spanning several episodes. We can therefore define *co-ordination* as 'a service characteristic which is manifested by coherent treatment plans for individual patients. Each plan should have clear goals and include interventions which are needed and effective: no more and no less. By *cross-sectional co-ordination* we mean the co-ordination of information and services within an episode of care. By *longitudinal* co-ordination we mean the inter-linkages between staff and between agencies (at the primary and secondary care levels) over a longer period of treatment.' (Thornicroft and Tansella, 1999b).

Why co-ordinate primary care with specialist mental health services?

Even if the usefulness of co-ordination is often taken for granted, it is better to specify and analyse its advantages, because this analysis will help in identifying the most effective models of co-ordination. The question of why to co-ordinate is therefore a necessary prior step to that of how to co-ordinate, which we discuss below. Table 17.1 describes key reasons why primary care and mental health services need to be co-ordinated.

The epidemiological imperative dictates that the *mass morbidity* of mental disorders among the general population, in all sites where this has been studied, vastly exceeds the capacity of specialist mental health services to provide care, and that general medical services, especially primary care health

Table 17.1 Reasons why primary care and mental health services need to be co-ordinated

---

- High general population rates of psychiatric morbidity beyond the capacity of specialist services (even in the best resourced settings)

- High rates of co-morbidity of mental and physical disorders and the need for individualised care, usually by the primary care doctor or team, to integrate information to support diagnosis, and to avoid gaps in treatment

- Primary care, in many settings, is the main provider of treatment to people suffering from severe, persisting and disabling mental illnesses, so it is not true that the primary care team largely concerns itself only with minor disorders

- The last 20 years have seen, in many economically developed countries, the relocation of mental health services to geographically widely distributed sites, much closer to the primary care level

- An increasing awareness of the need to establish the most cost-effective models of co-ordination to achieve the best value for the available resources

- A need to agree on local referral protocols and the selectivity of referral filters, which apply to the specific local circumstances

- To assist training activities across the interface between primary and secondary care

- To improve the management and outcome of difficult cases, for example, patients with poor adherence to treatment or patients requiring compulsory admission

- To reduce the stigma experienced by some patients in attending specialist mental health services

---

services where these exist, will be the main provider of care for these patients. Vázquez-Barquero *et al.* in this volume, and Goldberg *et al.* (1999) have summarised the now compelling evidence for this proposition.

Further, there is a substantial *co-morbidity* between physical and psychiatric disorders, and indeed about half of psychiatric cases report physical symptoms as the main reason for consultation, where patients describe somatic rather than psychological complaints (Üstün and Sartorius, 1995; Goldberg *et al.* 1999). In relation to the primary care level, several key questions arise: how to elicit, and integrate all the available initial information about the presenting physical and psychological symptoms and complaints (Del Piccolo *et al.* 1998); when to refer on to specialist services; and how to use information received from specialist assessments to improve understanding, treatment and management (Kendrick *et al.* 1991). The best point of integration of information from these multiple sources continues to be the 'truly personal physician' (Shepherd *et al.* 1966).

At the same time a substantial proportion of people suffering from *severe mental illness* only receive care from primary health care sources. In a North London survey, for example, 25 per cent of patients with schizophrenia had no contact with specialist services (Harvey *et al.* 1996). The implication of this is that some patients never cross the filter into the specialist services, as Simon describes in Chapter 8, this volume. The question of how best to provide services to the mentally ill in a whole local population is best addressed in a co-ordinated approach, jointly-planned by primary and secondary care staff.

The increasingly widespread distribution of *community-based mental health services* in multiple sites, on a smaller scale than was the case in days of the asylum, and for smaller catchment areas, makes both more necessary (to avoid overlapping provision), and more feasible the co-ordination of primary care services (because of the more manageable scale of forming close working relationships with a limited number of clinical staff in the vicinity) (Tansella and Bellantuono, 1986, 1991; Johnson and Thornicroft, 1993).

Co-ordination between primary care and specialist mental health services is also advisable to negotiate the selectivity of the filter between the two levels in a way that makes sense locally. Long-term case register monitoring of referrals over the last 15 years in South-Verona, for example, has shown that as the community mental health service has developed and consolidated, so the number and the proportion of first-ever patients (those without any previous contact with all mental health services) referred to specialist services from primary care rose steadily and trebled over the entire period. At the same time the number of self-referrals decreased commensurately (see Table 17.2). The role of GPs is far less in re-referring patients with a past history of contact with mental health services, as Table 17.3 indicates.

In terms of the *training* of primary care staff, even if Jenkins is correct in saying in her foreword to this volume that there is some evidence that the

Table 17.2 Referrals to the specialist mental health services for first-ever patients in triennial periods for 1982–96 in South-Verona

	By GPs		Self-referrals*		All	
	n	%	n	%	n	%
1982-84	107	10.2	498	47.7	1,044	100
1985–87	144	15.4	466	49.4	935	100
1988–90	134	18.8	296	41.6	711	100
1991–93	171	22.4	285	37.4	762	100
1994–96	304	30.8	287	29.1	986	100

Source: Tansella *et al.* (1979–98)
Notes:
* Includes referrals by relatives
NB Row totals do not add to 100 per cent because other sources of referral are not shown

effects of training endure (McGuire *et al.* 1978; Tylee, 1998), we still need to consider this as a reciprocal process, and the need to reinforce and update training in the context of a joint approach to serving the mental health needs of a given population. Chapter 13 by Gask in this volume details the pioneering work of David Goldberg in inspiring his colleagues in Manchester – both while he was there and later – to innovate and evaluate new forms of training for primary care staff in the recognition and treatment of mental disorders in primary care settings.

A final reason why primary care and mental health services will often need to be closely co-ordinated is that there is evidence that patients with psychiatric disorders find treatment in primary health care settings more easily accessible and less *stigmatising* (Tyrer, 1984). This may increase the proportion of patients who attend for appointments in primary care compared

Table 17.3 Referrals to the specialist mental health services for re-presentations of previously known patients out of contact for six months or longer, in triennial periods for 1982–96 in South-Verona

	By GPs		Self-referrals*		All	
	n	%	n	%	n	%
1982–84	19	2.7	327	46.9	696	100
1985–87	34	4.7	309	43.1	717	100
1988–90	25	3.6	293	42.6	667	100
1991–93	40	5.0	279	34.9	796	100
1994–96	78	7.7	265	26.3	1,006	100

Source: Tansella *et al.* (1979–98)
Notes:
* Includes referrals by relatives
NB Row totals do not add to 100 per cent because other sources of referral are not shown

with psychiatric out-patient clinics (Tyrer *et al.* 1984; Jackson *et al.* 1993). A further important advantage, for a limited number of more severely disabled patients, is that they may take advice from their own general practitioner, for example on prescribed medication, which they would not accept from staff at a dedicated mental health centre. This may be because the therapeutic relationship with the GP is longer-lasting or better established, or that the patient considers the GP to be essentially therapeutically orientated, while the psychiatrist occupies an ambivalent treatment and custodial role, or because the patient does not wish to identify him or herself as a 'psychiatric patient'.

In extreme or crisis situations this may mean that the GP can more easily persuade a patient to accept medication or even voluntary admission (a less restrictive alternative) than can a psychiatrist. The conjoint intervention of GP and psychiatrist, for example during a home visit, can be sufficient to render the intervention less intrusive for the patient and the advice more trustable. In addition, the primary care location of specialist services may also be more cost-effective because they reduce psychiatric admissions rates (Williams and Balestrieri, 1989; Tyrer *et al.* 1990), although this reduction was not apparent after one year in a study in Manchester, where a whole community mental health team was based in primary care (Jackson *et al.* 1993).

Framework for co-ordination: the hydraulic model

The totality of mental health service components may be considered as a series of interrelated elements, in which the behaviour of each effects (directly or indirectly) all the others. Such a view allows us to speak of the volume and the capacity of components and of the whole 'hydraulic' system (both for under and over-capacity), to calculate rates of flow between components, to build in control taps and safety valves for periods of expected and unexpected excess pressure, and to make allowance for overflow capacity in times of excess volume, for the 'leakage' of some patients out the system (when patients may be inappropriately lost to contact with services). Such a metaphor also allows us to consider the need for routine and emergency maintenance to avoid system breakdowns, and to build in sentinel events or alarm systems to warn of incipient system failures. While not wishing to overstretch this parallel, we do find that such a view helps to understand the links between service components (Thornicroft and Tansella, 1999a).

Once we have clarified that mental health services should be seen as a system, we can use this overall framework to consider three types of *interface*: (1) those *within the mental health service*, between its components, (2) those *within the health service*, between mental health and other services (both primary and secondary care), and (3) those *between health and other public services* including Social Services and the Housing Department. Figure 17.1 graphically displays first, some of the most important linkages between the

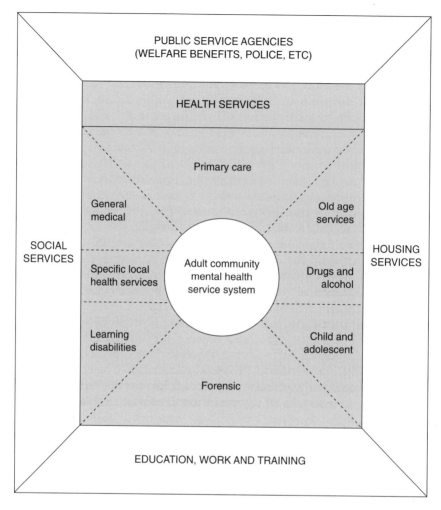

Figure 17.1 Key interfaces between the community mental health service and (1) other health services and (2) other public service agencies

Source: Thornicroft and Tansella (1999a).

core general adult mental health service system and eight other key health components, and second, it shows the four main categories of public service with which health services connect (from Thornicroft and Tansella, 1999a). It is in this wider perspective that the crucial interface between primary care and mental health services needs to be located.

The *permeability* of each interface may change over time and may differ for the direction of referral. Each facet between adjacent services can act as a filter in the same sense as that used by Goldberg and Huxley (1980, 1992) in their model of the pathways from the general population to primary and then to specialist psychiatric care. Although in clinical practice the existence of inter-actions between these services elements is well recognised, for example in terms of the transfer of patients from the criminal justice system to health facilities through prison or court diversion schemes, in theory such linkages are not usually described. Indeed the only interface which has been well characterised is that shown in Figure 17.1 between primary care and com-munity mental health services, known as Filter 3 in the Goldberg and Huxley scheme. As a consequence, there is little relevant research which quantifies the selectivity and the extent of patient flows across these other interfaces. It does seem clear, however, that the ground rules of engagement for these interfaces vary enormously, even within regions.

A number of factors at three levels affect the selective referral of patients from primary care to specialist services and back again (Goldberg and Huxley, 1992). At the *patient level*, referral is more likely for those who are male, younger, suffering from more severe disorders or who are socially isolated. At the *primary care level*, referral rates are higher for patients who are treated by older GPs, and for those registered at practices in urban areas. At the *specialist mental health services level* more referrals occur where mental health services are more accessible, especially where specialists offer consultations in primary care centres, and there is some evidence that this may also result in a greater proportion of women patients receiving specialist referral (Goldberg and Huxley, 1980; Goldberg and Huxley, 1992; Brown *et al.* 1988; Oiesvold *et al.* 1998). One particular characteristic of mental health services that affects referrals is the degree to which they are community or hospital based. A study in Verona, for example, showed that the total referral rates did not differ between South-Verona (which has a community-based service) and North-Verona (where a hospital-based service was provided at the time the study was conducted). However, in South-Verona 71 per cent of GP referrals were to the local public psychiatric service, while in North-Verona only 49 per cent were sent on to the local, hospital-based psychiatric services (Arreghini *et al.* 1991).

How to co-ordinate primary care with specialist mental health services

Three models have been described over the last two decades for how primary care and secondary care staff can work together. First, the *replacement model* in which the psychiatrist replaces the GP as the doctor of first contact for patients with psychiatric disorders, and which is exemplified by community mental health centres in the USA (Fink and Oken, 1976). Second, the *increased-throughput* model, which describes the idea that GPs should be encouraged to refer increasing numbers of cases to specialist services. Third, there are *consultation-liaison* models, which describe the movement of the psychiatrist out of the hospital into general practice settings, and which places greatest emphasis upon close links between the primary care and psychiatric teams. The first two models are not practical simply in terms of the limited capacity of specialist services, even in the best resourced health care systems (Williams and Clare, 1981).

The forms of consultation-liaison vary considerably between the *shifted out-patient* service, in which the psychiatrist carries out an ordinary out-patient clinic in primary care premises (Tyrer, 1984), to other more sophisticated varieties of co-ordination which can be shaped to meet specific requirements of local services (Gask *et al.* 1997). Simon (Chapter 8, this volume), has described the outcomes of recent models designed to improve co-ordinated care, most of which concerned the treatment of patients with depression. Gask *et al.* (1997) have described a 'pure consultation-liaison' model, which has four key components: (1) regular face-to-face meetings between the visiting psychiatrist and primary care staff, (2) referral of patients only after discussion at these meetings, (3) some cases are managed only by primary care staff, after direct discussion with the psychiatrist, and (4) there needs to be feedback to the primary care team by the psychiatrist after specialist assessment with treatment and management recommendations for the primary care staff to follow. As they indicate, formal evaluations of such specific services have not taken place, and future research will need to address the benefits in terms of outcomes for individual patients and the costs. A meta-analysis of studies comparing usual GP treatment and specialist care, in British primary health care settings, for example, has shown that overall outcomes were 10 per cent better for patients treated by psychiatric specialists (Balestrieri *et al.* 1988).

We need to develop a consultation-liaison model in a step-wise way that takes into account both details of the situation in each local area, including the available resources, specific aspects of the local services' traditions and methods of organisation, and the motivation of staff for change, and the expectations of each side of the primary–secondary care interface. For instance what a GP expects is not always clear to the psychiatrist, and may include the prompt provision of in-patient care, day care facilities, diagnostic investigations and procedures, highly specialised treatments, and respite from 'heart-sink' patients (Goldberg *et al.* 1999). The methods used so far to improve primary–secondary care co-ordination are listed in Table 17.4.

Implications of improving co-ordination in a public health perspective

A useful framework to structure possible implications of improving co-ordination between primary care and specialist mental health services is shown in Table 17.5. On one axis this shows the levels and filters of the Goldberg and Huxley (1980, 1992) pathways to care model, and on the other axis shows three major areas for action: clinical practice, health policy

Table 17.4 Methods used to enhance primary–secondary care co-ordination

- Shared care registers (Strathdee and Jenkins, 1996)
- Shared care plans (Burns and Kendrick, 1997; Goldberg *et al.* 1999)
- Protocols for management of patients in nursing homes and residential care
- Use of electronic referrals and transfer of the results of investigations
- Directories of local services for referral from primary and secondary care
- Crisis cards (Sutherby and Szmukler, 1997)
- Link worker schemes (Goldberg and Gournay, 1997)
- Joint training and skill sharing schemes
- Critical incident analysis, for example, following suicide

and research. These follow a time sequence in that the clinical actions can be implemented in the near future, the policy implications are likely to be less rapid as they must go through political processes, and the research implications may have the longest time scale, until the results of future studies become evident. The table suggests that the actions consequent upon what we already know in this field may be conceptually straightforward, but we acknowledge that the barriers to implementation are complex, and vary between the clinical, policy and research domains in each area, as well as in each country.

Our use of the Goldberg and Huxley model for this overview is a tribute to the enduring usefulness of their beautifully simple conceptualisation. In relation to the co-ordination of primary and secondary care this scheme locates two of our central points in this chapter: namely the need to compare different models of co-ordination within a strict evidence-based medicine approach, and to do so in a way that prioritises the outcomes of care for individual patients.

In a wider sense, the integrated pattern of co-ordination between primary and specialist care, which we have discussed in this chapter and which we try to summarise in Table 17.5, implies a *public health perspective*. This perspective adopts a 'systemic' view (where all service components are considered as parts of an integrated system of health care), rather than a 'segmental' approach (in which each service component is seen independently) to organising and delivering health services. In other words, co-ordination should be built-in as fundamental to our *thinking* about serving the public health, as well being central to how we organise services on the ground, rather than acting as a *post-hoc* afterthought, designed to minimise the disintegration of segmented service components (Thornicroft and Tansella, 1999a). It is in changing our thinking towards this public health approach, in so far as it effects

231

Table 17.5 Implications of improved co-ordination between primary care and mental health services

Implications for	Level 1 and Filter 1	Level 2 and Filter 2	Level 3 and Filter 3	Level 4 and Filter 4	Level 5
	Morbidity in the general population and illness behaviour	*Morbidity among attenders in primary care and GPs' ability to detect cases*	*Conspicuous morbidity (identified by doctors) and referral to specialist care*	*Total morbidity in specialist mental health services and decisions to admit to hospital*	*Morbidity of in-patient psychiatric wards*
Clinical practice	• Developing the capacity of 'natural' community networks to offer support in times of adversity to prevent the development of psychiatric symptoms	• Greater focus on training GPs in reducing disclosure thresholds of patients for life events and social problems • Improving the skills of primary care staff to detect cases	• Adherence of primary care staff to treatment guidelines and protocols • Developing locally agreed referral guidelines between primary and secondary care	• Shared care schemes • Joint case registers • Agreed prescribing responsibilities • Link worker schemes	• Information to GP when patients are admitted, when discharged, about what treatment has been given, its effects, and on the future care plan
National/regional health policy	• Public education on nature and treatability of mental illnesses	• Organising widespread training programmes for primary care staff to improve clinical skills and to detect mental illnesses • Incentives to treat mental illnesses	• Providing central guidance on acceptable guidelines and protocols	• Involving GPs in shared care planning • Clarifying responsibility for physical health care	• Clear guidelines on communications necessary with primary care when planning admission and discharge from hospital

Research				
• Studies of interventions that change illness behaviour or attendance rates at primary care, for example, for 'hard-to-engage' groups	• Research on specific strategies to promote positive attitudes to confiding psycho-social information among patients that find this difficult • Evaluating effects of large-scale training programmes	• Studies of factors which enhance fidelity to clinical guidelines • Comparing models of co-ordination e.g. consultation-liaison • Measuring outcomes of treatment	• Studies of shared care protocols • Studies of joint case registers of severely mentally ill patients • Identifying 'minimum effective dose' of direct specialist consultation in general practice	• Research upon the active ingredients of effective in-patient care

both primary and secondary care services, that David Goldberg's contributions have served as a deep and rich goldmine of inspiration. In dealing with research and the application of research findings it is useful to adopt the dictum 'go as far as you can see, because then you can see further', and in a sense David Goldberg has already gone very far, and helped us all to see further.

References

Arreghini, E., Agostini, C. and Wilkinson, G. (1991) General practitioners referrals to specialist psychiatric services: a comparison of practices in North- and South-Verona. *Psychological Medicine* 21, 485–494.

Balestrieri, M., Williams, P. and Wilkinson, G. (1988) Specialist mental health treatment in general practice: a meta-analysis. *Psychological Medicine* 18, 711–717.

Brown, R., Strathdee, G., Christie-Brown, J. and Robinson, P. (1988) A comparison of referrals to primary-care and hospital out-patient clinics. *British Journal of Psychiatry* 153, 168–173.

Burns, T. and Kendrick, T. (1997) The primary care of patients with schizophrenia: a search for good practice. *British Journal of General Practice* 47, 515–520.

Del Piccolo, L., Saltini, A. and Zimmermann, C. (1998) Which patients talk about stressful life events and social problems to the general practitioner? *Psychological Medicine* 28, 1289–1299.

Fink, P.J. and Oken, S. (1976) The role of psychiatry as a primary care speciality. *Archives of General Psychiatry* 33, 998–1003.

Gask, L., Sibbald, B. and Creed, F. (1997) Evaluating models of working at the interface between mental health services and primary care. *British Journal of Psychiatry* 170, 6–11.

Goldberg, D. and Gater, R. (1996) Implication of the World Health Organization study of mental illness in general health care for training primary care staff. *British Journal of General Practice* 46, 483–485.

Goldberg, D. and Gournay, K. (1997) *The General Practitioner, the Psychiatrist and the Burden of Mental Health Care*. Maudsley Discussion Paper Number 1. London, Institute of Psychiatry.

Goldberg, D. and Huxley, P. (1980) *Mental Illness in the Community*. Tavistock, London.

—— (1992) *Common Mental Disorders. A Bio-Social Model*. Routledge, London.

Goldberg, D., Mann, A. and Tylee, A. (1999) Psychiatry in primary care. In M.G. Gelder, J.J. Lopez-Ibor and N.C. Andreasen (eds) *New Oxford Textbook of Psychiatry*. Oxford University Press, Oxford.

Harvey, C., Pantelis, C., Taylor, J., McCabe, P., Lefevre, K., Campbell, P. and Hirsch, S. (1996) The Camden Schizophrenia Surveys, II. High prevalence of schizophrenia in an inner London borough and its relationship to socio-demographic factors. *British Journal of Psychiatry* 168, 418–426.

Jackson, G., Gater, R., Goldberg, D., Tantam, D., Loftus, L. and Taylor, H. (1993) A new community mental health team based in primary care. *British Journal of Psychiatry* 162, 375–384.

Johnson, S. and Thornicroft, G. (1993) The sectorisation of psychiatry in England and Wales. *Social Psychiatry and Psychiatric Epidemiology,* 28, 45–47

Kendrick, A., Sibbald, B., Burns, T. and Freeling, P. (1991) Role of general practitioners in care of long-term mentally ill. *British Medical Journal* 310, 508–510.

Kerwick, S., Tylee, A. and Goldberg, D. (1997) Mental health services in primary care in London. In S. Johnson, R. Ramsay, G. Thornicroft, L. Brooks, P. Lelliot, E. Peck, H. Smith, D. Chisholm, B. Audini, M. Knapp and D. Goldberg (eds) *London's Mental Health*, Kings Fund, London.

McGuire, P., Roe, P., Goldberg, D., Jones, D., Hyde, C. and O'Dowd, T. *et al.* (1978) The value feedback in teaching interview skills to medical students. *Psychological Medicine* 8, 697–704.

Oiesvold, T., Sandlund, M., Hansson, L., Christiansen, L., Gostas, G., Lindhardt, S., Saarento, O., Sytema, S. and Zandren, T. (1998) Factors associated with referral to psychiatric care by general practitioners compared with self-referrals. *Psychological Medicine* 28, 427–436.

Shepherd, M., Cooper, B., Brown, A.C. and Kalton, G.W. (1966) *Psychiatric Illness in General Practice.* Oxford University Press, London.

Strathdee, G. and Jenkins, R. (1996) Purchasing mental health care for primary care. In G. Thornicroft and G. Strathdee (eds) *Commissioning Mental Health Services*, pp. 71–83, HMSO, London.

Sutherby, K. and Szmukler, G. (1997) Crisis cards and self help crisis initiatives. *Psychiatric Bulletin* 22, 4–7.

Tansella, M. and Bellantuono, C. (1986) The view from abroad. Italy. In M. Shepherd, G. Wilkinson and P. Williams (eds) *Mental Illness in Primary Care Settings*, pp. 214–218. Tavistock Publications, London.

Tansella, M. and Bellantuono, C. (1991) Provision of mental health care in general practice in Italy. *British Journal of General Practice* 41, 468–471.

Tansella, M., Amaddeo, F. and Meneghelli, G. (1979–98) Statistics from the South-Verona Psychiatric Case Register, unpublished annual reports, Institute of Psychiatry, University of Verona.

Thornicroft, G. and Tansella, M. (1999a) *The Mental Health Matrix. A Manual to Improve Services.* Cambridge University Press, Cambridge.

Thornicroft, G. and Tansella, M. (1999b) Translating ethical principles into outcome measures for mental health service research. *Psychological Medicine* (in press).

Tylee, A. (1998) Education of primary care team, RCGP Senior Mental Health Education Fellowship and the Defeat Depression campaign. In R. Jenkins and T.B. Üstün (eds) *Preventing Mental Illness. Mental Health Promotion in Primary Care*, pp. 219–227. Wiley, Chichester.

Tyrer, P. (1984) Psychiatric clinics in general practice. An extension of community care. *British Journal of Psychiatry* 145, 9–14.

Tyrer, P., Seivewright, N. and Wollerton, S. (1984) General practice psychiatric clinics. Impact on psychiatric services. *British Journal of Psychiatry* 145, 15–19.

Tyrer, P., Ferguson, B. and Wadsworth, J. (1990). Liaison psychiatry in general practice: the comprehensive collaborative model. *Acta Psychiatrica Scandinavica* 81, 359–363.

Üstün, B. and Sartorius, N. (1995) *Mental Illness in General Health Care. An International Study.* Wiley, Chichester.

Williams, P. and Balestrieri, M. (1989) Psychiatric clinics in general practice. Do they reduce admissions? *British Journal of Psychiatry* 154, 67–71.

Williams, P. and Clare, A. (1981) Changing patterns of psychiatric care. *British Medical Journal* 282, 375–377.

World Health Organization (1973) *Psychiatry and Primary Medical Care.* Report of a Working Group. WHO Regional Office for Europe, Copenhagen.

—— (1990) *The Development of Mental Health Care in Primary Health Care Settings in the European Region.* Report of a Working Group. WHO Regional Office for Europe, Copenhagen.

INDEX

236

Bellantuono, C. 225
Benjamin, Sydney xix
benzodiazapines 22, 137
Birley, Dr J. 95
Blanchard, M.R. 130, 133
Bland, R.C. 4, 6
body dysmorphic disorder 97
Boyce, P. 39
brain aversion system (BAS) 19, 20, 21
Bridges, K. 106
Bristol Dementia Guideline Project 149
Brodarty, H. 188
Brooker, C. 92
Brooking, J. 94
Brown, G.W. 35, 40
BSI 71
bulimia 59
buspirone 137
Butler, R.N. 133
Butler, T. 89

Callahan, C.M. 110, 122
Canada, and mental health services 84
Canino, G.J. 4, 5, 6
Cantabria survey 7, 8–9
carers, and depression 137
Caspi, A. 39
Challenger, A. 84
Charleston, Carolina 198
Chitral, Pakistan 68
Chocron, L. 12
cholesterol reduction 59
Chronic Fatigue Syndrome 97
Churail 69, 70
Clayton, P.J. 39
Clear Vision Project 74
Clinical Interview Schedule (CIS) xvi,
 xxiv, 12, 151, 157, 158, 164
Clinical Outcomes Group (NHS) 147,
 149–50
clinical practice guidelines (CPGs)
 143–52; and computers 152, 162–4;
 development and evaluation 144–50;
 impact on GPs 163; internal 143; for
 psychological therapies 149–50; in UK
 146–50; in USA 144–6
Cloninger, S.C 39
CO_2 inhalation, and panic 23–4, 27
co-morbidity 11, 119, 184, 224, 225;
 see also somatisation
co-ordination of services 223–34;
 consultation-liaison model 229–30;

cross-sectional and longitudinal 223–4;
 framework for 227–9; implications of
 230–4; key interfaces 227–9; methods
 231; models of 229–30; need for
 224–7; public health perspective 231;
 see also collaborative care, training
Cochrane Collaboration Depression,
 Anxiety and Neurosis Review Group
 (CCDAN) 144
cognitive behaviour therapy 93, 95, 97;
 see also behaviour therapy
cognitive impairment 132, 134, 137,
 184; *see also* Alzheimer's disease,
 dementia, elderly patients
collaborative care 55–6, 107–13, 120–4,
 187–8, 191
Commander, M.J. 10
community health teams 118
community mental health teams
 (CMHTs) 195
community psychiatric nurses (CPNs):
 aftercare 93–4; background 93–6; as
 counsellors 94; and elderly patients
 135–6; evaluation of work 94, 95,
 96–7; as interface between primary and
 secondary care 95–6; and long-term
 mental illness 92, 94, 95; and
 non-psychotic illness 85–6; in primary
 care 97; training 92–3, 95, 96–7
community-based mental health
 programmes 73–8; evaluating needs
 73; research and evaluation 74–7;
 see also mental health services
component causes 38
Composite International Diagnostic
 Interview (CIDI) 4, 10, 12, 157, 184
computers 156–65; computerised records
 113; and decision support 163–4; and
 guidelines 162–3; self-administered
 computerised assessments 157–8,
 159–62, 164–5
continuing medical education (CME)
 201–2; *see also* training
Continuous Quality Improvement 110
coping 18, 19, 36, 37, 38, 45
CORE (Clinical Outcomes Research and
 Effectiveness) 149–50
Corney, R. 83, 84
cortisol 29–30
Coulehan, J.L. 55
counsellors/counselling, and qualifications
 83